Economics of Aquaculture: An Approach to Developing Economics

Economics of Aquaculture: An Approach to Developing Economics

Dr. Ashok Purohit

RANDOM PUBLICATIONS
NEW DELHI (INDIA)

Economics of Aquaculture: An Approach to Developing Economics

ISBN 978-93-5111-812-1

Published in 2016 in India by

RANDOM PUBLICATIONS

4376-A/4B, Gali Murari Lal, Ansari Road
New Delhi-110 002
Phone : +9111-43580356, 011-23289044, 011-43142548
e-mail: sales@randompublications.com,
info@randompublications.com, randomexports@gmail.com

Reprinted 2023

Type Setting by : Friends Media, Delhi-110089
Printed at : Replika Press Pvt. Ltd.

Preface

Aquaculture which is also known as aquafarming, is the farming of aquatic organisms such as fish, crustaceans, molluscs and aquatic plants. Aquaculture involves cultivating freshwater and saltwater populations under controlled conditions, and can be contrasted with commercial fishing, which is the harvesting of wild fish. Broadly speaking, the relation of aquaculture to finfish and shellfish fisheries is analogous to the relation of agriculture to hunting and gathering. Mariculture refers to aquaculture practiced in marine environments and in underwater habitats.

The economics of aquaculture is reviewed on two levels: micro and macro. Micro-economics in aquaculture deals mainly with the management measures and elements affecting the efficiency of operation at the farm level, while macro-economics addresses the assessment of social benefits and costs of an aquaculture project. If aquaculture is socially beneficial but unattractive to private investors, public support on credit, marketing, extension, training, and research may be appropriate, especially during the early stages of development. The importance of economic analysis is emphasized since it provides a basis not only in the decision making of the individual farmer, but also in the formulation of aquaculture policies. Thus, greater attention should be focused on the improvement of economic data for analysis.

– Author

Contents

1

Aquaculture

Aquaculture, also known as aquafarming, is the farming of aquatic organisms such as fish, crustaceans, molluscs and aquatic plants. Aquaculture involves cultivating freshwater and saltwater populations under controlled conditions, and can be contrasted with commercial fishing, which is the harvesting of wild fish. Broadly speaking, finfish and shellfish fisheries can be conceptualised as akin to hunting and gathering while aquaculture is akin to agriculture. Mariculture refers to aquaculture practised in marine environments and in underwater habitats.

According to the FAO, aquaculture "is understood to mean the farming of aquatic organisms including fish, molluscs, crustaceans and aquatic plants. Farming implies some form of intervention in the rearing process to enhance production, such as regular stocking, feeding, protection from predators, etc.

Farming also implies individual or corporate ownership of the stock being cultivated." The reported output from global aquaculture operations would supply one half of the fish and shellfish that is directly consumed by humans; however, there are issues about the reliability of the reported figures.

Further, in current aquaculture practice, products from several pounds of wild fish are used to produce one pound of a piscivorous fish like salmon. Particular kinds of aquaculture include fish farming, shrimp farming, oyster farming, algaculture (such as seaweed farming), and the cultivation of ornamental fish. Particular methods include aquaponics and Integrated multi-trophic aquaculture, both of which integrate fish farming and plant farming.

HISTORY

The indigenous Gunditjmara people in Victoria, Australia may have raised eels as early as 6000 BC. There is evidence that they developed about 100 square kilometres (39 sq mi) of volcanic floodplains in the vicinity of Lake Condah into a complex of channels and dams, that they used woven traps to capture eels, and preserve eels to eat all year round.

Aquaculture was operating in China circa 2500 BC. When the waters subsided after river floods, some fishes, mainly carp, were trapped in lakes. Early aquaculturists fed their brood using nymphs and silkworm feces, and ate them. A fortunate genetic mutation of carp led to the emergence of goldfish during the Tang Dynasty.

Japanese cultivated seaweed by providing bamboo poles and, later, nets and oyster shells to serve as anchoring surfaces for spores. Romans bred fish in ponds. In central Europe, early Christian monasteries adopted Roman aquacultural practices. Aquaculture spread in Europe during the Middle Ages since away from the seacoasts and the big rivers fish had to be salted in order to not perish. Improvements in transportation during the 19th century made fresh fish easily available and inexpensive, even in inland areas, making aquaculture less popular. Hawaiians constructed oceanic fish ponds. A remarkable example is a fish pond dating from at least 1,000 years ago, at Alekoko. Legend says that it was constructed by the mythical Menehune dwarf people.

In 1859 Stephen Ainsworth of West Bloomfield, New York, began experiments with brook trout. By 1864 Seth Green had established a commercial fish hatching operation at Caledonia Springs, near Rochester, New York. By 1866, with the involvement of Dr. W. W. Fletcher of Concord, Massachusetts, artificial fish hatcheries were under way in both Canada and the United States. When the Dildo Island fish hatchery opened in Newfoundland in 1889, it was the largest and most advanced in the world. Californians harvested wild kelp and attempted to manage supply circa 1900, later labelling it a wartime resource

21ST-CENTURY PRACTICE

About 430 (97 per cent) of the species cultured as of 2007 were domesticated during the 20th century, of which an estimated 106 came in the decade to 2007. Given the long-term importance of agriculture, it is interesting to note that to date only 0.08 per cent of known land plant species and 0.0002 per cent of known land animal species have been domesticated, compared with 0.17 per cent of known marine plant species and 0.13 per cent of known marine animal species. Domestication typically involves about a decade of scientific research. Domesticating aquatic species involves fewer risks to humans than land animals, which took a large toll in human lives. Most major human diseases originated in domesticated animals, through diseases such as smallpox and diphtheria, that like most infectious diseases, move to humans from animals. No human pathogens of comparable virulence have yet emerged from marine species. Harvest stagnation in wild fisheries and overexploitation of popular marine species, combined with a growing demand for high quality protein, encourage aquaculturists to domesticate other marine species.

SPECIES GROUPS

AQUATIC PLANTS

Microalgae, also referred to as phytoplankton, microphytes, or planktonic algae constitute the majority of cultivated algae. Macroalgae, commonly known as seaweed, also have many commercial and industrial uses, but due to their size and specific requirements, they are not easily cultivated on a large scale and are most often taken in the wild.

FISH

The farming of fish is the most common form of aquaculture. It involves raising fish commercially in tanks, ponds, or ocean enclosures, usually for food. A facility that releases juvenile fish into the wild for recreational fishing or to supplement a species' natural numbers is generally referred to as a fish hatchery. Worldwide, the most important fish species used in fish farming are, in order, carp, salmon, tilapia and catfish.

In the Mediterranean, young bluefin tuna are netted at sea and towed slowly towards the shore. They are then interned in offshore pens where they are further grown for the market. In 2009, researchers in Australia managed for the first time to coax tuna (Southern bluefin) to breed in landlocked tanks.

CRUSTACEANS

Commercial shrimp farming began in the 1970s, and production grew steeply thereafter. Global production reached more than 1.6 million tonnes in 2003, worth about 9 billion U.S., dollars. About 75 per cent of farmed shrimp is produced in Asia, in particular in China and Thailand. The other 25 per cent is produced mainly in Latin America, where Brazil is the largest producer. Thailand is the largest exporter.

Shrimp farming has changed from its traditional, small-scale form in Southeast Asia into a global industry. Technological advances have led to ever higher densities per unit area, and broodstock is shipped worldwide. Virtually all farmed shrimp are penaeids (*i.e.*, shrimp of the family *Penaeidae*), and just two species of shrimp, the Pacific white shrimp and the giant tiger prawn, account for about 80 per cent of all farmed shrimp. These industrial monocultures are very susceptible to disease, which has decimated shrimp populations across entire regions. Increasing ecological problems, repeated disease outbreaks, and pressure and criticism from both NGOs and consumer countries led to changes in the industry in the late 1990s and generally stronger regulations. In 1999, governments, industry representatives, and environmental organisations initiated a programme aimed at developing and promoting more sustainable farming practices through the Seafood Watch programme.

Freshwater prawn farming shares many characteristics with, including many problems with marine shrimp farming. Unique problems are introduced by the developmental life cycle of the main species, the giant river prawn. The global annual production of freshwater prawns (excluding crayfish and crabs) in 2003 was about 280,000 tonnes of which China produced 180,000 tonnes followed by India and Thailand with 35,000 tonnes each. Additionally, China produced about 370,000 tonnes of Chinese river crab.

MOLLUSCS

Aquacultured shellfish include various oyster, mussel and clam species. These bivalves are filter and/or deposit feeders, which rely on ambient primary production rather than inputs of fish or other feed. As such shellfish aquaculture is generally perceived as benign or even beneficial. Depending on the species and local conditions, bivalve molluscs are either grown on the beach, on longlines, or suspended from rafts and harvested by hand or by dredging. Abalone farming began in the late 1950s and early 1960s in Japan and China. Since the mid-1990s, this industry has become increasingly successful. Over-fishing and poaching have reduced wild populations to the extent that farmed abalone now supplies most abalone meat.

Sustainably farmed molluscs can be certified by Seafood Watch and other organisations, including the World Wildlife Fund (WWF). WWF initiated the "Aquaculture Dialogues" in 2004 to develop measurable and performance-based standards for responsibly farmed seafood. In 2009, WWF co-founded the Aquaculture Stewardship Council (ASC) with the Dutch Sustainable Trade Initiative (IDH) to manage the global standards and certification programmes.

OTHER GROUPS

Other groups include aquatic reptiles, amphibians, and miscellaneous invertebrates, such as echinoderms and jellyfish. They are separately graphed at the top right of this section, since they do not contribute enough volume to show clearly on the main graph. Commercially harvested echinoderms include sea cucumbers and sea urchins. In China, sea cucumbers are farmed in artificial ponds as large as 1,000 acres (400 ha).

AROUND THE WORLD

In 2004, the total world production of fisheries was 140 million tonnes of which aquaculture contributed 45 million tonnes, about one third. The growth rate of worldwide aquaculture has been sustained and rapid, averaging about 8 per cent per annum for over thirty years, while the take from wild fisheries has been essentially flat for the last decade. The aquaculture market reached $86 billion in 2009.

Aquaculture is an especially important economic activity in China. Between 1980 and 1997, the Chinese Bureau of Fisheries reports, aquaculture harvests grew at an annual rate of 16.7 per cent, jumping from 1.9 million tonnes to nearly 23 million tonnes. In 2005, China accounted for 70 per cent of world production. Aquaculture is also currently one of the fastest growing areas of food production in the U.S. Approximately 90 per cent of all U.S., shrimp consumption is farmed and imported. In recent years salmon aquaculture has become a major export in southern Chile, especially in Puerto Montt, Chile's fastest-growing city.

OVER REPORTING

China overwhelmingly dominates the world in reported aquaculture output. They report a total output which is double that of the rest of the world put together. However, there are issues with the accuracy of China's returns.

In 2001, the fisheries scientists Reg Watson and Daniel Pauly expressed concerns in a letter to *Nature*, that China was over reporting its catch from wild fisheries in the 1990s.

They said that made it appear that the global catch since 1988 was increasing annually by 300,000 tonnes, whereas it was really shrinking annually by 350,000 tonnes. Watson and Pauly suggested this may be related to China policies where state entities that monitor the economy are also tasked with increasing output. Also, until recently, the promotion of Chinese officials was based on production increases from their own areas.

China disputes this claim. The official Xinhua News Agency quoted Yang Jian, director general of the Agriculture Ministry's Bureau of Fisheries, as saying that China's figures were "basically correct". However, the FAO accepts there are issues with the reliability of China's statistical returns, and currently treats data from China, including the aquaculture data, apart from the rest of the world.

METHODS

MARICULTURE

Mariculture is the term used for the cultivation of marine organisms in seawater, usually in sheltered coastal waters. In particular, the farming of marine fish is an example of mariculture, and so also is the farming of marine crustaceans (such as shrimps), molluscs (such as oysters) and seaweed.

INTEGRATED

Integrated Multi-Trophic Aquaculture (IMTA) is a practice in which the by-products (wastes) from one species are recycled to become inputs (fertilizers, food) for another. Fed aquaculture (for example, fish, shrimp) is combined with inorganic extractive and organic extractive (for example, shellfish) aquaculture to create balanced systems for environmental sustainability (biomitigation), economic stability (product diversification and risk reduction) and social acceptability (better management practices).

"Multi-Trophic" refers to the incorporation of species from different trophic or nutritional levels in the same system. This is one potential distinction from the age-old practice of aquatic polyculture, which could simply be the co-culture of different fish species from the same trophic level. In this case, these organisms may all share the same biological and chemical processes, with few synergistic benefits, which could potentially lead to significant shifts in the ecosystem. Some traditional polyculture systems may, in fact, incorporate a greater diversity of species, occupying several niches, as extensive cultures (low intensity, low management) within the same pond. The "Integrated" in IMTA refers to the more intensive cultivation of the different species in proximity of each other, connected by nutrient and energy transfer through water.

Ideally, the biological and chemical processes in an IMTA system should balance. This is achieved through the appropriate selection and proportions of different species providing different ecosystem functions. The co-cultured species are typically more than just biofilters; they are harvestable crops of commercial value. A working IMTA system can result in greater total production based on mutual benefits to the co-cultured species and improved ecosystem health, even if the production of individual species is lower than in a monoculture over a short term period.

Sometimes the term "Integrated Aquaculture" is used to describe the integration of monocultures through water transfer. For all intents and purposes however, the terms "IMTA" and "integrated aquaculture" differ only in their degree of descriptiveness.

Aquaponics, fractionated aquaculture, IAAS (integrated agriculture-aquaculture systems), IPUAS (integrated peri-urban-aquaculture systems), and IFAS (integrated fisheries-aquaculture systems) are other variations of the IMTA concept.

NETTING MATERIALS

Various materials, including nylon, polyester, polypropylene, polyethylene, plastic-coated welded wire, rubber, patented rope products (Spectra, Thorn-D, Dyneema), galvanised steel and copper are used for netting in aquaculture fish enclosures around the world. All of these materials are selected for a variety of reasons, including design feasibility, material strength, cost, and corrosion resistance.

Recently, copper alloys have become important netting materials in aquaculture because they are antimicrobial (*i.e.*, they destroy bacteria, viruses, fungi, algae, and other microbes) and they therefore prevent biofouling (*i.e.*, the undesirable accumulation, adhesion, and growth of microorganisms, plants, algae, tubeworms, barnacles, mollusks, and other organisms). By inhibiting microbial growth, copper alloy aquaculture cages avoid costly net changes that are necessary with other materials. The resistance of organism growth on copper alloy nets also provides a cleaner and healthier environment for farmed fish to grow and thrive.

ISSUES

Aquaculture can be more environmentally damaging than exploiting wild fisheries on a local area basis but has considerably less impact on the global environment on a per kg of production basis. Local concerns include waste handling, side-effects of antibiotics, competition between farmed and wild animals, and using other fish to feed more marketable carnivorous fish. However, research and commercial feed improvements during the 1990s and 2000s have lessened many of these concerns.

Aquaculture may contribute to propagation of invasive species. As the cases of Nile perch and Janitor fish show, this issue may be damaging to native fauna. Fish waste is organic and composed of nutrients necessary in all components of aquatic food webs. In-ocean aquaculture often produces much higher than normal fish waste concentrations. The waste collects on the ocean bottom, damaging or eliminating bottom-dwelling life. Waste can also decrease dissolved oxygen levels in the water column, putting further pressure on wild animals.

FISH OILS

Tilapia from aquaculture has been shown to contain more fat and a much higher ratio of omega-6 to omega-3 oils.

IMPACTS ON WILD FISH

Salmon farming currently leads to a high demand for wild forage fish. Fish do not actually produce omega-3 fatty acids, but instead accumulate them from either consuming microalgae that produce these fatty acids, as is the case with forage fish like herring and sardines, or, as is the case with fatty predatory fish, like salmon, by eating prey fish that have accumulated omega-3 fatty acids from microalgae. To satisfy this requirement, more than 50 per cent of the world fish oil production is fed to farmed salmon.

In addition, as carnivores, salmon require large nutritional intakes of protein, protein which is often supplied to them in the form of forage fish. Consequently, farmed salmon consume more wild fish than they generate as a final product. To produce one pound of farmed salmon, products from several pounds of wild fish are fed to them. As the salmon farming industry expands, it requires more wild forage fish for feed, at a time when seventy five per cent of the worlds monitored fisheries are already near to or have exceeded their maximum sustainable yield.

The industrial scale extraction of wild forage fish for salmon farming then impacts the survivability of the wild predator fish who rely on them for food. Fish can escape from coastal pens, where they can interbreed with their wild counterparts, diluting wild genetic stocks. Escaped fish can become invasive, out competing native species.

COASTAL ECOSYSTEMS

Aquaculture is becoming a significant threat to coastal ecosystems. About 20 per cent of mangrove forests have been destroyed since 1980, partly due to shrimp farming. An extended cost–benefit analysis of the total economic value of shrimp aquaculture built on mangrove ecosystems found that the external costs were much higher than the external benefits. Over four decades, 269,000 hectares (660,000 acres) of Indonesian mangroves have been converted to shrimp farms. Most of these farms are abandoned within a decade because of the toxin build-up and nutrient loss.

Salmon farms are typically sited in pristine coastal ecosystems which they then pollute. A farm with 200,000 salmon discharges more fecal waste than a city of 60,000 people. This waste is discharged directly into the surrounding aquatic environment, untreated, often containing antibiotics and pesticides." There is also an accumulation of heavy metals on the benthos (seafloor) near the salmon farms, particularly copper and zinc.

GENETIC MODIFICATION

Salmon have been genetically modified for faster growth, although they are not approved for commercial use, in the face of opposition. One study, in a laboratory setting, found that modified salmon mixed with their wild relatives were aggressive in competing, but ultimately failed.

ANIMAL WELFARE

As with the farming of terrestrial animals, social attitudes influence the need for humane practices and regulations in farmed marine animals. Under the guidelines advised by the Farm Animal Welfare Council good animal welfare means both fitness and a sense of well being in the animal's physical and mental state.

This can be defined by the Five Freedoms:

1. Freedom from hunger and thirst

2. Freedom from discomfort
3. Freedom from pain, disease, or injury
4. Freedom to express normal behaviour
5. Freedom from fear and distress

However, the controversial issue in aquaculture is whether fish and farmed marine invertebrates are actually sentient, or have the perception and awareness to experience suffering. Although no evidence of this has been found in marine invertebrates, recent studies conclude that fish do have the necessary receptors (nociceptors) to sense noxious stimuli and so are likely to experience states of pain, fear and stress. Consequently, welfare in aquaculture is directed at vertebrates; finfish in particular.

COMMON WELFARE CONCERNS

Welfare in aquaculture can be impacted by a number of issues such as stocking densities, behavioural interactions, disease and parasitism. A major problem in determining the cause of impaired welfare is that these issues are often all interrelated and influence each other at different times. Optimal stocking density is often defined by the carrying capacity of the stocked environment and the amount of individual space needed by the fish, which is very species specific. Although behavioural interactions such as shoaling may mean that high stocking densities are beneficial to some species, in many cultured species high stocking densities may be of concern.

Crowding can constrain normal swimming behaviour, as well as increase aggressive and competitive behaviours such as cannibalism, feed competition, territoriality and dominance/subordination hierarchies. This potentially increases the risk of tissue damage due to abrasion from fish-to-fish contact or fish-to-cage contact. Fish can suffer reductions in food intake and food conversion efficiency. In addition, high stocking densities can result in water flow being insufficient, creating inadequate oxygen supply and waste product removal. Dissolved oxygen is essential for fish respiration and concentrations below critical levels can induce stress and even lead to asphyxiation. Ammonia, a nitrogen excretion product, is highly toxic to fish at accumulated levels, particularly when oxygen concentrations are low.

Many of these interactions and effects cause stress in the fish, which can be a major factor in facilitating fish disease. For many parasites, infestation depends on the host's degree of mobility, the density of the host population and vulnerability of the host's defence system. Sea lice are the primary parasitic problem for finfish in aquaculture, high numbers causing widespread skin erosion and haemorrhaging, gill congestion, and increased mucus production. There are also a number of prominent viral and bacterial pathogens that can have severe effects on internal organs and nervous systems.

IMPROVING WELFARE

The key to improving welfare of marine cultured organisms is to reduce stress to a minimum, as prolonged or repeated stress can cause a range of adverse effects. Attempts to minimise stress can occur throughout the culture process. During grow out it is important to keep stocking densities at appropriate levels specific to each species, as well as separating size classes and grading to reduce aggressive behavioural interactions. Keeping nets and cages clean can assist positive water flow to reduce the risk of water degradation.

Not surprisingly disease and parasitism can have a major effect on fish welfare and it is important for farmers not only to manage infected stock but also to apply disease prevention measures. However, prevention methods, such as vaccination, can also induce stress because of the extra handling and injection. Other methods include adding antibiotics to feed, adding chemicals into water for treatment baths and biological control, such as using cleaner wrasse to remove lice from farmed salmon.

Many steps are involved in transport, including capture, food deprivation to reduce faecal contamination of transport water, transfer to transport vehicle via nets or pumps, plus transport and transfer to the delivery location. During transport water needs to be maintained to a high quality, with regulated temperature, sufficient oxygen and minimal waste products. In some cases anaesthetics may be used in small doses to calm fish before transport. Aquaculture is sometimes part of an environmental rehabilitation programme or as an aid in conserving endangered species.

PROSPECTS

Global wild fisheries are in decline, with valuable habitat such as estuaries in critical condition. The aquaculture or farming of piscivorous fish, like salmon, does not help the problem because they need to eat products from other fish, such as fish meal and fish oil. Studies have shown that salmon farming has major negative impacts on wild salmon, as well as the forage fish that need to be caught to feed them. Fish that are higher on the food chain are less efficient sources of food energy.

Apart from fish and shrimp, some aquaculture undertakings, such as seaweed and filter-feeding bivalve mollusks like oysters, clams, mussels and scallops, are relatively benign and even environmentally restorative. Filter-feeders filter pollutants as well as nutrients from the water, improving water quality. Seaweeds extract nutrients such as inorganic nitrogen and phosphorus directly from the water, and filter-feeding mollusks can extract nutrients as they feed on particulates, such as phytoplankton and detritus.

Some profitable aquaculture cooperatives promote sustainable practices. New methods lessen the risk of biological and chemical pollution through minimizing fish stress, fallowing netpens, and applying Integrated Pest Management. Vaccines are being used more and more to reduce antibiotic use for disease control. Onshore recirculating aquaculture systems, facilities using polyculture techniques, and properly sited facilities (for example, offshore areas with strong currents) are examples of ways to manage negative environmental effects.

Recirculating aquaculture systems (RAS) recycle water by circulating it through filters to remove fish waste and food and then recirculating it back into the tanks. This saves water and the waste gathered can be used in compost or, in some cases, could even be treated and used on land. While RAS was developed with freshwater fish in mind, scientist associated with the Agricultural Research Service have found a way to rear saltwater fish using RAS in low-salinity waters. Although saltwater fish are raised in off-shore cages or caught with nets in water that typically has a salinity of 35 parts per thousand (ppt), scientists were able to produce healthy pompano, a saltwater fish, in tanks with a salinity of only 5 ppt. Commercialising low-salinity RAS are predicted to have positive environmental and economical effects. Unwanted nutrients from the fish food would not be added to the ocean and the risk of transmitting diseases between wild and farm-raised fish would greatly be reduced. The price of expensive saltwater fish, such as the pompano and combia used in the experiments, would be reduced. However, before any of this can be done researchers must study every aspect of the fish's lifecycle, including the amount of ammonia and nitrate the fish will tolerate in the water, what to feed the fish during each stage of its lifecycle, the stocking rate that will produce the healthiest fish, etc.

Some 16 countries now use geothermal energy for aquaculture, including China, Israel, and the United States. In California, for example, 15 fish farms produce tilapia, bass, and catfish with warm water from underground. This warmer water enables fish to grow all year round and mature more quickly. Collectively these California farms produce 4.5 million kilograms of fish each year.

AQUACULTURE ENGINEERING

DESIGN AND CONSTRUCTION FOR AQUACULTURE FACILITIES

Aquaculture draws on well-established engineering fields for most of the design and construction needs of its production facilities. Building earth ponds is similar to building roads — a knowledge of the characteristics of soils and the limits of safe design are the basis of good construction. Similarly, the buildings used for hatcheries and other support activities are no different from those common in the housing, agricultural and commercial sectors.

Sometimes ponds are lined with plastics or other impermeable materials, and here the techniques are similar to those for civil structures such as potable water reservoirs or sludge tanks. The design and installation of water control gates, including in unstable soils, benefits from the long experience in this field in the agriculture and irrigation sectors. An understanding of hydrodynamics allows ponds and tanks to be built with good water circulation, oxygen mixing and without 'dead spots' where sediments might accumulate and cause health problems to fish.

For installations in the sea, the situation is somewhat different and many of the important engineering solutions, such as for fish cages or suspended shellfish growout systems, have had to be developed by aquaculturists themselves. They have benefited however from the accumulated knowledge of seafarers in general and fishermen in particular, in the design and operation of mooring and buoyage systems. More recently, when fish farmers have turned their attention to how to operate fish cages in locations further offshore where seas are rougher, the experience of the oil exploration industry has proven very valuable.

MODERN TECHNIQUES

Techniques have been developed in recent years for the production of fish and other aquatic products in closed recirculation systems. To make these work, aquaculturists have needed to develop a knowledge of the biological processes operating — such as how bacteria can be used to neutralise and re-cycle the nitrogenous waste products produced by growing fish — and how to engineer the systems to meet the biological requirements. Knowledge of bio-engineering from the waste treatment and water treatment industries has made contributions to the development of closed aquaculture systems and there is probably more that could be usefully transferred from the sewage treatment sector to help solve problems in fish rearing.

Modern materials have brought many benefits to aquaculture. For instance, custom made plastic joints have simplified the construction of sea cages, and made them more reliable in high stress conditions. Experiments with huge free-floating or sunken net cages operated in the open ocean were begun several decades ago, for instance in the Caspian Sea. These showed some promise, but more reliable construction materials will make the farming of fish in such structures increasingly feasible. Modern materials and production methods have been important also, in the construction of plastic filter substrates for indoor recirculating systems. The fine detail of these has been found to make substantial differences to the efficiency of biological filters.

In shrimp farms, specially designed matting materials that stand upright on pond bottoms, with a structure that promotes the growth of the small animals and plants that the shrimp can thrive on, have recently been developed and shown to boost production.

ENGINEERING SKILLS

Engineering skills are important in the design of most aquaculture facilities and good engineering can affect the efficiency and economics of production. If capital costs can be minimised while still maximising productivity and reducing risk, the farming operation will be more profitable.

Aquaculturists have proven very innovative over the past fifty years, constantly developing new technologies to support their farming operations. As new production methods and species for farming are developed, the engineering solutions needed to support them will continue to evolve.

2

Aquaculture Extension

Aquaculture contributes significantly to the rural economy of most of the Asian and other developing countries by providing part- and full-time occupation to the farmers, fishermen and landless agricultural labourers. India and other developing countries of the South Asian region are endowed with ample water resources in the shape of freshwater ponds and tanks for fish culture, but these are not under effective and optimum utilization in spite of highly developed available technologies.

Research results have shown excellent production potential as well as economic viability of such technologies, but until these technologies are successfully transferred to the beneficiaries, the desired objective cannot be achieved. Like agriculture, aquaculture is also an agroclimatic-based technology which, when developed in one agroclimatic region, may need modifications and refinement for adoption to another region. Agriculture extension thus involves not only the extension of aquaculture technology, but also certain levels of adoptive research in a particular field environment before it is launched for large-scale extension.

It is a two-way education process in which both scientists and farmers contribute, receive and interact with the involvement of extension workers as a link between the two and a catalyst as well (model). In other words, it is a non-formal adult education programme for educating and training the rural mass to acquire suitable fish farming skills and capabilities with a view to boosting fish production efficiency and the socio-economic condition.

Aquaculture extension is basically an educational process by means of which scientific and technological knowledge of aquaculture is carried to the farmers to upgrade their existing operation and farm management skills. The philosophy behind this process is to change the altitude, enhance the skill and knowledge of the fish farmers to upgrade their aquaculture practice.

It also aims at binging maximum possible unutilized and under-utilized water areas under modern fish culture operation so as to raise the standard of living of the fish farmers through improving productivity and profitability. Apart from achieving its own target its overall objective is also to signifiantly contribute towards rural development by improving rural economy, creating additional gainful employment opportunities, fighting malnutrition and preventing rural exodus.

LAUNCHING AQUACULTURE TENSION PROGRAMME

Any aquaculture extension programme is designed based upon broad national consideration to achieve national goals and targets viz-a-viz local considerations to achieve short-term objectives such as application of composite fish culture in undrainable ponds to improve the aquaculture production level. A local aquaculture extension programme is relatively more definite in terms of scope and target. Like any other aquaculture extension programme, there should be three sequential steps for the dissemination of fish culture technology in undrainable ponds. They are as follows:

- Programme planning
- Programme implementation
- Programme evaluation

PROGRAMME PLANNING

While planning the dissemination of fish culture technology one should always bear in mind that the programme should be a self-regenerating production endeavour and once it is stimulated should continue on its own with a changed attitude and active participation of the recipient. This involves situation-specific strategies. The main components of programme planning are pre-adoption survey of the area, situation analysis, setting programme goals and finally designing strategies in a sequential manner.

Village Survey

Fish culture is basically a rural farming system and hence village survey is the most common method for identification of the difficulties faced by the farmers and to find out the scope and suitability of a specific technology needing to be transferred. The main objective is to get an overall picture of the village and the villagers, their attitude, values, together with their socio-economic conditions and also to locate and assess the available freshwater resources.

It also helps to identify the local institutions, village leaders, progressive farmers, school teachers, village level workers in order to design the most feasible extension strategy and also to establish a permanent rapport to strengthen the extension services.

At micro level it provides information about the socio-economic conditions of individual fish farmers, the pattern of fish farming and the technological gap. The village selected for the survey should be such that it may represent the locality. Regular contact with important and progressive farmers of the village should be maintained. They should be informed about the objectives of the survey proposed to be undertaken.

Interviews with these persons will provide an overall picture of available natural and human resources and possible areas for development. Finally detailed relevant information may be collected from individual pond owners/ fish farmers and fishermen through personal interviews/questionnaires.

Resource Inventory

- *Availability of water resources:* Various types of water resources are available for fish culture but usually all of them are not fully utilized. Large, medium and smaller types of water bodies are generally available in villages which may be suitable for fish culture. Many small water bodies are found fully shaded by large marginal trees and thereby lying unproductive. Some unconventional types of water areas with potentiality for intensive aquaculture are also available.
  Canal/road and village side small and large ditches, pits emerging due to construction of mud houses etc., are some of the unnoticed and untrapped potential aquaculture resources suitable for seed production and short-term fish rearing.
  Low-lying and swampy areas which are formed naturally due to human activities are also potential sites for undrainable ponds for fish culture.
- *Availability of human resources:* It is a well-known fact that the majority of the people in developing countries live in villages and most of the rural population depend upon agriculture, aquaculture, livestock farming and other allied activities for their livelihood. Human resources are the vital inputs in rural aquaculture development. Rural areas have vast potential of unutilized or underutilized human resources for both men and women, which can be effectively utilized in operating aquaculture.
- *Identification of possible constraints:* A village survey also offers an excellent opportunity to identify various constraints in the background of which an appropriate strategy can be suitably designed.

Financial

Farmers usually do not have surplus funds big enough to be diverted towards reclamation and renovation of existing watersheds as well as construction of new ponds. Initial expenditure for fish culture over fish toxicant, fish seed and supplementary feed is itself a considerably big amount to be exclusively borne by farmers themselves without any credit support. As such, possible sources for mobilizing credit facilities may be identified.

Improper Water Area Distribution Pattern

Like land distribution pattern, major water areas are usually found in the possession of medium and big farmers who bother least about fish culture and concentrate themselves mostly on agriculture, while small and marginal farmers have minimum water holdings at their disposal with adequate manpower potential to be utilized. In some areas most of the water bodies are vested to village institutions, local administrative bodies, etc.

Lack of Technical Knowhow

Several seasonal and perennial ponds without any proper embankments are found lying fallow in a derelict condition due to ignorance and lack of technical knowhow. In some cases farmers fail to follow-up the prescribed package of practices strictly and land themselves in a state of financial turmoil and lose confidence in the viability of newly developed fish farming technologies.

Lack of Stocking Materials and Other Material Inputs

Fish farmers usually face the biggest problem of unavailability of quality fish seed for stocking their pond. Paucity of quality fish seed in the locality force the farmers to stock their ponds without any consideration to proper stocking size, density, species, ratio, etc.

At times, they procure riverine fish seed which is usually mixed with the seeds of predatory and weed fishes. Other material such as fish toxicants are usually localised in its availability. All such problems are also vital for deciding area specific extension strategies.

Marketing Problem

It is a general practice that the fish is sold to middlemen at the pond site who invariably pay lower prices. Due to the perishable nature of the commodity and fear of exploitation by the fish wholesellers, farmers prefer to sell the crop at their pond/farm sites even at relatively lower rates. Information related to marketing practices will add to the scope of the extension programme so that farmers may be educated in marketing management to avoid such exploitation.

Lack of Transport and Efficient Communication System

In remote villages of India and many developing countries where fish culture technology needs to be extended, proper transport and communication facilities are lacking.

Social and Administrative Problems

Ponds remaining unutilized and lying in derelict conditions are common sights in rural areas in spite of a certain level of fish culture know how available with the farmers. In most cases such conditions exist due to family rivalry and non-cooperation among the members of the owners especially when the water areas are under multi-ownership. Poaching and deliberate poisoning of the ponds to destroy the crop are also serious social problems.

In some areas fish culture is supposed to be of a low-caste profession, thus many efficient upper-caste prople remain reluctant to come forward for this venture. Local administration such as Panchayats and Block Level Development Departments are also not always suitable geared enough to ensure rural aquaculture development.

Setting Programme Goals and Planning

In the light of resource inventory and possible limitations suitable target groups may be identified, programme goals may be set up and accordingly suitable extension strategy may be planned. Without such an early insight and planning, the programme may not have firm and realistic footing. Although the fish farmers are the usual target of any fish culture extension programme, all the fish farmers may not be suitable to be involved for immediate participation.

Target groups may be selected on a number of criteria including farming practice, production level, income, education, cultural background, nature, reputation in the society, initiative, liable to change their attitude, etc. Selection of suitable communication channels is also very important. Data collected during the pre-adoption survey provide the necessary information for such selection.

After these selections, programme goals may be set up. Goals indicate the direction towards which the programme is oriented. It also provides reference level for evaluating the programme achievements. Examples of goals in such extension programme may be on the following lines:

- Improving the socio-economic uplift of fish farmers and raising the standard of living;
- Bringing 100 per cent of the available undrainable ponds for composite fish culture.

Programme Implementation

"Plan the work and work the plan" is an appropriate term for any extension programme. Once the plan is laid, all possible efforts should be diverted to ensure that responsibilities are carried out, schedules are followed arid activities accomplished as per the plan.

Although the strategies and planning of the aquaculture extension programme are situation specific, some general steps may be cited as follows;

- Through heavy flow of information using mass media, publications, individual and mass contacts, etc., awareness and interest should be created among fish farmers.

- One or two demonstration centres may be set up and the technology of composite fish culture and seed production in undrainable ponds may be demonstrated to maximum possible farmers to let them realize the case of operation, production potential and profitability.
- A set of suitable farmers should be selected initially and be motivated and guided enough so that they strictly follow the different package of practices as per the schedule.
- Proper steps may also be taken to make available the critical material inputs at the pond/farm sites and if the programme permits, subsidy should be given as a token of initial attraction.
- If the availability of quality fish seed is found to be a limiting factor, fish seed may be distributed free of cost or at concessional rate to the farmers at the initial stage. Proper attention may also be paid for extending fish breeding and seed rearing programmes.
- Facilities for proper monitoring of water quality and fish health may be extended through the participation of nearby laboratories.
- Periodical netting for growth check/health inspection should be strictly followed and supervised.
- Self-explanatory/pictorial instruction booklets dealing with basic steps of composite fish culture, control breeding of common carp, techniques of pituitary gland collection, induced breeding of major carps, hatchery operation for carps, nursery and rearing pond managements, techniques of fish seed transport, etc., may be prepared, explained and distributed among farmers.
- *Ad hoc* training courses should be organized at the demonstration sites on different aspects of fish culture and fish seed production for participating and other interested farmers. Exhibition programme/Fish Farmer's Day should be organized time to time at different places in which live specimens of all the six carp species, other culturable air-breathing fishes, harmful predatory species, weeds, fish feeds, fish toxicants, etc., should be shown and the objective and goal of the programme may be exhibited through models, charts, posters, etc.
- At times a team of a few farmers may be selected on the basis of their leadership quality and performance and sent to visit important aquaculture centres, farms, research institutions, etc.
- Individual contacts through home visits is a very effective extension method. The extension worker must be very clear in this objective during the visit and must do sufficient preparation with regard to subject matter information he is going to deliver to the fish farmer and family members.
- Evening is the most suitable time for organizing an assembly of farmers. Necessary details about practices to be followed the next

day may be explained to them during such assemblies. Teaching aids may be used to make the communication effective.

Programme Evaluation

Programme evaluation is the process to determine the extent of success of the executed extension programme in the light of present objectives. It is an important management function in order to ensure effective implementation of the programme. It also helps in the identification of the deficiencies and weakness of the programme so that proper corrective measures may be taken to make it more useful in its future course.

Programme evaluation can be conducted once a year or at a specific period of the programme and finally at the concluding phase of the programme. The process of evaluation also depends upon the nature of the programme. A short term and less extensive localized extension programme may be evaluated by the extension workers themselves through the analysis of progress reports, field records, questionnaires, etc. However, broad-based and elaborate extension programmes can be evaluated by specialists in association with the extension workers to determine the effectiveness and impact of the extension programme.

It is convenient to fractionate the whole programme into smaller components for effective and easy evaluation. Fractionation may be done as follows:

- Resources (financial, personnel an material) made available.
- Objective of the programme in clear terms.
- Phases of the programme (evaluation should also be done phase-wise).
- Data collection from records and tabulation.
- Selection of ways, means and methods for the collection of data/ information from participating, non-participating fish farmers, village youths, prominent persons of the locality, etc.
- Sample selection
- Collection of data/information from target and non-target groups
- Tabulation of data
- Data analysis and interpretation of results

To measure the degree of success, certain values have to be associated with the information. Increased fish production level, profit through increased fish yields, knowledge of modern management techniques, fish breeding, fish seed rearing, increased number of ponds/water areas in the area, etc. are some of such measurable values for programme evaluation.

IMPORTANT CONSIDERATIONS

- Extension services can be made most effective by making the people understand, accept and adopt the new technology, as it is very much clear from statistical data that people remember 10 per cent of what they hear, 40–50 per cent of what they see and hear and 90 per cent of what they see, hear and do.

- Maximum potential for development of undrainable pond fish culture lies in developing countries where the prevailing literacy level is lowest.
- The personality profile of extension workers is of prime importance for the extension of any rural-based aquaculture technology. He must mould himself enough so that he may become technical by profession, social by temperament and preserve human values and missionary zeal of serving the rural poor. He should be simple, easily approachable and adaptable enough so that he can live among fish farmers. At the same time he must not have any inferiority complex while meeting with specialists and higher bureaucrats.
- The target groups of aquaculture extension programmes are usually socio-economically backward rural masses having a low level of literacy and technical knowhow and are reluctant to bring about quick changes in their attitude.
- Many extension departments and voluntary organizations are also of the opinion that the gains of socio-economic and technological development progrmames do net reach the rural poor and that the roots of this failure lies in the lack of organization of the poor themselves. Field workers experience very often instances of diversion of financial grants meant for production programmes for the small and marginal farmers into consumption subsidies. Similarly, there are numerous instances where free educational facilities are granted for children of rural poor, but they hardly avail the opportunity as they are treated as helping hands for supplementing family income. Most of the resources allocated for various welfare activities of the rural poor, however, are diverted into activities totally unrelated to mass welfare. The fact is that the poor are not only poor but are disorganized and hence they have very little influence in the process of decision-making and implementation of the programme. Under such conditions the concept of community fish farming may also be considered as an effective and ideal method for organizing at least a section of the rural poor/fish farmers/fishermen in cooperative and productive communication.
- Support services and credit facilities are the two important factors which play major roles in the aquaculture development programme. Lack of appropriate support services and proper credit facilities are the major drawbacks.

- Effective institutional support to provide the necessary technical services needed by the extension programme, such as site selection, pond designing, fish health check, pond environment monitoring, etc., are vital for programme implementation.

3

Sustainability Aquaculture

SUSTAINABLE AQUACULTURE

Aquaculture is currently one of the fastest growing food production systems in the world. Most of the global aquaculture output is produced in developing countries and significantly in low-income food-deficit countries. As defined by the united food nations Food and Agriculture Organisation (FAO), aquaculture is the "farming of aquatic organisms including fish, mollusks, crustaceans and aquatic plants. With stagnating yields from many capture fisheries and increasing demand for fish and fishery products, expectations for aquaculture to increase its contribution to the world's production of aquatic food are very high, and there is also hope that aquaculture will continue to strengthen its role in contributing to food security and poverty alleviation in many developing countries.

However, it is also recognised that aquaculture encompasses a very wide range of different aquatic farming practices with regard to species (including seaweeds, molluscs, crustaceans, fish and other aquatic species groups), environments and systems utilised, with very distinct resource use patterns involved, offering a wide range of options for diversification of avenues for enhanced food production and income generation in many rural and peri-urban areas.

WHAT IS SUSTAINABLE DEVELOPMENT

Though living resources are self-renewable, they have to be utilised rationally on a sustainable basis in harmony with the environment. Sustainable development is the management and conservation of the natural resource base and the orientation of technological and institutional change in such a manner as to ensure the attainment and continued satisfaction of human needs for present and future generations.

Such sustainable development (in the agriculture, forestry and fisheries sectors) conserves land, water, plant and animal genetic resources and it is environmentally non-degrading, technically appropriate, economically viable and socially acceptable.

NEED FOR SUSTAINABLE DEVELOPMENT

Aquaculture now accounts for roughly one third of the world's total supply of food fish and undoubtedly the contribution of aquaculture to sea food supplies will increase in the future. Aquaculture has potential to become a sustainable practice that can supplement capture fisheries and significantly contribute to feeding the world's growing population. Aquaculture is the fastest growing sector of the world food economy, increasing by more than 10 per cent per year and currently accounts for more than 30 per cent of all fish consumed.

Aquaculture, in common with all other food production practices, is facing challenges for sustainable development. Most aqua-farmers, like their terrestrial counterparts, are continuously pursuing ways and means of improving their production practices, to make them more efficient and cost-effective. Awareness of potential environmental problems has increased significantly. Efforts are under way to further improve human capacity, resource use and environmental management in aquaculture. COFI emphasized enhancement of inland fish production through integrated aquaculture-agriculture farming systems and integrated utilisation of small and medium-size water bodies.

Unsustainable aquaculture will only generate short and medium term profits for multinational corporations at the expense of long-term ecological balance and social stability. An unsustainable aquaculture development could exacerbate the problems and create new ones, damaging our important and already stressed coastal areas. Sustainable development alternatives are needed to ensure that in the future aquaculture can contribute to the growing need for seafood products. The sustainable development includes- "the management and conservation of natural resource base, and the orientation of technological and institutional change in such a manner to ensure the attainment and continued satisfaction for present and future generations. Such developments conserve land, water, plant and genetic resources as well they are environmentally non-degrading, technologically appropriate, economically viable and socially acceptable.

The promotion of sustainable aquaculture development requires that "enabling environments", in particular those aimed at ensuring continuing human resource development and capacity building, are created and maintained. The FAO Code of Conduct for Responsible Fisheries contains principles and provisions in support of sustainable aquaculture development. The Code recognises the Special Requirements of Developing Countries, and its Article 5 addresses in particular these needs, especially in the areas of financial and technical assistance, technology transfer, training and scientific cooperation.

There are a number of alternatives for sustainable development of aquaculture which include ecological aquaculture, organic aquaculture, composite fish culture, integrated aquaculture and closed recirculatory systems.

ECOLOGICAL AQUACULTURE

Ecological aquaculture has been defined as- "an alternative model of aquaculture research and development that brings the technical aspects of ecological principles and ecosystem thinking to aquaculture and concerns for the wider social, economic and environmental context of aquaculture".

There are few main principles of aquaculture:

- To preserve the form and function of natural resources
- To ensure trophic level efficiency
- To use native species so as not to contribute to biological pollution
- To share the practices and information on a global scale
- To ensure that system is integrated into the local economy and community in terms of food production and employment

Ecological aquaculture focuses on the development of farming systems that protect the environments in which they are situated and enhances the quality of these environments while at the same time maintaining a productive culture system.

ORGANIC AQUACULTURE

Sustainability is one of the main goals of organic food production.

Some of the basic principles of organic aquaculture according to the International Federation of Organic Agriculture Movements are as follows:

- To encourage natural biological cycles in the production of aquatic organisms
- Using various methods of disease control
- No use of synthetic fertilizer or other chemicals in production
- Use of polyculture technologies whenever possible

POLYCULTURE AND INTEGRATED AQUACULTURE

Polyculture and integrated aquaculture are methods of raising diverse organisms within the same farming systems, where each species utilises a distinct niche and distinct resources within the farming complex. This may involve the rearing of several aquatic organisms together or in conjunction with terrestrial plants or animals. Polyculture system can provide mutual benefits to the organisms reared by allowing for a balanced use of the available aquatic resources while integrated systems can increase the economic efficiency through improved conversion rates of input materials. The waste from one organism is used as input to another resulting in the optimal use of resources and less pollution overall. Although still experimental, other systems such as- integration of sea weed, fish and abalone culture and polyculture of shrimp and tilapia, have proved to be ecologically efficient methods for growing a variety of organisms and may increase profit at fish farms.

RECIRCULATING SYSTEM

Concerns for water conservation and reduced waste discharges have realised the use of closed recirculating aquaculture systems. This system is made up of three basic components: culture chamber, settling chamber and biological filter. Water enters the culture chamber, flows through the settling chamber and then moves through the biological filter to remove additional particulate matter. The water is then circulated back through the system culture chamber.

Recirculating systems conserve water and allow control of environmental factors (temperature, salinity and oxygen), predators and introduction and transfer of diseases. This system has less impact on environment because of their close nature - wastes and uneaten feed are not simply released in the ambient environment. In recirculating system, wastes are filtered out of the culture system and disposed of in a responsible manner.

In order for aquaculture to develop into an environmentally and socially responsible food production endeavour, following points should be recommended:

- Implement more ecologically sustainable practices
- Transition to use of closed systems and low discharge systems, especially those that provide total containment of fish and recovery or reuse of wastes
- Significantly decrease or eliminate the dependence on wild fisheries
- Develop sustainable aquaculture operations that provide long term social and economic benefits to communities

INTEGRATED FISH FARMING: RATIONALE AND SCOPE

INTRODUCTION

Nowadays, the economy is mainly based on the field of agriculture and software development in the area of Information Technology. For achieving rapid progress in rural area, our strategy must focus on; conserving natural resources, enhancing efficient use of resources, increasing productivity and profitability and improving quality and competitiveness through reduced unit cost of production.

Water is emerging as international challenge and its most efficient management as well as recycling has been given high priority in the plan of formulation. Recycling of crop residue as well as agricultural by products inclusion of nitrogen fixing legumes in rotation, bio fertilizers, vermicultres, agro forestry, nutrient solublising micro-organisms, efficient nutrient up taking plant varieties etc. are being strategies in the research mandate. Improved efficiency of farm machinery, agro- input and resource conservation technologies of minimum tillage are being researched to minimize the cost of production.

Integrated Fish Farming is one of the best examples of mixed farming. This type of farming practices in different forms mostly in the East and South East Asian countries is one of the important ecological balanced sustainable technologies. The technology involves a combination of fish polyculture integrated with crop or live stock production. On farm waste recycling, an important component of integrated fish farming is highly advantageous to the farmers as it improves the economy of production and decrease the adverse environmental impact of farming.

Integrated fish farming refers to the simultaneous culture of fish or shell fish along with other culture systems. It may also be defined as the sequential linkage between two or more culture practices. Generally integrated farming means the production or culture of two or more farming practices but when fish becomes its major component it is called as integrated fish farming. Fish culture can be integrated with several systems for efficient resource utilisation. The integration of aquaculture with livestock or crop farming provides quality protein food, resource utilisation, recycling of farm waste, employment generation and economic development. Integrated fish farming is well developed culture practice in China followed by Hungary, Germany and Malaysia. Our country, India, is organic-based and derives inputs from agriculture and animal husbandry. The integrated fish farming is accepted as a sustainable form of aquaculture. For integration we can use recycled effluents from agro-based industries as well as food processing plants.

Integrated fish farming serves as a model of sustainable food production by following certain principles:

- The waste products of one biological system serve as nutrients for a second biological system.
- The integration of fish and plants results in a polyculture that increases diversity and yields multiple products.
- Water is re-used through biological filtration and recirculation.
- Local food production provides access to healthy foods and enhances the local economy.

ECOSYSTEM OF INTEGRATED AQUACULTURE

The integrated fish farming includes:

- Process of trapping solar energy,

- Production of organic material by primary producers (autotrophs),
- Its utilisation by phagotrophs,
- Decomposition of autotrophs and phagotrophs by saprotrophs,
- Release of nutrients for autotrophs.

ADVANTAGES OF INTEGRATED FISH FARMING

- Efficient waste utilisation from different culture practice for fish production.
- It reduces the additional cost for supplementary feeding as well as fertilisation.
- It is an artificial balanced ecosystem where there is no waste.
- It provides more employment avenues.
- It reduces the input and increases output and economic efficiency.
- The integrated fish farming provides fish along with meat (chicken, duck, beef, pork etc.), milk, vegetables, fruits, eggs, grains, fodder, mushroom etc.
- This practice has potential to increase the production and socio-economic status of weaker section of our society.

TYPES OF INTEGRATED FISH FARMING

Basically the integrated fish farming is of two types:

1. Agri-based fish farming
2. Live-stock fish farming

The fish-cum live-stock farming is realised as innovation for recycling of organic wastes as well as production of high class protein at low cost.

4

Fish Business Analysis

Fishes form one of the most important group of vertebrates influencing man's life in various ways. Millions of human beings suffer due to hunger and malnutrition, and fishes form a rich source of food and provide a means to tide over the nutritional deficiencies of man.

In addition to serving as an important item of food, fishes provide several by-products to us. The importance of fish as food has been understood by man from antiquity.

Fishes are found abundantly in all natural waters. The importance of fish in diet lies in the chemical composition of the flesh, which is rich in protein and minerals like calcium, phosphorus and iron. Some fishes in addition have varying quantities of fat and oil..

In spite of the various advantages of fish, as a valuable source of food, its availability is rather restricted in India on account of the limited fishing industry. This fact can be best illustrated if we compare the annual catches of various countries expressed in metric tons. Japan 4.7; U.S.A, 2.9; USSR 2.6; China 2.5; Norway 2.1; Canada 1.07; UK 1.05. India with its large water resources has only about 1.10 m tons of fish catch per year.

The consumption of fish per person in India is about 1.52 kg/year, which is perhaps the lowest in the world. Although fishes are abundant in our seas, rivers and lakes, they have become popular only in those states which are bordered by the sea, or where large rivers and their tributaries flow. With a growing population and lack of facilities like transport and refrigeration. The interior regions of the country have little or no supply of fresh fishes.

The term aquaculture relates to the culture of aquatic organisms in fresh, brackish or sea water. Traditionally, fishes are netted from the sea or from rivers, lakes and ponds.

This is called capture fishery. The catch from fresh water has increased almost by five time whereas marine production has increased only by three times. India has a vast coastline and large number of fresh water resources has tremendous potential tor aquaculture. About 2.6

million hectares of brackish water are available in addition to many perennial rivers, lakes and ponds where aquaculture can be easily carried out. Aquaculture does not require skilled labour and even women folk and children with basic training can undertake the work effectively. Aquaculture also promises employment potential of up to 9 lakh people. If to accelerate aquaculture development, immediate steps are required to be taken by the centre and state agencies, including adequate financing through banks or other organisations.

The following sound steps should be initiated early to put aquaculture on a sound footing:

- Survey and demarcation of the inland water resources.
- Survey and demarcation of the brackish water resources.
- Survey and demarcation of the near shore sea water resources.
- Collection of suitable seed for stocking.
- Establishment of viable fish seed farms.
- Establishment of hatcheries.
- Rearing and culture of fish in reservoirs.
- Improved fishing methods.

An ordinary fish farmer can easily achieve production targets of at least 3 tonnes/ha/year after receiving some training. A few fish farms for aquaculture have been established recently. However, the need for more such farms is quite evident.

THE ORIGIN OF FISHES

Life originated in the sea is an accepted fact. Fishes have had a long history. There first emergence occurred about 430 million years ago. It is estimated that there are about 30,000- 40,000 species of fishes living today. They are second to insects in population and first among the vertebrates, mammals, birds, reptiles and amphibians put together.

The clue to the first fish is found in the geologic period, the Ordovician (360-400 million years ago). Fishes as we have seen belong to the sub kingdom or phylum Chordata. The evolution of fish type was gradual, and it is among the lower chordates, Amphioxus (lancelet), Assidians (sea squirt) and the Balanoglossids (acorn worms) we have to search the probable ancestor of the fishes.

GENERAL CHARACTERISTICS AND CLASSIFICATION OF FISHES

Fishes are cold blooded vertebrates that breathe by means of gills and live in water. They comprise about 30,000 to 40,000 species differing widely from each other in shape, size, habits and habitats. Fishes usually have a stream lined body but some are elongated and a few are dorsoventrally compressed. They have paired and unpaired fins supported by soft or spiny rays. Dorsal, caudal and the anal fins are un-paired while the pectoral and pelvic fins are paired.

Fishes have the following common characters, which are due to their permanently aquatic life:

- Organs of respiration are the gills.
- Locomotary organs are the paired and unpaired fins.
- An exoskeleton of scales is usually present but some species are naked secondarily.
- The notochord is partly replaced by cartilaginous or long vertebrae.
- Paired visceral arches are present. The first pair form the upper and lower jaws, the second forms suspensorium and the rest support the gills.
- There is no middle ear
- A swim bladder is usually present, but is secondarily lost in some species.
- Kidney is mesonephric (linked with reproductive system).

The skin of fishes is covered with protective scale and is abundantly coated with mucus. Organs of smell, sight, and hearing are found on the head.

Eyes are devoid of eyelids and the ears which are without external or middle parts are sunk within the skull bones. Most fishes lay eggs which hatch directly into larvae, although a few bring forth alive their young ones which develop for a period in the uterus of the mother.

Fishes of the present day world may be broadly grouped into three important subclasses: 1. Cyclostomes, 2. Cartilaginous fishes and 3. Bony fishes.

1. The cyslostomes are the primitive types of fishes (less evolved). They consists of lampreys and hagfishes which are the survivors of a very old and peculiar group.
2. The cartilaginous fishes are those with cartilageous comprise of sharks, rays and allied fishes in which the internal skeleton remains cartilagious throughout their life, bones being absent. One of the well known sharks of the Indian seas is Scoliodon. Sharks are the largest fishes living today.
3. The bony fishes, are those, in which bone is the chief t tissue of skeleton as compared to cartilage. In several i ways bony fishes are a higher group and embrace three i distinct subdivision, the lobefins, the lung fishes and the modem teleosts (a group of bony fishes).

FISHERIES OF INDIA

The topic of Indian fisheries is a wide one. It shall be dealt under following heads: marine fisheries, inland fisheries, fishing craft and gears and preservation, processing and uses.

MARINE FISHERIES

Fisheries related to sea are called marine fisheries. They are considered under coastal and offshore and deep sea fisheries.

Coastal

Marine fisheries resources of a country depend on a number of factors. The oceanographical features of a sea have a direct bearing on the fish fauna and the nature of fisheries. The chemical nature of the water, salt-contents and nutrients are intimately related to the production of plankton which form the food of fishes. Besides, the land beneath the seas (the continental shelter), its area and slope also, to some extent determine the facilities for fishing. It is estimated that more than 75 per cent of the total fish landings are from the west coast.

Off Shore and Deep Sea

Beyond the area of the continental shelf lies the expansive ocean, rich in various kinds of fishes. Some of them are surface or mid water dweller while others live in deeper waters or at the bottom of the sea. The exploitation of these fish fauna constitutes off-shore and deep sea fisheries. These were not given much importance in India owing to lack of mechanised or power boats and enterprising business. Besides, the economic conditions of fisher men did not permit large capital necessary for power-fishing. Deep sea fishery to be successful should have harbour and anchorage facilities, motor transport from landing place to centres of distribution and consumption, marketing and storage facilities, besides scientifically trained men.

INLAND FISHERIES

India has a large number of rivers, innumerable irrigation channels, tanks reservoirs, etc. All these bodies of water, both big and small, provide rich resources for inland fisheries. For convenience, these are considered under the following three sub headings.

Estuarine Fisheries

These fisheries are located in the mouths of the rivers Ganges, Mahanadi, Godavari, Krishna, Cauvery on the east coast and Narmada, and Tapti on the west coast Estuaries and estuarine lakes have saline waters and only those fishes which can withstand in salty conditions thrive best.

Riverine Fisheries

The major rivers of India the Indus, the Ganges, the Mahanandi, Kaveri, Krishna and the lesser ones -with their tributaries and canals, the inland lakes, streams, springs, pools, tanks provide varied habitats for the large population of fishes. In order of their economic importance these are major carps, cat fishes, line fishes, etc.

Pond Culture

Culturing of certain types of fishes in wells, garden ponds or domestic and temple tanks is an old practice in India. Realising the significant and nutritional values of fish in the diet of the people, various states established Fishery Departments, with the aim of exploiting the vast water resources by improving fish culture, techniques on scientific lines. During the last few decades the idea of rearing fish in large ponds and tanks on a systematic plan for commercial purpose has taken roots in several states.

Fishing Craft and Gear

The nets or gears and other devices for catching fishes are also numerous and ingenious. But both craft and gear were invented centuries ago and have remained static and have shown little or no change or improvement in India, unlike in other maritime countries. The fishing craft and gear can be considered under the following heads. They are: marine fishing craft and gear used in the sea, inland crafts and gears used in the rivers of inland and mechanised craft used both in the sea and inland.

Preservation and Processing

As fish is a highly perishable commodity various methods have been devised to preserve it. These include, drying, salting, smoking, canning, and the recent modem methods of freezing with ice or store in electrical refrigerator.

METHODS OF FISHING

Man has been using various methods to catch fish since the pre-historic times, and the fishing gear has undergone evolution in different parts of the world giving rise to various methods of the present day. The fishing gear along with the vessel, auxiliary equipment and men constitutes a "fishing unit". The size of a fishing unit is determined by the distance of fishing grounds from the shore, handling and disposal of catch as well as geographical factors.

The entire period between the launching of a fishing gear and launching it again after a gap is called a "fishing cycle", and includes the period for launching, hauling, emptying the net, repair and getting ready for the next launch. The number of fishing cycles per day depends upon the daily pattern of occurrence (density) of fishes, types of fishing methods used, geographical conditions of the fishing grounds and the fishermen.

It is difficult to enumerate all the fishing methods in use in various parts of India and there is no uniformity in the names given to various fishing gears used in commercial fisheries. Some of common methods are being enlisted here.

They are:

- Fishing without gear,
- Wounding gear,
- Stupefying methods,
- Line fishing,
- Fishing by baited springs,
- Fish screens,
- Fish traps,
- Trap for jumping fish,
- Dip net or lift net,
- Cast net (ghagaria jal),
- Triangular net,
- Purse net,
- Drug net,
- Gill and drift nets, and
- Electrical fishing.

CONSTRUCTION AND MAINTENANCE OF A FISH FARM

A fish culturist needs different types of ponds for rearing various stages of fish, and has to decide on the layout of his farm and its fish and its extent. The design of the fish farm and the number and size of the ponds depends on the species of the fish to be cultured. The primary consideration in constructing a fish farm is the site which has to be selected on the basis of soil, water supply and drainage.

LOCATION OF A FISH FARM

Success in fish farming and economy of the construction would depend largely on the selection of a suitable site tor the farm.

The main considerations are:

- Topography,
- Soil type, and
- Water supply.

LAYOUT OF THE FISH FARM

Before starting the construction, the layout plans have to be drawn for the location design and the number of various types of ponds. A fish farm consists of 4 or 5 type of ponds, each for a specific purpose.

They are:

- Hatching pits,
- Nursing ponds,
- Rearing ponds and
- Stocking ponds.

An ideal fish farm of 5 acres should have the following arrangement as mentioned in table.

Table. Arrangement for Different Types of Ponds in a 5 Acre (2 ha) Farm.

Sl. No	Type of Pond	No. of Ponds	Size in Feet
1	Hatching pits	6	8′ × 4′ × 2′
2	Nursery ponds	4	50′ × 50′ × 4′
3	Rearing ponds	12	40′ × 30′ × 4′
4	Stocking ponds	6	300′ × 80′ × 6′

For a good fish pond, the slope of embankment should be 2:1.

POND MAINTENANCE AND IMPROVEMENT

The productivity of the pond depends upon its soil base, and can be greatly enhanced by controlling the vegetation, cleaning the pond bottom, lining, and fertilizer application.

ARTIFICIAL FEEDING

Fish production can be increased by artificial feeding. The fish feed should be simple and cheap. Whole grain flour, rice bran, oil cake, and kitchen waste are generally used as fish food.

Fish meal, meat meal, meat and blood is also use two. The food can be kept in baskets or spread on the water.

Formulation of artificial feeds for any fish requires a knowledge of nutritional requirement at different life stages ranging from larval to juvenile to grow out adult phases.

Underfeeding can result in loss of production. Over feeding will cause a wastage of expensive feed and additionally a potential cause of water pollution, which is a major causative factor of loss of animals.

FISHING OR HARVESTING

This is done by draining the pond or netting. By draining, harvesting is complete and predators can be eliminated. Much less labour is required. The pond can be dried, cleaned, repaired. Soil can be enriched by fertilizer application. But all water is lost by draining.

However if the ponds are constructed in a row, loss of water can be avoided and ponds are drained by turns.

Fishes attain table size, normally within one year of rearing period. Final harvesting is done by drag net either during summer months when the water level depletes to the danger level or after the monsoon, or when the market demands goes up.

To have maximum catch of bottom dwellers from large and deep ponds, drag nets with pockets have been found to be more effective.

ECONOMIC VALUE OF FISHES

Fishes provide one of the cheapest protein foods. Economic value of fishes can be considered under the major heads: useful fishes and harmful fishes.

USEFUL FISHES

Fishes are useful in many ways; the most important among them are enumerated here.

Fishes as Human Food

Fishes have formed an important item of human diet from the time man appeared on earth. Fish diet provides proteins, fats, Vit, A and D. A large amount of phosphorus and other elements are also present in it. They have a good taste and are easily digestible. Several million tonnes of fish are captured every year by various methods such as spears, baited hooks, traps, nets, etc.

In the order of importance, the principal fresh water fishes consumed as food in India are listed here.

The major cultivated fishes allover the world are the fishes belonging to the carp family:

- *Major carps:* Calla calla, Labeo rohita, Labeo calbasu L. fimbriatus, Cirrhina mrigala, C. reba Barbus sp.
- *Cat fishes:* Wallago attu, Mystus seenghala, M. cavasius, BagarulS bagarius, Pangasius sp.
- *Herrings:* Hilsa ilisha, Clupea sF, Setipinna.phasa, Gadusia chapra.
- *Feather backs:* Notopterus chitala, N. notopterus,
- *Live fishes:* Clarias batrachus, Heterpneustes fossilis, chana SF, Anabas testudineus
- *Mullets:* Muglil corsule

- *Miscellaneous:* Labeo bata, L. goniu5', Schizothorax, Tor tor, Berillius, Suntius', Nandus candus, Colisa sp.
- *Exotic species:* Cyprinu5' carpio.

Fish as Food of Cattle

The scrap of canneries as well as entire fishes, that are not relished by man, are dried and ground in mill. This is called fish meal, and is used as artificial food for poultry, pig and cattle.

Fish meat is produced in several states like Bombay, Andhra Pradesh, Tamil Nadu, Bengal, Kerala chietly from sardines, mackerels, ribbon fish, etc. The fish is first cooked in large pots containing sufficient quantity of water on fire or on steam.

The cooked material is then pressed to remove moisture and dried in the sun on suitable platforms. The resultant product is then stored and if preserved in airtight containers after sterilisation retains it nutritive value for a long time. The fish meal contains about 60 per cent protein and a high percentage of calcium phosphate which is very valuable for cattle and poultry. The manufacture of fish meal can be undertaken as- a cottage industry requiring little expenditure.

Fish Manure

Fishes that are not fit for human consumption are used to prepare fish manure for the fields. During peak season, when there is a large supply of fish, or they are landed in spoiled condition, they are sun dried by spreading them on the beach. The dried fish is ground and converted to manure, which contains a high percentage of nitrogen and phosphate.

"Fish guano" is prepared from the material left over after extracting oil from the fish. Mostly sardines are used for preparing fish oil and the waste material forms the "fish guano". It contains 8.9 per cent nitrogen and phosphate and when mixed with soil forms a rich fertilizer for plants. It is several times richer than ordinary cattle manure

Fish Oil

The most important fishery industry's by-product is fish oil which is of too kirids: liver oil and body oil. The oil extracted from the whole body of the fish is called fish body oil while that obtained tram the liver of certain fish is called the fish liver oil. Liver oil contains Vit A and D, while the body oil contains them in traces only.

The refined oil from the liver of fishes has a medicinal value. The body oil has many uses such as in painting, varnishing, soap, candle, leather and steel industries. Liver oil contains 55 - 75 per cent fat, 5-10 per cent protein and rest is water.

Fish Glue and Isinglass

Liquid glue is prepared from the connective tissue of skin tram head and body of fish. The glue is used as an adhesive for paper, wood, leather and glass. The air bladder of fishes is used for preparing isinglass, which is a shinning powder and is used for clearing wines, bear, making edible jelly and in the preparation of adhesive material. The air bladder is removed from fish, washed in cold water and flattened by beating it on a piece of wood. The bladder is then dried in the sun and is exported for the preparation of isinglass.

Fish Leather

The skin of several fishes like the sharks and rays are used for making polishing and smoothing material.

The dried and treated skin is also used for preparing ladies shoes, money bags, suitcases, belts, etc.

Fish Fin

The fins of sharks are exported to China where they are used for preparing soap. Fins are also used for preparing decorative items.

Biological Control

Several species of fishes are larvivorous in habit, and feed upon insect larvae e.g. Chela, Punitivs, Berilius, Danio, Calisa, Raspora, Esomus, Ambassis, Aplocheilus sp. etc., several diseases are spread by mosquitoes, hence the larvivorous fish are introduced in the waters of the area. They feed upon larvae and help in reducing the population of mosquitoes.

For Manufacture of Artificial Pearls

The material obtained by scraping the silvery coating of the scales of certain fishes is used for polishing the hollow: glass beads. These beads are then filled with wax and marketed as artificial pearls, used in jewellery.

For Sports and Games

Fishing forms an important outdoor game for million people catch various species of trouts, salmen, carps and other species of fishes.

For Decoration

Several species of beautifully coloured fishes are kept in aquaria, ponds and lakes and used for ornamentation. They are bred and maintained by stockists who offer numerous varieties for this purpose, and earn their livelihood from this trade.

Industries

As the fish forms a rich source of food, millions of people are engaged in fishing industry and depend on fisheries for their livelihood in various ways. Besides those who directly catch the fish for marketing, there are equally large number of people engaged in subsidiary industries like refrigeration, preservation, canning and in manufacture of fish products and by-products.

HARMFUL FISHES

Some species of fish are the intermediate hosts of many parasites causing diseases in man and other animals. Sharks are extremely dangerous in the sea and injure fisherman and damage their nets. Certain species of fishes have poisonous sting or spine (*e.g.* string ray) and cause painful wounds which might prove to be fatal. Some electric fishes are capable of giving shock to man. Carnivorous fishes eat away the larvae of useful insects. Some species have poisonous flesh and may prove fatal to man.

COMPOSITE FISH FARMING

In order to obtain maximum yield of fish from a lake or reservoir, it is essential to culture fast growing compatible species of different feeding habits. Fish production by old traditional methods gives a low yield, but if several species are stocked together, in proper proportion in the same pond, so that the available ecological riches are exploited, the production increases several times. This is known as composite fish farming or mixed farming or polyculture. Stocking of three Indian major carps (Catla, Rohu and Mrigal) in the same pond is, ill excellent example of the correct selection of species for the maximum utilisation of the food from the different zones of the pond.

Experiments have also been conducted on integration of aquaculture like stock rearing to reduce the cost of fish production. In a fish-cum-duck rearing centre an average yield of 4323 Kg/ha/year was obtained without adding any fertilizer to the pond and giving any supplementary feed to the fish. In Fish-cum-pig culture yield was 7300 Kg/ha/year when pig dung 20000 Kg/ha was recycled through the pond.

Thus by applying modem methods of fish farming and using suitable combinations of fish species for mixed culture, an 'aqua-explosion in fish production can be achieved in the country. Though fish farming is mainly carried out in natural reservoirs and ponds, paddy-cum-fish culture is an innovation.

Rice plants, when they are few centimetres high are flooded with water to ensure constant and sufficient supply of moisture and nutrients to this cereal. At this stage if suitable fishes are introduced, both paddy and fish are reported to yield high production. This method is practised in Bengal and Kerala to some extent.

FISHERIES TODAY-GROWTH, EXPANSION AND TRADE

During the last 25 years, there has been steady growth and expansion in India to claim an important position in the world fish trade. The growth in population and demand for more fish compelled a more thorough and systematic survey in the early seventies. From 1972-83, the Indian Sea-food Industry, emerged out successfully, ranking as the seventh largest country in the world. According to a recent review, the annual quantity harvested from our seas is 92,000 tonnes, earning about 300 crore rupees in foreign exchange.

According to a survey (1983-84), India has over 20,000 mechanised vessels, 1,40,000 traditional crafts with facilities to land in 1,800 centres along its long coast. These facilities include harbour, landing, berthing, and out-fitting facilities, repair houses for boats, proper electricity and water supply, ice plants for refrigeration of fishes, and even roads to connect to the nearest towns and railway stations.

The Indian fisheries now employ 4 million employees who include fishermen and their families, technologists, processors, scientists, fishery biologists and exporters. With the expansion of fisheries markets, increase in production and export, the Government of India faced problems of resources and their quality marketing technology, fish and fisheries education and research, the overall control of sea food industry, etc.

The organisation and institutions that the Government has established to regulate and guide the several aspects of fishery industry and allied concerns are varied, as seen in the list below:

- Central Marine Fisheries Research Institute (Cochin, Kerala state) undertakes research in all aspects of marine fishes and fisheries.
- Inland Fisheries Research Institute (Barrackpore, W. Bengal) deals with the research on riverine, estuarine, lacustrine (lakes) fishes and their fisheries.
- Indian Institute of Fisheries (Cochin, Kerala state) doing research on ideal crafts and post-harvest technology.
- Institute of Nautical Engineering and Training (Cochin, Kerala state), trains personnels for operating fishing crafts and gears.
- Integrated Fisheries Project of India (Bombay, Maharashtra) concentration on fishes, their biology, exploration of fishing grounds.
- Institute of Fisheries Education (Bombay, Maharashtra) is designed for teaching and research, both theory and practice, on all aspects of

fisheries, resources, fishing grounds, crafts and gears, modernisation of boats, trawlers and equipment.

- Marine Products Export Development Authority (Cochin, Kerala state) is the national organisation responsible for the overall developments, regulation and controls of sea food industry as related to export.
- Export Inspection Agency (Cochin, Kerala state) to maintain quality, hygiene, sanitation level of products and inspection of processing plants and package products at export points.
- Fisheries Survey of India (Exploratory fisheries Project) Bombay, (Maharashtra state) to provide training and vital information required for a systematic exploitation of the Indian seas.

Besides the above organisations, study of fishes and fisheries biology has been introduced in colleges and universities in several states of India both in graduate and post graduate courses. There has been a rapid progress in the fisheries industry. Within the last four decades, the industry has reached a top position in exports.

In the world sea food trade, India stands first in the prawns and shrimps export tonnage and second largest in marine fisheries, among developing nations, while seventh in the world. Further, the seas have opened up employment for millions of people. Most of all, thousands of fishermen and their families to have benefited from fishing industry, their earnings have grown and their socioeconomic conditions have improved.

FISH FARMING

Fish production is a complex process that involves interaction between various eco-biological factors such as soil, water, air, light, heat, micro-organisms, micro flora and fauna, plants, animals and human beings. Basically it is a biomass production which takes place in a pond or aquatic ecosystem. In the fish production it is mainly the interaction between the fish reared and the pond ecosystem which is organised by human beings.

The success in fish farming depends on how best one can organise these interactions between the variations of each of the eco-biological factors in such a way that maximum production of fish takes place in a given pond system. The complex process in the fish production involving combinations of many things living, non-living and environmental factors results in unlimited variations in management practices. Therefore, no single practice can be considered the ideal one and the management practices should be decided at times on the spur of the moment according to the variations resulting from the above mentioned combinations. However we can reduce most of the practices in the fish farming into few principles which if followed will ensure success and satisfaction.

At the time of planning for fish farming if one is mindful of all these principles he can establish the fish farm in such way that all the operations during fish farming can be carried out with least expenditure in terms of time, labour and energy.

PRINCIPLES IN FISH CULTURE

Over the years extensive study of the possible variations occurring due to the various combinations of the production factors in relation to the fish growth and development has highlighted certain principles which should be kept in mind by anyone who would like to venture into fish production. These principles are mainly related to the food chain system in the nature, the oxygen balance in the aquatic system, stocking combinations between various species of fish, stocking density, living space needed, the supplementary feeding, soil and water management, health and hygiene and efficient management of the operations. They are explained here one by one.

At the same time it is not possible to describe all the practical aspects of each of the principles. The fish farmer will have to evolve appropriate practices for each of these principles explained here. Like in all other enterprises fish production also requires a fairly good knowledge of the principles which is certainly necessary for evolving suitable management practices.

SHORTER FOOD CHAIN

To explain the principle of shorter food chain we must first of all understand the process of biomass production and food chain cycle in the nature. Biomass production whether it is in the farm land, animal husbandry farms, forest, wild life sanctuaries or in water bodies such as ponds, lakes, reservoirs and seas is essentially a process of transformation of solar energy into some form of biomass or biochemical compounds in a specific ecosystem.

This process takes place in the nature basically through a set of biochemical reactions together called photosynthesis. During the photosynthesis the available sun energy is traped first into simple carbohydrates like glyceraldehyde (the first compound formed from the combination of carbon dioxide, water and solar energy in the carbohydrate metabolism during the photosynthesis) by the chlorophyll present in the green plants.

From the simple carbohydrate compounds a little more complex carbohydrate compounds such as arabinose, manose, ribose, glycogen, sucrose, fructose are formed. Later still more complex carbohydrate molecules like cellulose, fatty acids are formed. Further in combination with the other elements such as nitrogen, phosphorus, potassium, magnesium, calcium, etc., absorbed from the soil by the plants compounds like amino acids, proteins, vitamins, hormones and other very complex biochemical compounds are formed. Green plants or plants with chlorophyll are consumers of solar energy, carbondioxide and water. This is the primary level of consumption and production and hence plants are called primary consumers and producers. The secondary consumers are those who consume what is produced by the primary producers. They are the animals and human beings who feed on plants and are known as herbivores and produce the biomass at their own levels. They are also called secondary producers.

Those who consume the animals to produce some biomass are called carnivores. They are the tertiary consumers and producers. Some, of course are called omnivores as they can consume both plants and flesh of the animals. Human beings and some animals are in general are omnivores. Finally, all the consumers and producers at all levels die and are decomposed by the micro-organisms known as decomposers. After the decomposition the elements and compounds that made up the plant, animal and human body are disbursed and merge with different forms of visible and tangible material existences such as soil, water, air, light and heat.

Again some of these same elements and compounds are reassembled into plants, animals and human beings and the cycle starts again one becoming the food for second and the second becoming the food for the third, etc., forming a long chain of food cycle.

Thus all the living and non-living beings (eco-biological factors) are linked together through predator-prey relationship in this chain of food production which follows a general pattern food chain cycle of primary consumers-producers (plants), herbivores or secondary consumers-producers (animals) and carnivores or the tertiary consumers-producers (animals and humans) which are decomposed and back again to primary producers. This process though looks simple is a very complex relation food-web with various cross linkages.

The food chain cycle is also an energy cycle in which the energy is being fixed in varying quantities at different stages. At the primary production level maximum energy fixation take place but as we move in the food chain cycle from one link to another much energy is lost by the time it reaches the last consumer-producer link. Only a fraction of that energy which is fixed at the primary level is available at the tertiary level. At every consumer-producer level the quantum of energy fixed is much less than the energy consumed by them. More the linkages in a food chain cycle lesser will be energy or biomass production or availability at the end of it. In other words shorter the toad chain cycle the more will the energy or biomass. Therefore, in an efficient fish culture the food chain system is made short as possible so that minimum loss of the energy is ensured to maximize fish production. This is done mostly by growing herbivorous fish instead of carnivorous.

In a natural fish pond system the plants are consumed by some of the fishes (herbivores) while the other fishes feed on the animal organisms (carnivores). Herbivorous fishes feed on the plants in the pond or supplied from out side. Among the carnivorous fishes some big ones eat up the small ones of different fishes and even of the same species.

In an artificial fish rearing system if we depend on the carnivorous fish then the fish production chain is longer and the energy available in the form of total fish harvested will be much less. Therefore, it is highly advisable to go for production of herbivorous fishes rather than carnivorous. Because, by this way at least one step in the chain of fish production can be reduced. Besides the total production of fish per unit area per unit time is more through herbivorous fishes.

Productivity at the primary level is dependent on light, carbon dioxide, temperature and nutrient elements. Of these factors balance of dissolved nutrients is the easiest to be controlled in the fish production. The pond soil differs from the land soils in several aspects mainly because it remains always waterlogged and aeration is almost absent in it u: like in the land soil. In a pond soil only in the top 2-5 cm of soil, nutrient-ion-exchange will take place and below this layer the soil is unaerated and has negligible involvement in the production cycle.

Ponds receive dissolved nutrients and sedimentary particles from their catchment area, carried by precipitated rain water run off. The quantity and quality of the dissolved nutrients depend on the nature and extent of catchment area and the amount of rainfall run-off. The character and productivity of the pond soil is influenced by the nutrients dissolved in it. Hence, the production of minute plants and animal organisms in ponds are also influenced by the nutrients in the pond soil. Diffusion of nutrients throughout the pond is faster than in land soil.

The productivity of the pond also depends on the type of fertilizers used. For example, the use of phoshatic fertilizers increase the development of the phytoplankton. Even the concentration of phosphatic fertilizers alter the species composition of the phytoplankton. At lower concentration, diatoms are common but with increase in concentration of the phosphate green algae become more prevalent and eventually giving way to blue-green algae at the higher concentration. At the same time too much of the phosphate lowers the production due to the effect of auto-shading and prevention of the penetration of sunlight.

Primary production is also dependent on light energy and hence maximum light energy utilisation is an important aspect in the fish production. The amount of light penetrated into the pond water, absorbed and utilised depends on the amount of light reflected back which again is guided by the angle of incidence of the sun rays on the surface of the pond water. Some of the light is absorbed by the water as heat energy while other may be absorbed by plants and suspended particles in the pond water. In turbid waters in which more suspended particles are present more light is absorbed or scattered. However, proper light penetration is only to a depth of 1.2 to 1.8 metres (4-6 ft).

In deeper ponds the lower layers of water being poorly lighted, and consequently devoid of plants, having more incidence of decaying material and oxygen being depleted generally may not support fish growth as much as it does at the middle and top layers of water. Therefore, the primary producers at the upper light-reaching layers should supply enough food for the herbivorous fishes and provide oxygen to support total biological respiration during darkness and also during the less favourable climate such as warm, overcast or rainy days.

OXYGEN BALANCE

As already mentioned the amount of the oxygen dissolved greatly influences the fish production or the carrying capacity of the pond. There is an inverse correlation between the temperature and the amount of oxygen dissolved in the water as is clear from the table given here.

Table. Solubility of Oxygen Under Different Temperatures.

Temperature C°	Solubility of Oxygen (mg/litre)	Temperature C°	Solubility of Oxygen (mg/litre)	Temperature C°	Solubility of Oxygen (mg/litre)
0	14.63	13	10.53	26	8.12
1	14.23	14	10.29	27	7.84
2	13.84	15	10.07	28	7.70
3	13.46	16	9.86	29	7.54
4	13.11	17	9.65	30	7.45
5	12.77	18	9.46	31	7.45
6	12.45	19	9.27	32	7.33
7	12.13	20	9.08	33	7.21
8	11.84	21	8.91	34	7.09
9	11.55	22	8.74	35	6.98
10	11.28	23	8.54		
11	11.02	24	8.42		
12	10.77	25	8.26		

From the table it is clear that the oxygen dissolved at lower temperatures is higher than that dissolved at the higher temperatures. But when heavy infestation of aquatic weeds and dense blooms of plankton are present the situation becomes much more complex. On the one hand they are additional source of oxygen but they also consume quite a lot of oxygen during day and night.

At night besides their consumption of oxygen they also release carbon dioxide during their respiration (the dark reaction). At times during the day especially in the evening hours there may be very high amount of oxygen dissolved in the water.

Similarly at other times during the light especially early morning hours there may be very low level of oxygen present in the water. In other words there exists a high rate of fluctuation in the amount of oxygen dissolved in water within a period of twenty four hours.

In case of dense algal bloom the net production of oxygen (production minus consumption by the algal bloom) may become lesser. In some cases of dense algal bloom the oxygen consumed will be more than the oxygen produced. And at times the daily net production of oxygen may fall below zero. The day and night fluctuation of the oxygen production is an inevitable phenomenon. However, within this there can be an ideal condition of oxygen balance. But the magnitude of this fluctuation varies with different climatic conditions. These fluctuations are clear from figure given here.

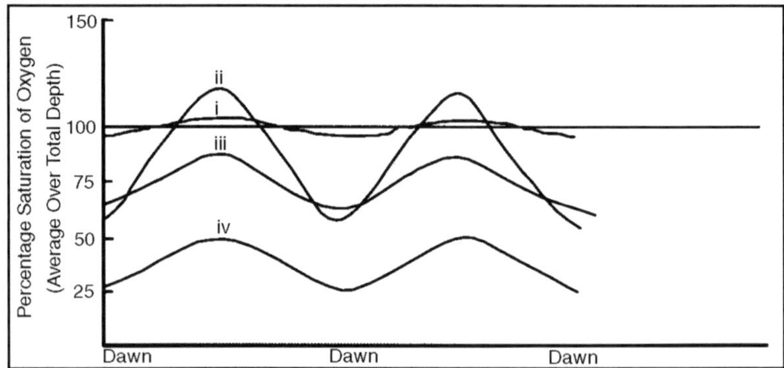

Curve 1 represents and ideal condition in sunny periods, when there is a daily addition of oxygen produced by photosynthesis. Curve II represents the critical condition in sunny period when all the oxygen produced by photosynthesis is used up by weed and plankton for their respiration. The average oxygen content lies slightly lower than the satuarated level because it rarely reaches the full saturation point in pond ecosystem. Even if there is some natural circulation of water in the pond fully saturated conditions are rarely seen. The Curve II also indicates that even in the critical stage the percentage of oxygen in the ponds is better in the night because of lower temperature and consequently higher oxygen solubility. Difficulties arise when there is a series of cloudy days.

The total amount of oxygen produced is less and the fluctuation shifts down ward to Curves III and IV. At Curve III there is still enough oxygen at night to maintain a fish population but at curve IV most of the oxygen fluctuations are below the critical level for fish survival and mass mortality usually occurs. In the pond ecosystem the oxygen dissolved even at the maximum level will always be lower than the saturation level. This is because in the ponds practically there is no water circulation or very little circulation.

FEEDING HABITS

Different fishes have different feeding habits. Some fish feed on very minute plants as small as micro-organisms, others feed on green algae or blue green algae, yet some others feed on weeds and grasses (grass carp). Some as already mentioned feed on plants (herbivores) while others feed of organisms of animal origin (carnivores). Some feed on dead and decaying material (catfish and Mrigal) while others eat only tresh material. Some accept supplementary feeds while others may be shy of taking supplementary feeds. In the supplementary feed also some will prefer feeds of animal origin while others prefers feeds of plant origin. Some are phytoplankton feeding (silver carp) while others are zooplankton feeding (bighead carp). Fishes like tilapia, catfish, and eel are omnivores.

Again some fish (catla and silver carp) feed mostly on the upper layers of the pond water, while others (rohu and grass carp) feed at the middle layers and other fishes (mrigal and common carp) feed at the bottom layers of the water in the pond. Hence, the selection of the fish for rearing in the pond is done based on the principle of feeding habits of specific species of fish. This leads to the next principle of optimum stocking combination.

STOCKING COMBINATION

The stocking combination refers to the species mix and the proportion in the combination of species selected for rearing in a given pond. Obviously stocking combination takes into consideration the feeding habit of the fishes selected and the amount of natural feed both plant and animal types growing in the pond. The intensity of natural feed depends on the fertility of the pond whether natural or artificial. In the tropical fertile ponds there is always a chance of abundant grass and weed growth besides the algal bloom.

The temperature of the water and the climate of the area also should be taken into consideration in stocking the pond. Some fishes grow in tropical areas while others grow better in temperate and cold climates. Taking all these into consideration we can have a variation of single species to six species mix at various proportions. Obviously each fish farmer will have to decide from his experience and from the experience of others the optimum combination of species and the proper proportion of the species in his pond. However, few examples are given here as guide lines to the practice of this principle.

Generally two, three, four and six species culture are found to be more productive:

- *Two species*: Tilapia and catla are stocked in 50 per cent each. Tilapia is an omnivorous fish and multiplies fast while catfish feeds on all kinds of dead and living material, also the fry of tilapia and thus keeping the population of the tilapia under control.
- *Three species*: Catla 40 per cent, rohu 30 per cent and mrigal 30 per cent is an example of three species combination. Catla feeds at the surface layers, rohu at the middle layers and mrigal at the bottom layers.
- *Four species*: Catla 30-40 per cent, rohu 20-30 per cent, in deeper ponds and 10-15 per cent in shallow ponds, mrigal 15-2Q per cent and common carp 20-25 per cent is an example of four species combination.
- *Six species combination*: Catla 10-.15 per cent, silver carp 20- 30 per cent, rohu 15-20 per cent; in moderately deep ponds (above 2.00 m) and 10 per cent in shallow ponds (less than 2.00 m) mrigal 15-20 per cent common carp 20-25 per cent and grass carp 5-15 per cent is an example of six species combination.

Similarly, there may be several other combinations that can be tried according to the ingenuity of the fish farmer.

STOCKING DENSITY

Normally fish production increases with the increase in the number of fish stocked per unit area to a maximum and then starts decreasing when no supplementary feeding is provided and the total crop is dependent only on the naturally generated feed. If supplementary feeding is given we can in crease the fish production further but again up to a certain extent only. After that the production decreases. In other words we cannot increase the number of fish stocked beyond certain number and there is always an optimum stocking rate beyond which there will be decrease in production. Stocking beyond certain number will cause competition for space, feed, oxygen, light and create aggressive interaction among the fish.

Further there will be excessive accumulation of excretory matter in the pond. In the running water the excretory matter flow down the stream. But in the stagnant pond they settle down to the bottom of the pond. Stocking density and stocking ratio of the fishes should be on the basis of the quantity of water and the amount of oxygen production. Normally the thumb rule is to provide at the rate of one cubic metre volume of water per fish to move and to feed around. In other words, 10,000 fish per hectare pond of one metre depth. If the depth is increased we can go for combination of fishes feeding at the surface, middle and bottom. In that case the pond should have a depth of 2-3 metres (6' 4" to 10').

LIVING SPACE

Experience in many places have proved that the bigger the pond greater will be the size of the fish produced even if the same stocking density is maintained. For example, keeping the same stocking density of 500 fish per 0.1 hectare pond rear 500 fish in a pond of 0.1 hectare and in another 1000 fish in 0.2 hectare. At the time of harvesting after providing equal period of growing period we can see that the fish in the second pond have grown bigger. The reason is that there is direct correlation between the total space available to each fish to move around. In the second pond each fish gets an area of 0.2 hectare to move around and to feed whereas in the first one each fish gets only half the area of the second to move and feed around. We must remember again that the stocking rate in both are the same.

Greater surface area provides greater chance of dissolution of oxygen into the water and the excess carbon dioxide being released into the atmosphere. Moreover, ponds with greater surface area is prone to greater wind action resulting in the dissolution of atmospheric oxygen into the water and also for the mixing up of the bottom layer with the top layer of water. Large ponds being exposed to wind action and evaporation of the water from the surface is subjected to greater cooling effect.

In the smaller ponds greater area is lost to the bunds though from the management aspect, they are better than bigger ponds. However, large ponds are more difficult to fill in with water and to empty at the end of the cropping. Harvesting is also difficult in bigger ponds.

The best is to have sufficiently large enough pond to ensure maximum growth of the fish and also small enough to ensure better and efficient management of the pond. Normally, pond size ranging between 0.4 to 1.00 hectare are found to be meeting both the standards. However, greater emphasis should be given to better management, supplementary feeding, adequate oxygen maintenance, generation of natural feed and hygienic conditions than the surface area.

SUPPLEMENTARY FEEDING

The sixth principle deals with the supplementary feed and the percentage of protein in it. Under the normal conditions pond ecosystem fish production is directly correlated to the amount of fish feed available to the fish. Rearing high yielding breeds of fish necessarily require proportionately higher amount of feed. This demand cannot be met by the natural generation of feed in the pond alone. Because the natural generation of feed in the pond system cannot cope with the feed requirement for an intensive rearing of fish for commercial purposes. Hence, providing protein rich supplementary feed is essential for intensive fish rearing.

The feed conversion ratio in fish as high as 1:2; for every two kg of feed the production fish can be one kilogram which is quite high compared to all other domestic animals. Besides fish require minimum 40 per cent protein during its growth from fingerling (90 days) to marketable size. Of course the protein requirement is as high as 70-75 per cent during the fry stage (0-15 days) which comes down gradually to 40-45 per cent as the fry grow into fingerling size (15-90 days). When we consider the conversion ratio of protein alone it amounts to 1:1 in fast growing fish (one kg protein in feed is converted to one kg of flesh in fish). Supplementary feeding increases the growth rate of fish and thus increases the yield. It has been observed that supplementary feeding of nerigal and common carp with a mixture of rice bran and oil cake the increase in growth rate was ten times more than the ones grown without supplementary feed. Feeding with, additional amount of grass and weeds increases the growth rate in grass carp.

Feeding should be done on small platforms at different places in the pond. This will ensure least wastage and maximum utilisation of feed. It also helps to find out the amount of feed required at different stages of growth of the fish, to know whether the amount provided is sufficient or not, whether, the fish is eating the given feed or not, etc., if not eaten it may be an indication of the health and physiological conditions of the fish, etc. By observing the fish during feeding one can get a fairly accurate idea of the health and physiological condition of the fish.

SOIL AND WATER MANAGEMENT

The principles of water management implies maintenance of water depth within the optimum range during the monsoon and summer seasons, maintaining the water quality whether, fresh water with pH around 7.00 or brakish water if brackish water fish culture is followed and maintaining the clarity of the water. The optimum range of depth is 1.20 to 2.1 metre or 4 -7 ft. In any case water depth should not be less than 1.20 metres. By clarity of water, it is meant that the '?later should be free from suspended particles which make water turbid. Clarity is important for the sun light to penetrate into the depth of the pond. Shading should be avoided to ensure maximum utilisation of the sun light.

The temperature of the water should be maintained within an optimum range. The optimum range is about 15 to 30° C for the warm water fish though from the point of oxygen dissolution lower temperature is preferred. But at less than 15°C the physiological activities, such as feeding, maturing, breeding and hatching are affected. The water should also be protected from the flood water during monsoon and run off water from the surrounding areas. The water also should be free from excessive vegetative growth as well as deficiency of the same. Application of both organic manures and chemical fertilizers should be done regularly so that there is sufficient dissolved nutrients in the water. At the same time too much of the dead and decayed organic matter should not present in the pond.

The soil management consists in first of all maintenance of the stability of the sides of the pond. By no means the sides should collapse. Secondly, the pond should hold whatever water impounded. In other words, there should no leakage of water. Though in mud walled ponds the seepage cannot be avoided it should be reduced to the minimum. The bunds around the pond should be strong and avoid all the chances of erosion and breakage. Soil is the vessel in which the pond water is held and obviously the vessel should be maintained in the best of the conditions possible.

Once the stability of the soil is ensured the next important point is to maintain the optimum chemical and fertility conditions of the pond soil. Basically, the pH of the soil indicates the chemical condition of the soil. The optimum pH of the pond soil is between 6.5 to 7.5 which is chemically neutral. However, in saline alkali soils where brakish water fish culture is carried out this will not be applicable. Here the effort will be to maintain the salinity or alkalinity conditions. Salinity refers to the presence of the chlorides of calcium, magnesium and sodium in the soil and alkalinity refers to the amount of sodium present and is capable of exchanging with calcium, magnesium, etc.

Soil in the pond condition remain always under sub-merged and saturated condition and hence completely devoid of aeration. This is called anaerobic condition of the soil in which only the aquatic plants will grow. In most cases proper addition of sufficient amount of organic manures and lime we can maintain the optimum condition of the soil required for the fish growth. At the same time accumulation of dead and decayed matter beyond a certain limit in the soil is detrimental to fish growth. Heavy accumulation of organic matter can be controlled by stocking more common carps which eats up the dead and decayed material in the pond and help in maintaining balance of organic matter in the pond soil.

HEALTH AND HYGIENE

The principles involved in the health and hygiene in fish farming are prevention of the disease and maintenance of sanitation. Outbreaks of communicable diseases are the result of interactions between the three factors; the pathogen, a susceptible host and predisposing environmental condition in the pond. Under high level intensification the risk of contracting the disease will be more. Hence, the key to health maintenance involve three sequential steps: a. prophylactic measures, b. fish health monitoring, and c. treatment for specific diseases. Prophylactic measures include sanitation of ponds using disinfectants like, bleaching powder or quick lime prior to stocking. Similarly, prophylactic measures, if needed, against parasites and other microbial pathogens are also done prior to stocking and during trial netting.

QUICK AND EASY MANAGEMENT

The last but not the least principle in the fish farming is to ensure facilities to perform quickly and easily all the day to day management operations. For example daily feeding, aerating if needed, maintenance of water flow, manuring and fertilization, emptying of the pond and refilling, control of flood water or run off water, control of silting, prevention of over heating the pond, control of parasites and predators, breeding hatching, fry and fingerlings raising, netting for sampling or harvesting, etc., should be planned in such a way that these operations can be done smoothly with minimum labour, time and energy. Otherwise, fish production will become un- wieldy and uneconomical.

Eventually, one will be forced to wind up the enterprise. Because the planning is done differently by different people under different conditions. Only the principle can be reiterated saying that all the operations should be done with minimum labour, time and energy. How they are planned to be done depends on the owner of the fish farm, the environmental conditions and the resources available. Planning all the daily, weekly, monthly and seasonal operations for the quick and easy management is perhaps the most important and foremost in the planning of fish farming. The principle involved is "use minimum time, labour and energy" for the fish farming. This is done by arranging all the infrastructures in the line of a smooth flow of operations. Fish farmer should get a full knowledge of the various implications and imperatives before he can plan all the operations in a smooth running way.

RECYCLING

Fish production as already mentioned takes place in an ecosystem and in any ecosystem biomass or organic matter recycling along with water cycling is a fundamental process that sustains the ecosystem as well as form a base for all individual organisms to evolve. It is same as food chain cycle. In the pond system which is predominantly a water ecosystem the same type of recycling is very much operative. The principle is recycle as much and as many items as possible in the pond as well as outside into the fish-production-chain cycle.

In the pond all types of organisms of plant and animal origin grows at the bottom, middle and at the top layers of the water. Usually there will "be weeds and grasses growing on the banks and bunds of the pond. There should be fishes that consume planktons, microscopic plants and animals, fishes that consume algae, blue-green algae, weeds, insects, worms, beetles, etc. Thus all the organisms could be recycled in the food chain of fish production.

In an agro-ecosystem the farmer may have rice bran, wheat bran, oil cake, fish and meat meal, etc. These are recycled as feed for the fish. There may be cow dung or any other animal dung available in the farm itself. There may be compost already made or being made in the pond area or in the agricultural farm in which the pond is situated. These recycles as organic manure for the pond. It may happen that a poultry or a piggery or a duckery or a goat or sheep pen may be there in the farm. If so all the their wastes such as animal wastes (faeces), slaughter wastes, meat wates, feather wastes, visceral organs, etc., should be recycled as manure for the pond and feed for the fish. What all things in whichever way can be recycled depends mainly on the ingenuity of the fish farmer. The same resources may be recycled in different ways by different people. However, the principle is "Recycle as many things as possible in as many ways as possible."

PLAN ACCORDING TO THE AVAILABLE RESOURCES

"Plan according to the available resources" is a principle that is applicable in the planning of any enterprise. However, it cannot be omitted either among the principles enumerated here as it should be kept in mind by every fish farmer while he is planning for the fish farm. The natural resources available (land, water, climate, biomass generation, feeds, fertilizers, types of fry and fingerlings, etc.) vary from places to place. In some areas plenty of water is available in the form of submerged land, streams, high rain fall, etc. But in some other places there may be very poor water source or medium level water source.

In some other place the soil and file topography are quite suitable or rather suitable or not suitable for fish ponds. In some other place the natural feed generation may be very high, medium or low. Yet in another place the fry and fingerlings are easily available or not available. Similarly the financial resources, marketing possibilities, infrastructural facilities like road, transport, electricity, communication, etc., too vary from place to place. In some places there may be facilities for processing and canning of the fish produced. Further there may be possibilities for export to other states or to other countries.

In some place there may be plenty of raw material like rice or wheat bran and/or oil cake available at cheaper rate; in some other place plenty of fish and animal slaughter waste available. Under such conditions even if other resources are scarcely manageable there exists still a high possibility of fish production. Thus, even if some of the resources are under constrain but some other key sources are available one can go for fish farming.

CONSERVATION AND MANAGEMENT OF AQUATIC RESOURCES

The activities of the Department aim at promoting effective management and conservation of production systems through complementary work on the two sub-sectors of capture fisheries(marine and inland) and aquaculture. The Department is *inter alia* involved in organising inter-governmental and technical forums to analyse and resolve the numerous issues raised by FAO members.

It collects and distributes key statistics on the sector activity, develops normative documents such as the Code of Conduct for Responsible Fisheries (CCRF), binding legal agreements, guidelines, manuals and information systems.

It also provides, on request, technical assistance to FAO members in developing management strategies and plans, national assessment and management capacity, control and surveillance, food safety, trade etc. The Committee on Fisheries (COFI) oversees FAO efforts and provides the inter-governmental forum of choice for debating on key issues.

BACKGROUND TO DEPARTMENT'S ACTIVITIES

The effective management and conservation of the living aquatic resources used by fisheries and aquaculture are necessary to ensure their contribution to sustainable development, poverty eradication and food security. The effectiveness and performance of conservation and management measures is conditioned by given social, economic, institutional and political circumstances. The sectoral governance of fisheries and aquaculture encompasses complex social, institutional and political processes. It has international, national and local dimensions and clearly requires legal, social, environmental, economic and political considerations.

It involves interactions between the governments and civil society (sensu lato, including in particular fishers, fishfarmers, industry and private sector in general, as well as other stakeholder groups) for allocation of resources and power. Its components include the principles, arrangements (including customary ones), institutions, instruments (*e.g.*, international treaties), rules (*e.g.*, national laws) and processes used to decide, control and exert oversight on the sectors activities and their impacts.

The UN Law of the Sea Convention (1982), complemented by other related international agreements, establishes the global framework for the governance of marine capture fisheries.

The FAO Code of Conduct for Responsible Fisheries (CCRF), adopted by FAO members in 1995 and complemented by the CCRF Technical Guidelines, is considered to be the basic foundation on which to promote sustainable fisheries and aquaculture development for the future. The CCRF and Guidelines pay due attention to the environmental aspects of the sector and contains provisions relevant for the implementation of the Convention on Biodiversity (CBD). The CCRF covers all fishery and aquaculture practices as carried out in freshwater and marine environments.

Focus on the governance of fisheries has increased during recent decades, because of the growing realisation that fish stocks, in different parts of the world, were being increasingly harvested beyond their optimal level and the fishery sector was in economic and social difficulty.

The need for controlling better, limiting, and in most cases reducing access to wild resources (including stocks, space, seeds) and minimizing damage to productive environments, for example, aquatic pollution and habitat degradation, is widely recognised.

Management and conservations responsibilities rest with the States under their sovereign rights. To some extent, however, they can be devolved at a lower (*e.g.*, local) or higher (*e.g.*, regional) level. At regional level, regional fishery bodies have a fundamental role to play. At both sub-national and regional levels, insufficient capacity to implement effective management measures is a central issue. Major efforts are still needed, worldwide to deal with shared resources.

The future challenges in fisheries and aquaculture management rest *inter alia* on the capacity to control access to resources resolving conflicting claims, integrate concerns and policies across sectors and geographical scales, develop sustainable development ethics, implement precautionary, livelihood and ecosystem approaches, coordinate management of sub-sectors (*e.g.*, within an ecosystem, a watershed or a coastal area). While many of the basic concepts, principles and issues may be similar in the national exclusive economic zones and the international waters of the high seas, the systems of rights and duties and, hence the management systems will differ.

FISHERY: AQUATIC SPECIES

A fishery is an organised effort by humans to catch fish or other aquatic species, an activity known as fishing. Generally, a fishery exists for the purpose of providing human food, although other aims are possible (such as sport or recreational fishing), or obtaining ornamental fish or fish products such as fish oil. Industrial fisheries are fisheries where the catch is not intended for direct human consumption.

Regardless of purpose, however, the term fishery generally refers to a fishing effort centered on either a particular ecoregion or a particular species or type of fish or aquatic animal, and usually fisheries are differentiated by both criteria. Examples would be the salmon fishery of Alaska, the cod fishery off the Lofoten islands or the tuna fishery of the Eastern Pacific. Most fisheries are marine, rather than freshwater; most marine fisheries are based near the coast. This is not only because harvesting from relatively shallow waters is easier than in the open ocean, but also because fish are much more abundant near the coastal shelf, due to coastal upwelling and the abundance of nutrients available there.

FISHERIES HISTORICALLY

Fisheries have been important parts of human life and food production throughout history. Fish acts as one main food in people's everyday life as well as food security of the nation. Fisheries have become a part of human cultures and mythologies, providing a community identity and a subject for artists throughout the ages. Partially, this is because fisheries are irretrievably wrapped up in humanity's perpetual fascination with the sea, and partially, because they have been a major source of food and income for many communities throughout the ages.

One of the world's longest lasting trade histories is the trade of dry cod from the Lofoten area to the southern parts of Europe, Italy, Spain and Portugal. The trade in cod started during the viking period or before, has been going on for more than 1000 years and is still important. In India, the Pandyas, a classical Dravidian Tamil kingdom, were known for the pearl fishery as early as the 1st century BC. Their seaport Tuticorin was known for deep sea pearl fishing. The paravas, a Tamil caste centred in Tuticorin, developed a rich community because of their pearl trade, navigation knowledge and fisheries.

Fisheries in the Present Day

Today, fisheries are estimated to provide 16 per cent of the world population's protein, and that figure is considerably elevated in some developing nations and in regions that depend heavily on the sea. Fisheries are a huge global business and provide income for millions of people. Fisheries have been and continue to be culturally important for many communities as well.

According to the Food and Agriculture Organisation of the United Nations, total world capture fisheries production in 2000 was 86 million tons. The top producing countries were, in order, the People's Republic of China (excluding Hong Kong and Taiwan), Peru, Japan, the United States, Chile, Indonesia, Russia, India, Thailand, Norway and Iceland. Those countries accounted for more than half of the world's production; China alone accounted for a third of the world's production. Of that production, over 90 per cent was marine and less than 10 per cent was inland.

There are large and important fisheries worldwide for various species of fish, mollusks and crustaceans. However, a very small number of species support the majority of the world's fisheries. Some of these species are herring, cod, anchovy, tuna, flounder, mullet, squid, shrimp, salmon, crab, lobster, oyster and scallops. All except these last four provided a worldwide catch of well over a million tonnes in 1999, with herring and sardines together providing a catch of over 22 million metric tons in 1999. Many other species as well are fished in smaller numbers, both locally and globally.

Fishing Methods

Fishing methods vary according to the region, the species being fished for, and the amount of income and technology available to the fisher. A fishery can consist of one man with a small boat hand-casting nets, to a huge fleet of trawlers processing tons of fish per day. Some common commercial techniques today are trawling, seining, driftnetting, handlining, longlining, gillnetting, and diving.

Trawling Method

Trawling is a method of fishing that involves actively pulling a fishing net through the water behind one or more boats.

Structure of a Trawl Net

When two boats are used (pair trawling), the horizontal spread of the net is provided by the boats, with one warp attached to each boat. However, single-boat trawling is more common. Here, the horizontal spread of the net is provided by trawl doors (also known as "otter boards"). Trawl doors are available in various sizes and shapes and may be specialised to keep in contact with the sea bottom or to remain elevated in the water. In all cases, doors essentially act as wings, using a hydrodynamic shape to provide horizontal spread. As with all wings, the towing vessel must go at a certain speed for the doors to remain standing and functional. This speed varies, but is generally in the range of 2.5-4.0 knots. Nets for trawling in surface waters and for trawling in deep water and over the bottom. Note the "tangles" with all of the marine life caught up in them.

The vertical opening of a trawl net is created using flotation on the upper edge ("floatline") and weight on the lower edge ("footrope") of the net mouth. The configuration of the footrope varies based on the expected bottom shape. The more uneven the bottom, the more robust the footrope configuration must be to prevent net damage.

Environmental Impacts of Trawling

Although trawling today is heavily regulated in some nations, it remains the target of many protests by environmentalists. Environmental concerns related to trawling refer to two areas: a perceived lack of selectivity and the physical damage which the trawl does to the seabed.

Selectivity of Trawling

Reports of the lack of selectivity of trawling have been present since it started (about the 1600's) and it became used more widely (about 1900). Trawl nets may be non-selective, sweeping up both marketable and undesirable fish and fish of both legal and illegal size. Any part of the catch which cannot be used is considered as by-catch. size selectivity is controlled by the mesh size of the "cod-end" - the part of the trawl where fish are retained. Fishermen complain that a mesh size which allows undersised fish to escape also allows a proportion of legal-landing sized fish to escape as well. There are a number of "fixes", such as tying a rope around the "cod-end" to prevent the mesh from opening fully, which have been developed to work around technical regulation of size selectivity. One problem is when the mesh gets pulled into narrow diamond shapes (rhombuses) instead of squares.

The capture of undesirable species is a recognised problem with all fishing methods and unites environmentalists, who do not want to see fish killed needlessly and fishermen, who do not want to waste their time sorting unsellable fish from their catch.

A number of methods to minimize this have been developed for use in trawling. Bycatch reduction grills or square mesh panels of net can be fitted to parts of the trawl, allowing certain species to escape while retaining others. Trawling for shrimps has specifically been cited as having high levels of bycatch in various parts of the world.

Ecological Damage

Because bottom trawling involves towing heavy fishing gear over the seabed at a speed of several knots, it is destructive to the ocean bottom. The primary sources of impact are the doors, which can weigh several tonnes and create furrows when dragged along the bottom, and the footrope configuration, which usually remains in contact with the bottom across the entire lower edge of the net. Depending on the configuration, the footrope may turn over large rocks or boulders, disturb or damage sessile organisms or rework bottom sediments. Published research has shown that benthic trawling destroys the cold-water coral Lophelia pertusa, an important habitat for many deep-sea organisms. The primary focus of dispute over the impact of trawl gear is on the magnitude and duration of these impacts. Opponents of trawl gear argue that the impact of trawl nets is widespread, intense and long-lasting. Defenders of trawl gear maintain that impact is mostly limited and of low intensity compared to natural events.

Pelagic trawling is a much "cleaner" method of fishing, in that the catch usually consists of just one species. However, some cases of it have been attacked for depleting resources which are important sources of food for certain sea birds. An instance of this was the RSPB linking a population crash of sea birds in the North Sea to pelagic fishing for sand eels, which are food for many seabird species. This led to political pressure for the closure of this fishery; the seabird populations subsequently improved. However, a second population crash of seabirds which occurred with no effect on the stocks of sand eel, cast doubt on this link.

Other uses of the Word "Trawl"

The noun "trawl" has many possibly confusing meanings in commercial fisheries. For example, two or more lobster pots that are fished together may be referred to as a trawl. In some older usages "trawling" meant "long-line fishing"; that usage occurs in Rudyard Kipling's book Captains Courageous. (This use is perhaps confused with trolling, where a baited line is trailed behind a boat)

The word "trawling" has come to be used in a number of non-fishing contexts, usually meaning indiscriminate collection with the intent of picking out the useful bits. For instance, in law enforcement it may refer to collecting large records of telephone calls hoping to find calls made by suspects. The word "trawling" occurs frequently in general literature and is used to mean searching through literature for information more often than it means catching fish.

Hand-line Fishing

Handlining is one of the oldest forms of fishing and is still common. The method consists of a single fishing line with a weight and one or more lure-like hooks are attached. The line is jigged or moved up and down in a series of short movements, most often close to the sea floor. The motion attracts the fish, which are normally caught while trying to eat the lure but also as they move close to jigged the lure. The line is then hauled onboard and the fish removed. Handlining are most often used to catch groundfish and squid but also other species are sometimes caught, including pelagic species.

Long-Line Fishing

Long-line fishing is a commercial fishing technique that uses hundreds or even thousands of baited hooks hanging from a single line. Swordfish, tuna and Patagonian toothfish are commonly caught by this method. It is also practiced on a smaller scale in New Zealand, where a twenty five hook maximum is prescribed by law.

Longlines can be set to hang near the surface, for instance in tuna fisheries, or on the sea bottom, such as in the Patagonian tooth fish fishery.

Long-line fishing is controversial because the lines can lead to significant bycatch, often of endangered species such as sea turtles, petrels and albatrosses. Methods to mitigate such incidental mortality have been developed and successfully implemented in some fisheries. These include the use of weights to ensure the lines sink quickly, the deployment of streamer lines to scare birds away from the baited hooks as they are deployed, setting lines only at night with ship lighting kept low (to avoid attracting birds), limiting fishing seasons to the southern winter (when most seabirds are not feeding young), and not discharging offal while setting lines.

ECONOMICS AND MANAGEMENT OF AQUATIC RESOURCES IN COLLABORATION

Between March and May 2000 the Centre for the Economics and Management of Aquatic Resources in collaboration with the Ghanaian Department of Fisheries conducted a survey of 64 fishing villages along the Ghanaian coast. This sample represents 33 per cent of the villages listed in the latest Canoe Frame Survey (1995) conducted by the Department of Fisheries. These villages are spread amongst 4 regions. With no information on the variability of the population it was decided to select one third of all the villages in each region on a random basis.

In order to gain a complete picture of conflicts within the coastal zone, interviews were also conducted with inshore-vessel owners and a number of industrial fleet operatives. Ghanaian artisanal canoe communities are organised around the Chief Fisherman. A complex set of procedures has to be undertaken before any interviewing can take place and no interviewing can be conducted with permission from the Chief Fisherman. Consequently we targeted the Chief Fishermen who on most occasions was accompanied by a number of other village elders, usually comprising his right-hand man and the most skilful or successful fisherman in the village.

On a number of occasions large groups of women traders and other fishermen were present at the meeting. For reasons of simplicity and speed a number of tools were adapted from the extensive PRA 'toolbox' to help build PISCES (Participatory Institutional Survey and Conflict Evaluation Study) developed specifically for use with artisanal fishing communities to gather information on institutional arrangements.

AN OASIS OF CALM IN A SEA OF TROUBLES

Theory would suggest that given the economic context within which Ghanaian fisheries are operating, the open-access nature of the resource and the inherent instability of pelagic stocks, conflict should be widespread and the fisheries management institutions under considerable pressure. Initial analysis, however, suggests that this is not the case.

At the time of writing data collection was still continuing in Central and Western Regions. The summary results below are therefore preliminary results on regions already completed. Villages as institutions. From the results so far, Ghanaian coastal villages appear to be stable and differ little in their organisational structure along the entire length of the coast. The village chief is at the top of the hierarchy, the Chief Fishermen, first point of call for all fisheries matters sits beneath the Chief.

Although by law the Ghanaian coastal line is open access (to Ghanaian citizens), in practice, a complex set of local laws and a system of reciprocity and responsibility govern inshore waters. 91.7 per cent of villages questioned confirmed that although anyone could fish off the beach, in practice, they must seek permission or announce their intentions to the Chief Fisherman, this includes residents and migrants. The remaining 8.3 per cent stated that anyone could fish off the beach, and did not qualify their answer. No one reported ever having a request to fish denied.

Once permission has been granted by the Chief Fisherman he then becomes responsible for the welfare of the fisherman and his kin. This system of 'responsibility' is not unique to Ghana and acts as a kind of insurance scheme. There are many internal migrant fishermen in Ghana-some are migrants that seasonally move from one area to another, others are migrants that have been settled in a village for generations but, because they are from a different language group, are still classed as migrants.

The distinction between natives and migrants to so powerful than in one village in Western Region, there are two separate landing sites: the Fante-line and the Ewe-line highlighting the two distinct groups that have fished from the village for many years. The institutionalisation of fisheries management. The local institutional structure of Ghanaian fisheries has, on the face of it, changed very little over the past centuries, and it is perhaps this stability and consistency that helps it remain comparatively peaceful.

However, economic reforms have caused many significant negative changes to the national organisation of fishing in the past five years but in some areas have also ironically tended to bolster the local structures rather than threaten them. The most significant positive change has been the introduction of the Community Based Fisheries Management Programme (CBFM) under the auspices of the Fisheries Sub-sector Capacity Building Project. The success of the CBFM would appear to be largely due to the fact that rather than radically changing the status quo, it has strengthened the existing structures.

The Fisheries Sub-sector Capacity Building Project is a joint venture between the Government of Ghana and IDA/World Bank. Started in October 1995 its main objectives were to improve the long-term sustainability of Ghanaian fisheries. Within this main objective was also the aim to improve the capacity of the Department of Fisheries, address the issue of lack of an active management regime, weak institutional and legal frameworks for fisheries and a growing financial and resource crisis in the industry. In order for the sustainability of Ghanaian fisheries to be improved management plans were needed and for these to be successful they would need the full approval of local communities. The Project will run until 2001 when the funding will finish and the Government of Ghana will be responsible for seeing its continuation.

As part of the CBFM, committees have been formed in each community and their first task was to draw up a list of by-laws governing fishing activity there. By drawing up their own by-laws and submitting them to the District Assembly for ratification, local norms would be lent weight and legitimacy. This has a two-way function.

Firstly the community feels that its laws are valued because they are recognised by a higher authority and secondly, it engenders a sense of trust and liaison between the communities and the District Assemblies. The make-up of the committees varies but as a rule consists of the chief fisherman and representatives of the various stakeholders. Typically this would include the indigenous and migrant fishermen, the fish processors, fishmongers and fishtraders, vessels, gear and engine owners, and a representative from the Fishermen's Service Centre. During the course of the field work the villages in a number of districts in Central Region were going through the process of ratifying the by-laws which had recently been gazetted.

The drawing up of by-laws has allowed existing norms to be institutionalised and has allowed 'best-practice' in fishing to be argued out amongst the fishermen and agreed up in a formal setting. A good example of this is the by-law that bans children from the beach during school hours (recognising that schooling is a very important part of village development) and the by-law that formally bans fishing with dynamite (an extremely contentious issue up to this point). Conflicts and conflict management.

In the regions so far covered, violent conflict between fishermen was very rarely mentioned. Day-to-day squabbles and difficulties are, however, common. Interestingly, the pricing of fish is regarded as a conflict, although it could be argued that this is an essential and integral part of how markets work and is a sign of competition not conflict.

However, because the ethos of the survey was for the communities to identify what they considered to be conflicts, we have let it stand. Two other conflicts often attracted heated debate: the incursion of semi-industrial trawlers into water less than 30 metres deep (reported by 25 per cent of villages) and fights among women over access to catches and credit facilities (reported by 29.2 per cent of villages). Although there was scant reference to a rising number of canoes or fishermen related to the presence of conflict, two examples stand out in particular. One was a fishing community in Accra which suffers from its proximity to the city centre and all the urban poverty problems associated with it. Here the Secretary to the Chief Fisherman mentioned that the landing beach was no longer able to cope with the number of canoes and there were many conflicts over landing canoes and off-loading catches.

The other was Mumford, a well documented fishing village also reported problems with lack of landing facilities exacerbated by the increased number of canoes present in the village. Based on the answers recorded, conflict in Ghanaian coastal artisanal fisheries can be divided into a number of categories: conflict that results from outside influences, conflict that results from the internal allocation of resources and that which could probably be better described as competition.

The typology below attempts to categorise the most frequent problems encountered, it should be noted that at the margins some conflicts could happily sit in a number of boxes. Those conflicts caused by outside influences are the hardest to solve because they involve elements beyond the immediate control of the village.

Because violent conflict is almost unheard of, it is perhaps useful to establish a conflict scale for Ghana that better distinguishes between the various degrees of day-to-day squabbles. Conflict management at the village level is highly structured and organised and it is perhaps a reflection of this that conflicts are few and far between. All villages in the survey reported that any conflict between fishermen is reported first to the Chief Fisherman who then, along with his panel of elders, comes to a decision on the issue. In the case of damage to nets or boats caused by other canoe owners, the culprit is usually made to pay 2/3 of the damages (recognising thus that fishing is a dangerous activity and incidents are rarely deliberate). Although these cases may take a while to resolve-establishing fault and liability-they are not considered to be onerous. The conflicts that do take longer to resolve are those between different types of vessel-trawlers damaging the nets of canoe fishermen cause a frequent problem.

Even when there are a number of witnesses and broad daylight has enabled the collection of the name and registration details of the offending vessel, the cases can take months to resolve. Such cases are reported to the relevant local fisheries office that then deals with them.

Trawler owners often deny all responsibility for the damage and communication and transport difficulties between the administrative centres and the villages further lengthens the process. Other factors arose that, whilst not identified as conflicts by the villagers, were identified as making life in the villages more difficult. Two examples of these are the incidence of erosion and the rising costs of inputs.

Sea erosion was frequently mentioned in villages in Greater Accra and Volta region to the east of Tema harbour. Sea erosion in the Bight of Benin is serious; current large scale project funded by international agencies are working to building sea defences to protect the coastline. Local lore suggests that without these sea defences Keta Lagoon (a significant water body close to the Togo border) will disappear into the sea in five years time. The building of Tema harbour was the most frequently cited reason for erosion in the east of the country.

The knock-on effects of the Akosombo Dam, built on the Volta River are also cited for disrupting flooding patterns in the river delta (this has resulted in decreasing water levels in lagoons) and the disappearance of certain fish species at the mouth of the river.

The rising price of inputs was universally mentioned as one of the hardest issues to contend with. Given that changing economic circumstances affect how communities deal with the day to day running of their lives, it is hardly surprising that there is a perceived link between increased economic hardship and conflict.

Only increased funding of a monitoring and enforcement capacity and negotiation with the trawler owners is going to be able to better deal with this problem. This is supposed to be covered under the remit of the FSCBP, but as it liable to be a long-term goal. The root cause of the trawler issue-declining catches and rising costs pushing the trawlers into illegal areas-has a number of long-term solutions.

However, the trawler sector is facing severe economic pressures and any measures are probably too painful to contemplate at this juncture and beyond the capacity of the State (economically and politically) to implement currently.

The Community Based Fisheries Management Programme (CBFM) would appear to have had positive benefits to the communities. By using the existing institutional structure, the CBFM has enabled more formalised management to be introduced to communities without upsetting what was clearly a system that worked well to begin with.

The only communities that appeared indifferent to the CBFM were those in urban areas (principally Accra). The reason given for this attitude is that fishermen in these communities tend to be better educated and have greater access to media and other information. They are more cynical of government promises of how things will get better in the future and more likely to rebuff any attempts by the government to interfere. Outside urban areas, the CBFM was the reason cited for the decrease in conflict or the satisfaction with the conflict management system in place.

The gazetting of local by-laws was looked upon favourably by all those spoken to. So, in terms of transaction cost analysis, it could be argued that providing local institutions with a more 'legitimate' basis both within their own community and in the district as whole has helped maintain transaction costs at a stable level. In those communities where the incidence of conflict has declined, the CBFM may even have helped reduce transaction costs.

There is, however, a corollary to this argument. Although the CBFM has had a number of positive benefits, it has also inserted bureaucratic systems into institutions that worked quite happily without them before. Further research needs to be done on this issue, but it would be interesting to see if CBFM has actually increased the transaction costs of some communities in terms of time spent at CBFM meetings, costs incurred in travel to meetings and the added costs of bureaucracy involved.

ADOPTION OF CONSERVATION AND MANAGEMENT MEASURES

When considering the adoption of conservation and management measures, the best scientific evidence available should be taken into account in order to evaluate the current state of the fishery resources and the possible impact of the proposed measures on the resources. Research in support of fishery conservation and management should be promoted, including research on the resources and on the effects of climatic, environmental and socio-economic factors. The results of such research should be disseminated to interested parties.

Studies should be promoted which provide an understanding of the costs, benefits and effects of alternative management options designed to rationalise fishing, in particular, options relating to excess fishing capacity and excessive levels of fishing effort. States should ensure that timely, complete and reliable statistics on catch and fishing effort are collected and maintained in accordance with applicable international standards and practices and in sufficient detail to allow sound statistical analysis. Such data should be updated regularly and verified through an appropriate system. States should compile and disseminate such data in a manner consistent with any applicable confidentiality requirements.

In order to ensure sustainable management of fisheries and to enable social and economic objectives to be achieved, sufficient knowledge of social, economic and institutional factors should be developed through data gathering, analysis and research. States should compile fishery-related and other supporting scientific data relating to fish stocks covered by subregional or regional fisheries management organisations or arrangements in an internationally agreed format and provide them in a timely manner to the organisation or arrangement.

In cases of stocks which occur in the jurisdiction of more than one State and for which there is no such organisation or arrangement, the States concerned should agree on a mechanism for cooperation to compile and exchange such data. Subregional or regional fisheries management organisations or arrangements should compile data and make them available, in a manner consistent with any applicable confidentiality requirements, in a timely manner and in an agreed format to all members of these organisations and other interested parties in accordance with agreed procedures.

PRECAUTIONARY APPROACH

States should apply the precautionary approach widely to conservation, management and exploitation of living aquatic resources in order to protect them and preserve the aquatic environment. The absence of adequate scientific information should not be used as a reason for postponing or failing to take conservation and management measures. In implementing the precautionary approach, States should take into account, *inter alia*, uncertainties relating to the size and productivity of the stocks, reference points, stock condition in relation to such reference points, levels and distribution of fishing mortality and the impact of fishing activities, including discards, on non-target and associated or dependent species, as well as environmental and socio-economic conditions. States and subregional or regional fisheries management organisations and arrangements should, on the basis of the best scientific evidence available, *inter alia*, determine:

- Stock specific target reference points, and, at the same time, the action to be taken if they are exceeded; and
- Stock-specific limit reference points, and, at the same time, the action to be taken if they are exceeded; when a limit reference point is approached, measures should be taken to ensure that it will not be exceeded.

In the case of new or exploratory fisheries, States should adopt as soon as possible cautious conservation and management measures, including, *inter alia*, catch limits and effort limits. Such measures should remain in force until there are sufficient data to allow assessment of the impact of the fisheries on the long-term sustainability of the stocks, whereupon conservation and management measures based on that assessment should be implemented. The latter measures should, if appropriate, allow for the gradual development of the fisheries. If a natural phenomenon has a significant adverse impact on the status of living aquatic resources, States should adopt conservation and management measures on an emergency basis to ensure that fishing activity does not exacerbate such adverse impact.

States should also adopt such measures on an emergency basis where fishing activity presents a serious threat to the sustainability of such resources. Measures taken on an emergency basis should be temporary and should be based on the best scientific evidence available.

LEVEL OF FISHING PERMITTED IN MANAGEMENT MEASURES

States should ensure that the level of fishing permitted is commensurate with the state of fisheries resources. States should adopt measures to ensure that no vessel be allowed to fish unless so authorised, in a manner consistent with international law for the high seas or in conformity with national legislation within areas of national jurisdiction.

Where excess fishing capacity exists, mechanisms should be established to reduce capacity to levels commensurate with the sustainable use of fisheries resources so as to ensure that fishers operate under economic conditions that promote responsible fisheries. Such mechanisms should include monitoring the capacity of fishing fleets.

The performance of all existing fishing gear, methods and practices should be examined and measures taken to ensure that fishing gear, methods and practices which are not consistent with responsible fishing are phased out and replaced with more acceptable alternatives. In this process, particular attention should be given to the impact of such measures on fishing communities, including their ability to exploit the resource.

States and fisheries management organisations and arrangements should regulate fishing in such a way as to avoid the risk of conflict among fishers using different vessels, gear and fishing methods.

When deciding on the use, conservation and management of fisheries resources, due recognition should be given, as appropriate, in accordance with national laws and regulations, to the traditional practices, needs and interests of indigenous people and local fishing communities which are highly dependent on fishery resources for their livelihood. In the evaluation of alternative conservation and management measures, their cost-effectiveness and social impact should be considered.

The efficacy of conservation and management measures and their possible interactions should be kept under continuous review. Such measures should, as appropriate, be revised or abolished in the light of new information. States should take appropriate measures to minimize waste, discards, catch by lost or abandoned gear, catch of non-target species, both fish and non-fish species, and negative impacts on associated or dependent species, in particular endangered species.

Where appropriate, such measures may include technical measures related to fish size, mesh size or gear, discards, closed seasons and areas and zones reserved for selected fisheries, particularly artisanal fisheries. Such measures should be applied, where appropriate, to protect juveniles and spawners. States and subregional or regional fisheries management organisations and arrangements should promote, to the extent practicable, the development and use of selective, environmentally safe and cost effective gear and techniques.

States and subregional and regional fisheries management organisations and arrangements, in the framework of their respective competences, should introduce measures for depleted resources and those resources threatened with depletion that facilitate the sustained recovery of such stocks. They should make every effort to ensure that resources and habitats critical to the well-being of such resources which have been adversely affected by fishing or other human activities are restored.

EFFECTIVE LEGAL AND ADMINISTRATIVE FRAMEWORK

States should ensure that an effective legal and administrative framework at the local and national level, as appropriate, is established for fisheries resource conservation and fisheries management. States should ensure that laws and regulations provide for sanctions applicable in respect of violations which are adequate in severity to be effective, including sanctions which allow for the refusal, withdrawal or suspension of authorisations to fish in the event of non-compliance with conservation and management measures in force.

States, in conformity with their national laws, should implement effective fisheries monitoring, control, surveillance and law enforcement measures including, where appropriate, observer programmes, inspection schemes and vessel monitoring systems. Such measures should be promoted and, where appropriate, implemented by subregional or regional fisheries management organisations and arrangements in accordance with procedures agreed by such organisations or arrangements.

States and subregional or regional fisheries management organisations and arrangements, as appropriate, should agree on the means by which the activities of such organisations and arrangements will be financed, bearing in mind, *inter alia*, the relative benefits derived from the fishery and the differing capacities of countries to provide financial and other contributions. Where appropriate, and when possible, such organisations and arrangements should aim to recover the costs of fisheries conservation, management and research.

States which are members of or participants in subregional or regional fisheries management organisations or arrangements should implement internationally agreed measures adopted in the framework of such organisations or arrangements and consistent with international law to deter the activities of vessels flying the flag of non-members or non-participants which engage in activities which undermine the effectiveness of conservation and management measures established by such organisations or arrangements.

Financial Institutions

Without prejudice to relevant international agreements, States should encourage banks and financial institutions not to require, as a condition of a loan or mortgage, fishing vessels or fishing support vessels to be flagged in a jurisdiction other than that of the State of beneficial ownership where such a requirement would have the effect of increasing the likelihood of non-compliance with international conservation and management measures.

FISHERIES AND AQUACULTURE PRODUCTS

Fisheries and aquaculture products are globally important sources of much needed, high quality, aquatic animal proteins, and invaluable providers of employment, cash income, and foreign exchange. Fisheries products are the world's most widely traded foods, with commerce dominated by the developing countries.

Fisheries products are the primary protein sources for some 950 million people worldwide, and are an important part of the diet of many more. In comparison to other sectors of the world food economy, however, the fisheries and aquaculture sectors are poorly planned, inadequately funded, and neglected by all levels of government. This neglect occurs in a paradoxical situation: fishing is the largest extractive use of wildlife in the world; and aquaculture is the most rapidly growing sector of the global agricultural economy.

Our vision is one in which the USAID is a world leader in channeling high quality, "needs directed" kinds of technical assistance in fisheries and aquaculture to developing countries, mainly in the form of capacity-building though education and training opportunities, but also in applied research. Considering the status, priority issues and future trends we have identified in this study, we recommend seven strategic approaches and investments to USAID:

- USAID needs to substantially increase its programmatic emphasis and enlarge its financial and human resource commitments to global fisheries and aquaculture.
- USAID needs to play a central role in mobilising America's considerable human and institutional resources in fisheries and aquaculture to assist developing countries.
- USAID needs to bridge the "digital divide" to develop solutions to fisheries and aquaculture issues in developing countries.
- USAID should prioritise the improved management of coastal marine and inland fisheries by providing technical assistance to evolve innovative fisheries management schemes in developing countries, including but not limited to, property rights, co-management, and the use of marine protected areas; plus assist in the development of more accurate and reliable fisheries data reporting systems.
- USAID needs to substantially increase its support to develop more comprehensive, sustainable, ecologically and socially compatible, and economically viable aquaculture systems in developing countries that

have the long-term goals of poverty alleviation and food security.

- USAID should prioritise its assistance to fisheries and aquaculture activities that are more integrated, comprehensive, community-based, and use "systems approaches"-such as ecological and integrated farming/fishing systems research and extension approaches-in both rural and urban settings. The current agriculture emphasis of USAID is on plant commodity research, not on comprehensive, agro/aqua-ecosystems research/extension approaches. We urge the USAID to support long-term, applied research and development that makes expanded use of participatory ecological and social science tools to empower community control of fisheries and aquaculture systems; and to better integrate aquaculture and fisheries activities into the comprehensive management of natural and social resources of its missions, target nations and regions.
- USAID needs to develop comprehensive strategic and implementation plans and regular impact assessments of an expanded fisheries and aquaculture portfolio. USAID missions and regions should include fisheries and aquaculture into their strategic plans for the comprehensive management of natural resources-or they will be incomplete-especially in regards to USAID plans for involvement in the issues of water allocation and quality, and plans for the management of marine and inland coastal areas.

We believe our case for increased strategic engagement and substantially increased investments in priority issues of importance to the future sustainability of global capture fisheries and aquaculture by all levels of the USAID bureaucracy (headquarters, regions, missions, etc.) cannot be overlooked. America has an accelerating trade deficit in fisheries products that now exceeds $9 billion per year-a deficit surpassed only by those in oil and automobiles-and the US remains the 4th largest exporter of fisheries products in the world (~$2.8 billion). The lack of US engagement in international fisheries and aquaculture not only compromises America's financial position: and an important part of our Nation's food security is at risk; and our domestic fisheries and aquaculture industries are rapidly losing their competitive position.

STATUS, TRENDS AND ISSUES IN FISHERIES AND AQUACULTURE

We suspect that living in true harmony with the natural world, in a manner sustainable over the long run, is something no modern human society has yet learned how to do. The survival of the natural world, however, and likely our survival as a species, depends on our learning to do this. It will be a unique experience in human history.

MARINE FISHERIES RESOURCES AND POTENTIAL

Reported global production of marine capture fisheries increased from 17 million tons in 1950 to about 80 million tons in the mid-1980s, oscillating since then between 78 and 88 million tons (excluding discards), representing 60 per cent of the overall fisheries production including aquaculture in 2001. The annual rate of increase of marine catches decreased to almost zero in the 1990s, indicating that the world oceans have reached their maximal production under the present fishing regime. An estimated 25 per cent of the major marine fish stocks for which information is available are underexploited or moderately exploited. Stocks or species groups in this category represent the main source for the potential expansion of total marine catches. About 47 per cent of the main stocks or species groups are fully exploited and are therefore producing catches that have reached, or are very close to, their maximum sustainable limits. Thus, nearly half of world marine stocks offer no reasonable expectations for further expansion.

Another 18 per cent of stocks or species groups are reported as overexploited. Prospects for expansion or increased production from these stocks are negligible; and there is an increasing likelihood that stocks will decline further and catches will decrease, unless remedial management action is taken to reduce overfishing. The remaining 10 per cent of stocks have become significantly depleted, or are recovering from depletion and are far less productive than they used to be (or than they could be) if management can return them to the higher abundance levels commensurate with their pre-depletion catch levels.

Recovery usually implies drastic and long-lasting reductions in fishing pressure and/or the adoption of other management measures to remove conditions that contributed to the stock's overexploitation and depletion. In most areas, overfishing is certainly a significant factor responsible for the declines. The information available tends to confirm the estimates made by FAO in the early seventies that the global potential for marine fisheries is about 100 million tons of which only 80 million tons were probably achievable for practical reasons. It also confirms that despite local differences, overall, this limit has been reached.

Developed countries are faced with fully or overexploited stocks so their management objectives concentrate on stock rebuilding and capacity reduction, although most countries also have significant aims regarding markets and social conflict. The most urgent objective is to scale fleet sizes so that they become commensurate with sustainable exploitation of the resources. Management plans also increasingly recognise the need for a policy that integrates fisheries with management of the coastal zone or inland waters.

Developing countries tend to concentrate on fisheries development in terms of new resources and technology. Although it is recognised that some stocks are overfished, objectives are concentrated more on enhancing and diversifying fisheries rather than on limiting fishing efforts.

This is perhaps because the underlying concern for many countries is the relatively important role fisheries play in employment and food security for some of their poorest people. More specific aims include building infrastructure (particularly for processing to reduce post-harvest losses and increase the value added); fishery enhancement, through restocking; and reducing social conflicts, not only among different fishing groups but also between fisheries and other sectors. The principal policy challenge is to bring the capacity of the global fishing fleet back to a level at which fish stocks can be sustainably harvested. Fisheries based on clearly defined rights of access will need to become more common: experience shows that when these rights are not merely in place but are understood and observed by users, conflicts tend to be minimized. The need is to blend innovation, research, conservation and educational awareness into a goal of aquatic sustainability, and to demonstrate this via successful commercial enterprises. The "great trends" of the past 20 years in marine fisheries worldwide are the:

- Globalisation of both production and labour in marine fisheries,
- The overcapacity of fleets both nearshore and offshore, resulting in dramatic and widespread declines in catches per unit efforts,
- The movement of the bulk of the world's fishing capacity from the developed to developing countries, resulting in
- Declining catches and economic hardships worldwide in small scale artesanal and inshore fisheries resulting in less fish for poor consumers, and
- Infant success with various property rights schemes and use of protected areas to sustain stocks.

Inland Fisheries Resources and Potential

Four current strategies in the use of inland waters for fisheries can be distinguished:

- Food fisheries based on wild stocks;
- Enhancement of food fisheries in smaller water bodies and reservoirs;
- Recreational fisheries, which are becoming more common in many areas of the world, and, where they develop, tend to supplant commercial food fisheries; and
- Locally very intense exploitation of juvenile or small adults for stocking into other water bodies and/or aquaculture ponds, or for the ornamental fish trade.

In 2001, inland capture from 129 countries reached 8.7 million tons. Regionally, Asia dominates inland capture, accounting for nearly 66 per cent (about 5.8 million tons) of the total in 2001, with Africa second at 24 per cent (nearly 2 million tons). In comparison, the remaining regions are relatively insignificant. The capture from inland waters is very diverse. Apart from fish, other groups included in inland capture that are tabulated by weight are freshwater shrimps and prawns, frogs, terrapins, turtles, crayfishes, mussels, mussel shells, pearl oyster shells, swamp crabs, marine worms, manatees and green seaweeds.

There is an enigma concerning the status of inland fishery resources. On the one hand, it is widely accepted and well documented that freshwater resources and environments are deteriorating rapidly and widely. On the other hand, harvests from freshwater environments are stable or on the upswing among countries that account for 93 per cent of the total inland capture.

The increases are due to three factors:

1. Enrichment of aquatic systems from land based human activities that until now have been a counterweight to habitat losses and pollution;
2. Enhancements of inland fisheries (*e.g.*, stocking, introductions) that increase the output per unit of area; and
3. The increased number of reservoirs with capture fisheries enhancement activities.31 Inland fisheries enhancement methods, often combined with conventional fisheries management practices, are widely applied, and are becoming a central theme in the management of inland waters in developing countries The exact contribution of enhancements to the total inland capture fisheries production is, however, difficult to estimate.

INLAND CAPTURE IN DEVELOPING COUNTRIES

About two-thirds of inland capture is from developing countries and about one-fourth is from China. The countries in Africa and Asia that are among the top 20 in inland capture production also rank low in the Human Development Indices.

This comparison underlines the need to sustain inland fisheries in the countries where inland capture is relatively important in its own right, where inland capture contributes significantly to food security, and where levels of human development are lowest.

In contrast, inland recreational fisheries are pre-eminent in most developed countries; however, almost every country with inland waters has some recreational fisheries that often play an important role in subsistence. Indications are that freshwater recreational effort is perhaps one-half of the food fishing effort from a worldwide perspective.

Output from inland food fisheries will continue to increase slowly overall. In the short term most of the gains will be realised where enhancements are already common, namely in Asia.

In Africa, where enhancements have been slow to be implemented, output may actually decrease due to overfishing and a deteriorating environment in the most populous countries, but increase as enhancements become more widely implemented. Likewise, in Latin America, inland fisheries enhancements are practiced and are growing, but the demand for inland fish is weak in many countries, while in others degradation of the environment is causing a decline in production.

Degradation of the environment is the main underlying issue, and the consequent loss of fishery habitat is the pre-eminent concern. A closely related concern is that loss of habitat that, along with the intense and widespread exploitation of fishery resources, negatively impacts aquatic biodiversity. In practical terms, the resiliency of resources to fishing, and often the quality of the resources, is lessened.

Additionally, in most countries the main challenges to maintaining and enhancing inland fish production and small-scale aquaculture and their associated social and economic benefits are increasing competition for resources and insufficient institutional and political recognition.

Reporting and Statistical Issues in Fisheries

Without reliable statistics, effective fisheries management and policy-making are impossible. During the last decade, financial support for the development and maintenance of national fishery statistical systems have decreased sharply in real terms, while statistical requirements have been increasing dramatically for by-catch and discards, fishing capacity, illegal fishing, vessels authorised to fish in the high seas, economic data (costs, revenues, prices, subsidies), employment, management systems, inventories of stocks and fisheries, aquaculture, etc.

Despite FAO's efforts, the available fisheries data are not fully reliable. The outcome is far from perfect in terms of coverage, timeliness, and quality. Statistics from artisanal and subsistence fisheries are still a concern, and many key statistics are missing, *e.g.*, economic and social data, discards, fishing capacity, etc. The result is that the general trends are probably reliably reflected, but the annual figures and the assessments involve a degree of uncertainty, and small changes from year to year are probably not statistically significant. Illegal, unreported and unregulated fishing is found in all capture fisheries, irrespective of the location, species targeted, fishing gears employed or level and intensity of exploitation. Working with the countries is the only way to improve fishery statistics, primarily to meet national needs with regard to food security and fisheries management. Unlike capture fisheries, the separate monitoring of aquaculture is relatively new in most countries, and often there are less well-established systems of data collection as compared to capture fisheries.

Actual inland capture fisheries production is considerably greater than the amounts reported to FAO. The factor is at least two overall, but may be as high as three in some instances.

There is an urgent need for better data on inland fisheries that can be interpreted in both economic and ecological terms. Although the cost of improving inland fishery data collection may be high, failure to fully account for inland capture also is costly in terms of lost opportunities to increase food security and other economic and social benefits from enhanced management of inland fisheries resources.

China's marine capture fishery production for 1995-1999 has been overstated in Chinese statistics submitted to and published by FAO. The chapter states that as a consequence of this, global marine capture fishery production-excluding Peruvian anchoveta-has likely been declining since 1988 rather than remaining fairly constant as indicated by the statistics. According to the authors, this would have led to understating the degradation of world fisheries, and produced unfortunate policy and investment decisions. However, the FAO maintains that despite likely errors in the data sets, the main global trends have not been masked, and that the most important conclusions have emerged, nevertheless. These findings, together with similar ones emerging at regional and national level, have been the foundation for the governance and institutional changes observed since 1990.

Aquaculture Status and Potential

Aquaculture is more akin to farming and animal husbandry than to fishing, as it involves the rearing and management of living aquatic resources in a restricted environment. Tenure of production facilities, and property rights to the produce, are as important to the success of aquaculture as land tenure is to agriculture.

Aquaculture has been developed to serve a variety of purposes:

- Producing high nutritional value food for human consumption;
- Contributing to rural income and employment through farming and related activities;
- Enhancing capture and sport fisheries;
- Cultivating ornamental species for aesthetic purposes;
- Controlling aquatic weeds or pests hazardous to humans or crops; and
- Desalination and other forms of soil recuperation.

Meeting basic human needs for protein foods in the future will be a difficult challenge. Approximately 1.3 billion people live on less than a dollar a day-the cost of a half a pint of beer-and half of the world's population lives on less than 2 dollars a day.

Since 1950, there's been a 100 per cent increase in the per capita demand for fish, a 40 per cent increase for grain, and 33 per cent for wood. If world fish consumption will increase from 16 kg (1997) to 19-20 kg by 2030, total human use of aquatic foods will increase to 150-160 million tons. Capture fisheries can provide no more than 100 million tons, so the bulk of the increase will need to come from aquaculture.

In 2001, 48.4 million tons of aquatic products (including plants) valued at US$ 61.5 billion were produced, with half of the production being finfish. Aquaculture is growing more rapidly than all other animal food producing sectors.

Worldwide, the sector has increased at an average compounded rate of 9.2 per cent per year since 1970, compared with only 1.4 per cent for capture fisheries and 2.8 per cent for terrestrial farmed meat production systems. Over half of global aquaculture production originated from marine and brackish coastal waters, while the remainder (45 per cent) was from freshwater.

Aquaculture will soon overtake cattle ranching as a global food resource, possibly signaling a basic shift in diets. Over the last century, the world relied heavily on two natural systems-oceanic fisheries and rangelands-to satisfy a growing demand for animal protein, but that era is ending as both systems are reaching their productive limits.

Between 1950 and 1990, beef production, four-fifths of it from rangelands, nearly tripled, climbing from 19 million to 53 million tons before leveling off. Since 1990, there has been little growth in either beef production or the oceanic fish catch. Additional production of beef or seafood now depends on placing more cattle in feedlots or more fish in ponds.

PRODUCTION EFFICIENCIES OF AQUACULTURE

Comparisons of energy and production efficiencies of aquaculture versus an array of fisheries and terrestrial agriculture systems confirm that aquaculture is an efficient mass producer of animal proteins for a crowded, coastal planet. Production efficiencies of edible mass for aquaculture range from 2.5 to 4.5 kg dry feed/kg edible mass compared with 3.0 to 17.4 for conventional terrestrial animal production systems.

Beef cattle require over 10 kg of feed to add 1 kg of edible weight, whereas catfish can add a kg of edible weight with less than 3 kg of feed. To produce 1 kcal of catfish protein about 34 kcal of fossil fuel energy is required-lobster and shrimp capture fisheries use more than 5 times this amount of energy. Energy costs for even the most intensive salmon cages are less than lobster and shrimp fishing, but are comparable to beef production in feedlots. Aquaculture also has a comparable advantage in water efficiency, since a comparatively smaller amount of water for aquaculture is required. For example, catfish ponds managed using multiple harvest strategies use 1.50 m3 of water per 1 kg of product while conventional soybean production takes 1.63 m3 of water to produce 1 kg.

In a world of land and water scarcity, the advantages of aquaculture over capture fisheries and other land-based protein production systems to produce low-cost animal protein are clear. However, care must be taken to ensure that aquaculture is not viewed as a panacea-since most analysts agree that aquaculture will never completely replace capture fisheries-and that increased aquaculture production will not be associated with higher rates of environmental damage and harvest rates of forage fish species used to produce fish meals and oils, which would lead to a net loss of fish production (*e.g.*, the capture for fish meals and oils would exceed the amount of fish produced for consumption).

There are many cases where aquaculture expansion has fueled the hope of fragile coastal and inland rural communities that have undergone unprecedented changes in their traditional ways of life. Aquaculture has provided significant multiplier effects on the local economies increasing both direct and indirect personal spending in these coastal communities. And yet, communities in many parts of the world actively oppose aquacultural development because such development is perceived as a threat to local social and/or ecological systems.

If intensive aquaculture operations-no matter how advanced technically-have no community roots; and feeds, seeds, supplies, equipment and human expertise are procured from great distances from the sites of production; community opposition will continue to occur. In these cases it is easy to see why some community members view aquaculture development as "all we get is your pollution".

Planning for aquaculture development as community development and environmental enhancement must thereby encompass regional planning processes to accommodate aquaculture's vital support industries (inputs), and for the use of aquaculture resources and wastes in agriculture or in environmental enhancement projects (outputs). Regional planning for "ecological aquaculture" developments will have much higher positive impacts on jobs and the environment, and will eventually dissolve the opposition from communities who will see the newcomers as one of their own.

Aquaculture production systems, aquatic environments, and the feeds to produce fish must be environmentally benign and ecologically sound in order for the advantages of aquaculture as a food production system to be embraced and supported. Indeed, the expansion of aquaculture can never be justified on the destruction of the world's capture fisheries. The future protein needs of millions of people-and the sustainability of aquaculture itself-depend on the conservation, good management and recovery of the world's capture fisheries and the environments on which they depend.

CONSERVATION THROUGH CONSUMER ACTION

To assess public attitudes regarding a variety of ocean issues, between 1996 and 2001, SeaWeb has worked with professional market research firms. The results reported here represent a subset of the opinions expressed by survey respondents. In all cases, the surveys were conducted using industry-standard market research techniques and included sample sizes that allowed for accurate calculation of statistical significance.

Most Americans care about the oceans and believe that the health of oceans is threatened. Fifty-nine per cent of those responding to a 1999 poll rated the overall health and quality of the oceans as "only fair" or "poor," while less than one-third thought the oceans are in "good" or "excellent" condition. The same poll showed that over half believe that the condition of the oceans is deteriorating, having gotten worse in recent years. An even larger percentage 'Äì nearly three-quarters 'Äì evaluate the condition of coastal waters as negative. Coastlines are where the majority of people interact most directly with oceans.

Studies consistently show that the public--caring most about human health--views pollution with greatest concern and as the topmost threat to ocean health.

- From among a range of environmental problems--water pollution, rain forest loss, development, overconsumption, etc.--people consider most urgent those with the most direct impact on human health, namely water pollution and toxic wastes.
- The 1999 poll gave people a list of specific ocean issues--ranging from oil spills, corporate farm run-off, and improperly treated sewage to coastal development, commercial overfishing, and damage from boating/jet skis--and asked respondents to rank them. Deterioration of coral reefs was a middle tier concern, ranked well below pollution concerns but above such concerns as damage from boating and recreational overfishing. While this places coral reefs in a context of other concerns, it is difficult to know whether people would have themselves volunteered reef loss in the survey.
- In 1996, while testing messages that would help communicate more effectively about oceans, SeaWeb found that people connect to the need for ocean conservation mostly through two themes--a sense of responsibility to future generations and concern for human health.

Making the case for coral reef conservation could use examples that fit these themes.

Communicating about specific threats to coral reefs and solutions is complicated by public confusion about reef systems. Approximately four in ten Americans either believe that fish breeding grounds and coral reefs are found throughout the oceans (versus only in certain places, as is the case) or do not know.

TOWARDS CORAL REEF CONSERVATION AND CONSUMER ACTION

However, there is strong support for establishing marine reserves. Respondents in the 1999 poll included protection of ocean life and habitats--and coral reefs specifically--as some of the top goals for marine protected areas. These were placed well above such other goals as responsible management for oil exploration/drilling and commercial fishing, maintaining clean areas for swimming and diving, and providing recreational areas for boating. Nearly three-quarters of the public would support prohibiting the collection of tropical fish and corals from protected areas.

The public clearly is concerned about the state of the world's oceans. The public believes that humans can do lasting damage to the oceans, and supports efforts to strengthen ocean protection. However, many do not believe that their personal actions have much impact on ocean health. On the other hand, taking environmental action as a consumer—for example, recycling motor oil, cleaning up litter, eating only environmentally safe fish, and buying non-overfished seafood–is more popular than other kinds of individual action (such as contacting politicians and joining an environmental group).

Indeed, there are substantial numbers of people willing to modify their purchasing behaviours to help oceans. For example, many strongly support actions to protect oceans, even if it meant paying more for seafood. Sixty-two per cent of respondents in one survey said they would not eat fish classified by the government as overfished, and 44 per cent would only eat fish caught or farmed in a way that protects oceans.

Americans are increasingly connecting to conservation through consumerism and there is growing momentum to use consumer markets to drive ocean conservation.

- The Marine Stewardship Council has developed a certification programme for sustainable fisheries.
- Various organisations, like the Monterey Bay Aquarium, National Audubon Society, and the Chefs Collaborative have developed seafood-buying guides for consumers, chefs, and restaurateurs.
- SeaWeb has started the Seafood Choices Alliance as a trade association to provide the seafood sector with the information it

needs to make sound choices and provide the best options for its customers.

For coral reefs, there are two areas of consumer concern--food fish and marine ornamental fish, coral and live rock. To address the consumption of fish, the Seafood Choices Alliance and other organisations are working to create a sustainable food fish industry. To address the trade in ornamentals, the Marine Aquarium Council seeks to create a sustainable trade through certification of marine ornamental fish. In addition to formal opinion polling, SeaWeb conducted an informal survey of 77 aquarium hobbyists attending a conference of the Marine Aquarium Societies of America.

The results of this survey suggest that there is great interest in using purchasing behaviour to support reef stewardship. Most respondents indicated they want to support an industry based on quality and sustainability. Some hobbyists currently seek out suppliers of healthy animals, and are "very interested" in the source and collection methods of the fish they purchase. More importantly, they are willing to pay more for fish that are certified as being caught and handled in an environmentally responsible way. While based on a small, self-selected sample of hobbyists, these results point to a positive atmosphere for providing information that would allow marine aquarists to make environmentally sound choices.

THE FUTURE OF MARINE FISH RESOURCES

Marine fisheries supply a major source of protein to the world's population, and they support an industry worth over $85 billion annually. People have fished since the dawn of human history, and overfishing impacts were apparent even in some primitive societies at relatively low population density. It was during the 20th century that fishing expanded rapidly to the global scale as a result of motorised vessels, inexpensive oil, refrigeration, increasingly global commodity markets, and heavy government subsidies to increase fleets. Marine fisheries now use 24-35 per cent of primary production on continental shelves and in major upwelling areas, including bycatch (marine animals caught in the nets inadvertently)-a figure similar to the roughly one-fourth of the land's potential net primary production appropriated by humans. Fishing has transformed the world's oceans. Humans are now a dominant force of nature in the seas as we are on land, and we often affect marine fish resources negatively with such practices as:

OVERFISHING IMPACTS RESOURCES

Overfishing-this takes place when fish supplies fall below standard levels due to excessive fishing; it can be categorised into three main types: growth overfishing, recruit overfishing, and ecosystem overfishing. Destructive fishing practices-utilising destructive fishing practices such as bottom trawling, where the fishermen suspend large nets from boats to drag the bottom of the oceans and end up with other marine animals and organisms such as corals in their nets, as well as threaten biodiversity by killing animals unnecessarily and damaging the ocean environment.

Polluting the ecosystem-*e.g.*, directly with litter, boat exhaust, and oil spills, and indirectly with phosphates and nitrates from agricultural run-off.

STATUS OF GLOBAL MARINE FISHERIES

Currently, fishing pressure appears to be near-if not beyond-the ocean's capacity to provide. Estimates based on fisheries catch data, which were corrected for over-reporting by China, suggest that global fish catch peaked in the late 1980s, and this number has remained flat or begun to decline since. The Food and Agricultural Organisation of the United Nations (FAO) conducts the most comprehensive analysis of global fish stocks every four years, and recently reported that "the maximum wild capture fisheries potential from the world's oceans has probably been reached." The situation is reminiscent of society's reaching the point of peak oil-although fishery production is at least partially a renewable resource.

Half the World's Stocks

What about individual fish stocks? In 2008, the FAO estimated that roughly half of the world's 523 assessed fishery stocks are "fully exploited," meaning that they are harvested at rates near their maximum sustainable limits, while another 28 per cent are "overexploited or depleted," meaning that they are being harvested at rates not sustainable in the long term. Even these numbers are uncertain and possibly conservative since they do not include many small-scale commercial and artisanal tropical fisheries; furthermore, these numbers do not include stocks that have already collapsed and been abandoned.

Entire Ecosystems are Affected by Fisheries

Fishing impacts have fallen especially hard on slow-growing predators. Typically, deep-sea fisheries, such as those targeting Chilean sea bass (Dissostichus eleginoides) and orange roughy (Hoplostethus atlanticus), have undergone an initial boom followed by collapse. In addition, many sharks, which are slow growing and have very low reproductive rates, have been reduced by more than 75 per cent in recent decades.10-13 Impacts are not restricted to such species, nonetheless. At the community level, a wide range of data sources conclude that average abundance, size, and habitat quality have declined substantially in many regions of the world ocean in recent decades.

MARINE BIODIVERSITY AND FISHERY PRODUCTION

Long-simmering controversy about the state of world fisheries came to a head in 2006, when the scientist Boris Worm and colleagues reported the first comprehensive quantitative analysis of links between marine biological diversity and ecosystem services to human society. They concluded that disparate sources of data-from theory, controlled experiments, observed historical trends, and fishery catches-show a consistent pattern: marine ecosystems with fewer species, whether naturally or because of human impacts, have lower average productivity and stability. The greater fish productivity in more diverse ecosystems probably results in part from climate or resources that affect both diversity and productivity; however, such effects are less likely to explain the lower frequency of and faster recovery from collapse in diverse ecosystems. Although mechanisms remain speculative, the correlations of diversity with productivity and resilience probably result in part from a more efficient use of resources by diverse communities with broader functional capacity, and to the "portfolio effect," whereby a diverse group of stocks (whether fish or financial instruments) is more stable in the face of environmental fluctuations than any single stock.

The primary message of Worm and his colleagues that links biodiversity to ecosystem services was overshadowed, however, by another point made in the press release associated with the paper's publication, which was that if current trends continue, all currently fished marine species will have collapsed (fallen below 10 per cent of their maximum historical harvest) by the middle of the 21st century.

This claim generated worldwide attention and proved highly controversial. Much of the controversy centered on the use of catch data as a proxy for fish abundance. Critics pointed out, correctly, that catches may fail to track fish abundances because of changing markets, social factors, and management regimes.

Declining Catches are an Indication of Declining Stocks

While such factors can obscure population trends for individual stocks, however, no compelling evidence has been suggested that globally averaged catch data significantly misrepresent trends in global fish abundances. Indeed, one analysis concluded, "declining catches are an indication of declining stocks. Assuming otherwise would imply that all fishers or regulatory agencies in large marine ecosystems like the Mediterranean drastically reduce fishing of a species without the stock being in decline. Except for the World Wars, we are not aware of any such case." This same analysis showed that the number of new stocks entering global fisheries declined steadily over recent decades and that if current trends continue, the world's reservoir of unexploited fishable stocks will be exhausted by 2020. This general trend is consistent with the FAO's conclusion. It seems reasonable, therefore, to conclude that we are at the threshold, or even beyond, the world ocean's capacity to provide fish and that significant changes are necessary to maintain this service over the long term.

THE FUTURE OF MARINE FISHERIES

While evaluating the future of fisheries depends in part on what we as a society want from the oceans, several issues complicate the more optimistic predictions:

How much harvest is too much?

- Continued harvest stability is questionable. The theoretical target of MSY is exceeded in fisheries routinely- sometimes severely so; yet, it is still poorly understood how such sustained high harvest levels affect stock stability in the face of natural and anthropogenic (*i.e.*, human-derived) disturbances. Increasing evidence shows that both individual fish populations, and the more complex ecosystems in which they are included, can respond in a non-linear fashion to exploitation and other pressures; but these may cross a tipping point into a new stable state that is resistant to attempts to restore it to the original state.
- Demand will continue to increase. Global human population is increasing rapidly; it is likely to roughly double before stabilising at an estimated nine billion. The average per capita resource use is increasing even faster, which means that the human population's already large demand for fish and other resources will undoubtedly increase a great deal in the coming decades.
- Current fishery projections are not all-inclusive. The more optimistic projections of the future of world fisheries are typically based on extrapolating a handful of examples of well-managed fish stocks within the territorial waters of rich, stable, and well-governed western democracies. This is a non-representative sample of the world's fisheries, nonetheless, and there will surely be formidable hurdles to spreading good management models through the rest of the world- particularly in the face of growing human population, per capita resource use, environmental change, and probable political instability resulting from global climate change interacting with these factors.

Indeed, the future of marine fisheries can be seen as a microcosm of the future of human society generally. Some basic questions include:

What can we do to ensure stock stability?

- How important is abundant and inexpensive food, and the jobs associated with providing this food in the short term-relative to the many other tangible and intangible benefits that we receive from healthy ecosystems over the longer term? It is increasingly clear that many of these benefits cannot be achieved simultaneously.

- How important is the availability of abundant fish now relative to long-term maintenance of a functioning ecosystem that can provide fish (and other ecosystem services) to our grandchildren and beyond?
- What sacrifices, if any, are we willing to make now to ensure the long-term stability of that resource?

A recent consideration of how values influence the conflicting attitudes towards fishery management divided the major stakeholders in ocean ecosystems into consumptive users (*i.e.*, fishers), government, and non-governmental organisations (NGOs); however, they could as reasonably be characterised into present users and future users. When we consider the interests of "users" of the ocean two, three, or four generations down the line, the interests of fishers and governments and others become much more closely aligned. Policies that maximize fish production now-but endanger the production of fish and other important ecosystem services in the next generation-would not benefit tomorrow's fishers or any of the other citizens represented by governments and NGOs.

Potential Solutions

As is true of environmental challenges generally, there is unlikely to be a single solution to making world fisheries sustainable. Effective marine conservation and management will involve several parallel approaches, among which three central proposed solutions should be mentioned.

Ecosystem-based management (EBM) recognises and seeks to incorporate the complex interactions of fish stocks with one another and with the broader ecosystems that support them into fishery management. A related, more specific concept is the ecosystem approach to fisheries (EAF)-a form of fisheries governance that draws its conceptual basis and operational approaches from both conventional fisheries management and ecosystem management. The basic elements of both approaches involve maintaining single-species exploitation rates lower than would produce MSY and avoiding by-catch of non-target species.

Thus, both EBM and EAF depart from traditional fisheries management, which focuses on maximizing productivity of individual stocks in isolation. Because complex indirect interactions are the rule in ecosystem dynamics, and are often unpredictable, EBM ascribes particular importance to precautionary measures that aim to avoid depleting stocks. Ecosystem-based management has been mandated by the Great Barrier Reef Marine Park Act of 1981, in Australia, the Magnuson-Stevens Fishery Conservation and Management Act

(1996, reauthorised 2006) in the USA, and the International Convention on the Conservation of Antarctic Marine Living Resources.

Marine spatial planning is related to the concept of ecosystem-based management, and focuses specifically on better integrating management of the sundry, and often conflicting, human activities in the sea.

Many of the challenges facing the oceans derive in part from uncoordinated governance. For example, fishing, mining, oiland gas extraction, marine mammal conservation, shipping, and other activities in U.S., territorial waters are regulated by more than 20 separate agencies in isolation from one another.

Fixing this situation was a key recommendation of both the U.S., Commission on Ocean Policy and the similar Pew Commission reports in 2004. Zoning has been used routinely on land for many years. Marine spatial planning can strategically site compatible activities together and separate incompatible ones, and it seeks to accommodate the plethora of potentially conflicting human uses such as recreation, fishing, and energy generation in an optimal way. Ultimately, marine spatial management must also coordinate with activities on land to develop adjacent coastal watersheds responsibly; to reduce inputs of toxic contaminants and nutrients; and to mitigate and adapt to human-induced climate change.

Improved incentive systems for sustainable fishing include, most recently, an exploration of dedicated access such as catch-share programmes, as well as more effective governance at national and local levels. Fundamentally, managing fisheries involves managing the people that fish, which can involve both sticks (such as the restrictions historically used in management) and carrots (such as financial incentives to switch to less damaging gear). The latter involves appropriate incentive systems for making fishing sustainable.

One such promising approach that is gaining momentum involves Limited Access Privilege programmes (LAPP's), also known as "catch shares," in which a secure share of fish is allocated to an individual fisher, community, or association. The rationale is that because the shares are allocated before the season begins, fishers know how much fish they are allowed to harvest that year, and so there is incentive to do it efficiently, rather than in the counterproductive and expensive race to get the most fish possible that results under the often complicated, historic regulations. On the other hand, LAPPs limit access by definition, and therefore, these entail many difficult decisions about how shares are allocated, as well as the potential impacts of consolidating effort on both the environment and fishing communities.

Finally, no account of the future of fish would be complete without considering the rapidly growing global aquaculture industry, which accounted for more than a third of total global fishery production in 2006. Although aquaculture has been suggested frequently as a solution to the environmental impacts of ocean fishing, and it will surely be part of such a solution, the answer is not simple.

Many farmed fish proposed for large-scale ocean ranching-notably salmon and tuna-are carnivorous. These operations can cause even greater harm than wild capture fisheries because such apex predators require large quantities of food, which comes from forage fish harvested from the ocean, and also because of their prodigious waste output, and the risk of disease and parasitism they pose to wild relatives. Moreover, farmed tuna are taken as juveniles from wild populations but are not recorded as catch in capture fishery statistics. Thus, if aquaculture is to be part of a sustainable long-term solution, rather than part of the problem, it will need to focus on species low on the food chain such as catfish and tilapia, avoid transmitting diseases and genetic defects to wild fish, and produce minimal waste and habitat destruction. As in wild capture fisheries, achieving these goals requires effective management and policies that can adapt to a rapidly changing world.

5

Procurement Policy for Sustainable Fish Purchasing

Seed, feed and fertilizers are the three major inputs of undrainable pond culture systems. Paucity of quality fish seed is even now considered as one of the major constraints in the development of freshwater carp farming. This is mainly due to the large-scale development of this farming system creating ever-increasing pressure on carp seed industry. However, construction of large and small-scale carp hatcheries has provided enough support to this industry during recent years. Ideally, a farm should be self-sufficient with nursery and rearing ponds so that after meeting their own demand the surplus seed can be sold for additional farm income.

Small, seasonal, undrainable village ponds are most suitable for this purpose. Procurement of feed is not a problem as most of the feed materials are village-based agro-industrial products and by-products and are readily available in villages and local markets. Only some feed additives are needed to be procured from towns. Animal manures are incidental to village-based allied agricultural and animal husbandry activities while fertilizers are readily available in the local markets throughout the year.

PROCUREMENT OF SEED

Except common carp, all the other five Indian and Chinese major carps, *viz.* catla, rohu, mrigal, silver carp and grass carp, cultivated under composite fish culture do not breed in pond conditions although they attain full gonadal maturity.

However, they breed in bundh type tanks. The successful development of the technique of induced breeding through hypophysation ensures breeding of both Indian and Chinese major carps in captivity. Therefore the stocking materials are procured from three different sources, *viz.* collection by traditional methods from rivers, by induced breeding of carps and by breeding in bundh-type tanks.

COLLECTION OF SPAWN FROM RIVERINE SOURCES

The technique of spawn collection from rivers essentially consists of operating fixed filtration nets in marginal areas of flooded rivers during monsoon months, when the Indian major carps normally breed.

Success of operations mainly depends on proper sites, suitable nets, monsoon flooding patterns, availability of sufficient brood stock and the success of spawning.

Spawn Net and its Operations

These are funnel-shaped nets made of fine mesh (1.5 to 3.0 mm) handloom nettings The posterior end has a small round opening fixed on a bamboo ring. A small trough-like receptacle (gamcha) is tied to the ring where live spawn is collected.

The net is fixed in marginal waters where depth of water is negotiable without any aid. River margins with gradual slopes are the most suitable sites. Water flow in the range of 20 to 60 cm/sec is desirable.

Fig. Collection of Riverine Spawn

Site Selection

A premonsoon survey should be conducted to collect the following details, based upon which the suitable site is selected.

- The topography and terrain and river bank features in the vicinity of a site to determine the extent of area available for operating nets at different flood levels.
- Topography of dry beds and bank features to know the likely current pattern of the river at different levels of flooding.
- The distribution and composition of the fish fauna in the selected stretch of the river for assessing the resident population of Indian major carps.

- Location of tributaries, streams, etc., along with their confluence with the main river as these may be connected with the breeding grounds.
- The accessibility of the site.

  Spawn availability is mostly associated with receding phases of floods.

Collection Operation

To assess the availability of spawn, initially 2–3 spawn nets should be operated constantly at suitable sites and the whole battery of nets should then be introduced as soon as the spawn become available.

The nets should be fixed along the river margins with the help of bamboo poles and are adjusted according to changes in flood level. At every four hours, the nets should be removed, cleaned and refixed. The flowing spawn are collected in the receptacle (gamcha) from where they are scooped every 15 to 30 minutes, depending on the amount of spawn being collected.

The collected spawn along with the bigger fishes, debris, etc., should be scooped from the receptacle (gamcha) and transferred to aluminium containers (hundies) half filled with water. The collection should then be sieved through round meshed mosquito netting to segregate spawn from debris and larger fishes and the spawn should be conditioned in hapas (cloth compartments fixed in water) before they are transported. Measurement of spawn should be done by special sieve cups. Usually early spawn measures about 500 individuals/ml. The seed collected from rivers are generally a mixture of seeds of major carps, minor carps, predatory fishes, etc.

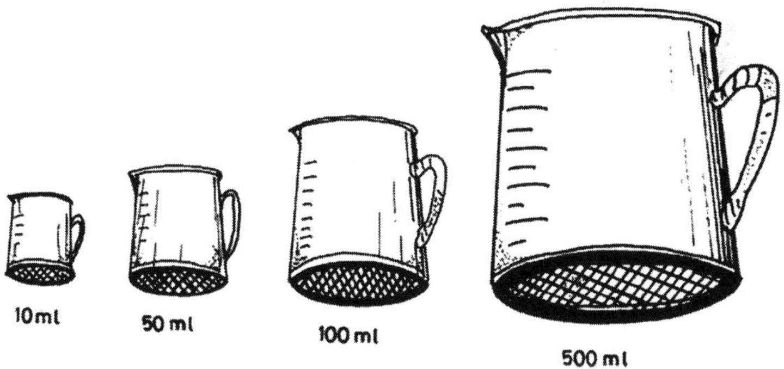

Fig. Sieve Cup for Measurement of Spawn/Fry

BUNDH BREEDING

Bundhs are special types of perennial and seasonal tanks or impoundments where riverine conditions are simulated during monsoon months. The bundhs are ordinarily of two categories, *viz.*, a perennial bundh commonly known as "Wet bundh" and a seasonal one called "Dry bundh".

Wet Bundh

A typical "Midnapore type" of wet bundh is generally located in a gradual slope of a catchment area with an inlet towards the high land and an outlet at the opposite side towards the lower end to regulate the inflow and outflow of water respectively during heavy showers.

The wet bundh contains a deeper area which retains water throughout the year and where adequate stocks of brood fishes are maintained.

During heavy rains, a major portion of the bundh is submerged and excess water, if any, is drained through the outlet which is guarded by bamboo fencing (locally termed as "Chhera").

The shallow areas of the bundh (moans) serve as breeding ground for fishes present in the bundh. The wet bundh varies in shape and size from place to place.

Generally, the ponds covering a water body of 1–2 ha with catchment area ranging from 20–100 times are considered as wet bundhs, but a bundh could be as large as 300 ha.

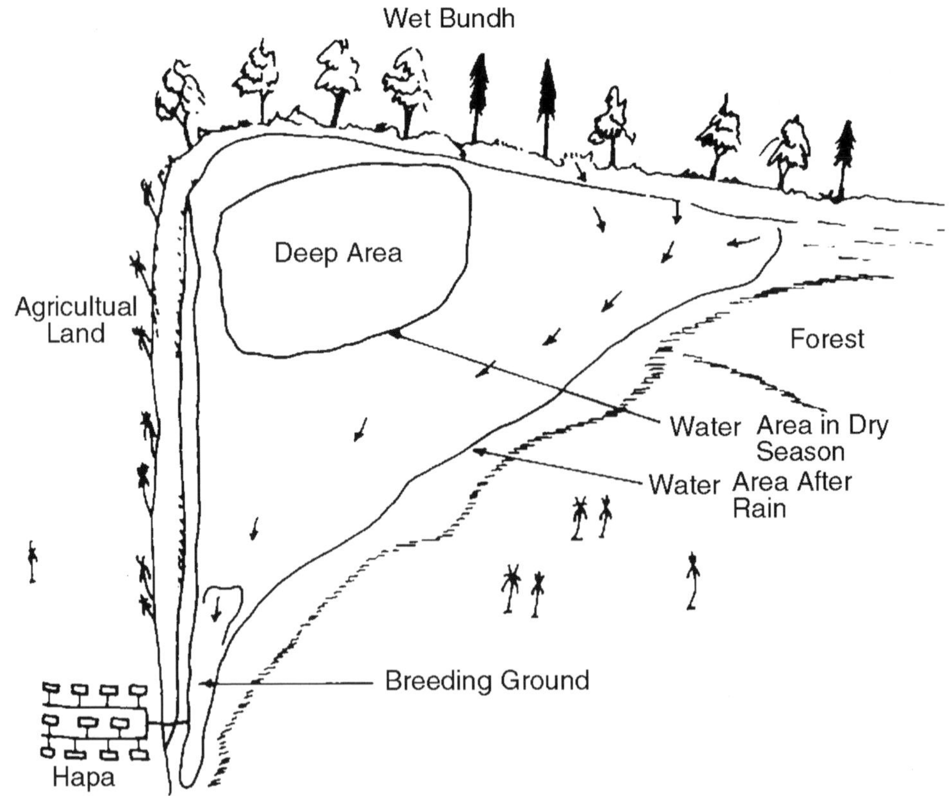

Fig. Bundh for Breeding (Wet Type)

Fig. Bundhs for Breeding (Dry Type)

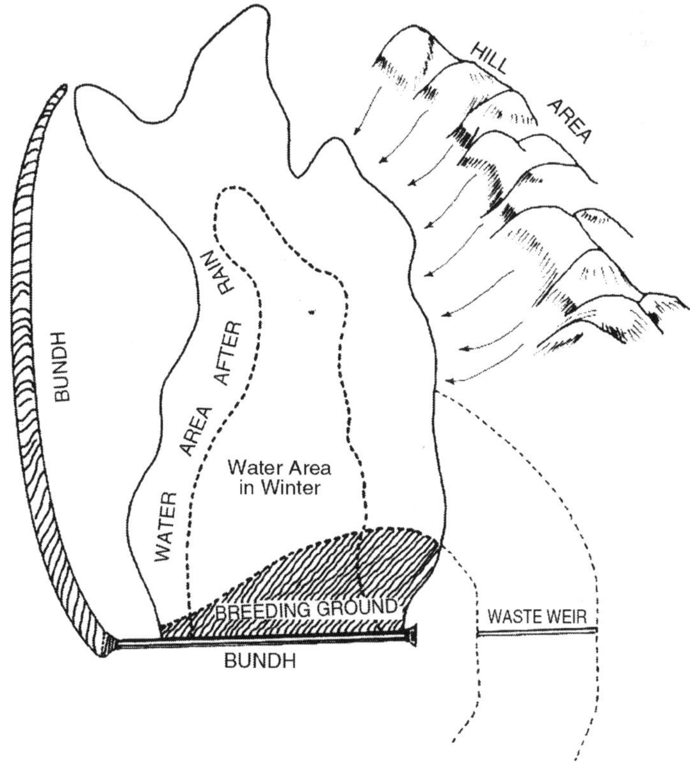

Fig. Bundhs for Breeding (Dry Type)

Dry Bundhs

This type of dry bundh consists of only one shallow depression (or one shallow pond) and a catchment area located in a gradual slope. The upper high land area is considered as a catchment area. The shallow depression or pond is enclosed by embankments on three sides which impounds freshwater from the catchment area during the monsoon season. There should be provision for an outflow for drawing excess water from the pond during heavy rains. The outlet is guarded by fine bamboo fencing. Such bundhs remain more or less dry during the greater part of the year.

In the West Bengal Province of India, a catchment area more than five times the size of the bundh is considered most suitable, whereas in Madhya Pradesh the recommended ratio is 1:25 (Dubay and Tuli, 1961). Dry bundhs of Madhya Pradesh are comparatively bigger in size (0.2 to 2.5 ha) than those of West Bengal (0.1 to 0.5 ha).

In a modified bundh, adjacent ponds are constructed along the gradient of the catchment area. The upper one where the premonsoon rain water is collected from upland catchment area serves as a "reservoir" and the lower one is used for breeding purposes. A deeper tench is dug along the lower extremity of the breeding bundh so that the breeders can take shelter before and after spawning.

The reservoir and breeding bundhs are arranged in a sequence along the gradient so as to facilitate the flow of water which is controlled through a system of sluice gates. Premonsoon rain water is collected from the catchment area to fill up the reservoir. The water-holding capacity of the reservoir is generally more than that of the breeding ground bundh.

Breeding Operation

Wet Bundh

With the onset of monsoon the fresh rain water from the catchment area enters into the bundh and the latter is inundated. The excess water flows out from the bundh creating a water current. The breeders present in the deeper area of the bundh migrate to shallow areas where they start breeding.

Dry Bundh

Rain water which accumulates in the catchment area during premonsoon showers flows in to fill up the pond seasonally. Thereafter, the brood fishes from a perennial pond are introduced into the seasonal ponds to breed, preferably on cool rainy days. Spawning usually commence during and after heavy showers when the bundh as well as the catchment area are flooded with fresh rainwater.

In a modified method adopted in Bankura and Midnapore districts of West Bengal, some fresh water is released from the reservoir into the breeding bundh. Gravid carps from the perennial ponds are then transferred to the breeding bundh. Generally, the ratio of male and female spawners is maintained at 1:1, but sometimes this proportion is not strictly followed. The spawners are allowed to remain for 10–12 hours in order to get acclimatised to the environment.

A few sets of males and females are then selected and taken out from the bundh and placed in separated mosquito net hapas, which are cloth compartments fixed in water with the help of poles at its four corners The selected female breeders are taken out of the hapas and injected intramuscularly with fresh pituitary extract. The females are administered an initial dose of the extract at the rate of 3 mg/kg body weight and thereafter kept again in mosquito net hapas. After 4–5 hours, the second dose (8 mg/kg) of extract is injected to the female. At the same time the males are given the initial dose of the extract at the rate of 3 mg/ kg of body weight.

The injected spawners are then released into the breeding bundh. After administration of the second dose of extract to the females, the inlets and outlets of the bundh are lifted to allow the entry of a steady flow of water from the reservoir into the breeding bundh soon after breeding takes place. In one such bundh 5–6 breeding operations can be taken up in one season, subject to availability of spawners and fresh water. Before starting the next breeding operation in the same bundh, the water is completely drained out and it is allowed to dry.

Exotic carps such as grass carp and silver carp have also been induced to breed in the dry bundhs of West Bengal by applying pituitary extract and under regulated water.

Collection of Eggs

Egg collection is taken as soon as the embryo starts twitching movements. To collect eggs, the water level of the bundh should be lowered by opening the outlet. Eggs are generally netted by a piece of thin cotton cloth (gamcha) or a piece of mosquito netting cloth. In such areas a series of earthen pits are constructed with water flow facilities. Fertilized eggs are allowed to hatch in these pits and the spawn are collected after three days. Spawn are usually sold at the bundh site.

INDUCED SPAWNING BY HYPOPHYSATION

As an alternative method, use of hormones for inducing spawning in Indian major carps has been in practice for the last three decades. The gonadotropic hormones secreted by the pituitary gland of fish play an important role in the process of maturation and spawning. This is due to the fact that the pituitary gonadotropic hormones which induce spawning are not released in sufficient quantities from the pituitary gland (hypophysis) to the general blood circulation so as to trigger spawning. Therefore, for induced spawning, the hypophyseal hormones extracted from the pituitary of donor fish are injected into the sexually matured fish under favourable water and climatic conditions during the monsoon season.

Pituitary Gland of Major Carps and its Collection

The pituitary gland or hypophysis of Asiatic major carps is a small, pear-shaped, whitish soft body, situated on the ventral side of the brain below hypothalamus, which is connected to the pituitary gland by a funnelshaped structure, the infundibulum. The quantum of gonadotrophic hormones in the pituitary vary with the season and maturation stages of the fish and hence the degree of success achieved in induced spawning depends very much upon the condition of the pituitary gland of donor fish.

Based on a series of experimental trials it has been found that the maximum success in induced spawning is possible with extracts prepared from gland collected during May/June, *i.e.* the period just before spawning.

Thus the pituitary glands for the induced spawning programme should preferably be collected from the freshly killed fully matured specimen of both the sexes of the same (homoplastic) or allied species (heteroplastic) during May/June when the potency of the gland remains at its peak. Well preserved iced fish are also suitable for this purpose. Common carp, a perennial breeder, has been found to be an excellent donor fish as the potency of the gland remains more or less high throughout the year. Both male and female donor fish are suitable for gland collection.

COLLECTION OF GLAND

The commonly adopted method of gland removal is by chopping off the skull with a sharp butcher's knife or a hand saw. The brain thus exposed is lifted up by detaching the optic nerve. Excess of watery fluid and the blood is soaked by absorbant cotton and then the membrane covering the gland is cautiously removed by using a needle and a pair of forceps. The gland thus exposed is picked up very carefully avoiding any damage Broken or damaged glands lose their potency due to hormonal drainage.

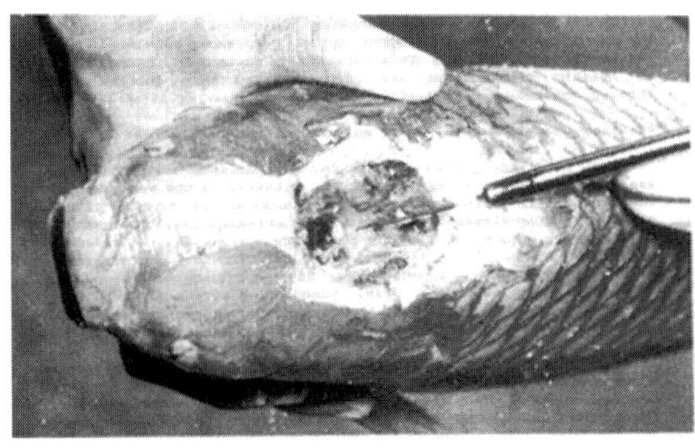

Fig. Collection of Pituitary Gland

In India, in fish markets where a large number of fish heads are sold separately and the consumers strongly dislike dissected fish heads for consumption, the glands are taken out from behind the head through the foramen magnum. The technique of removing glands by this method is simple and quick. Behind the head there is a big hole in the brain case known as the foramen magnum. The brain tissues are removed through this foramen magnum and then by close examination the gland is located embedded in the floor from where it is scooped out carefully with the help of a small scooper.

PRESERVATION AND STORAGE OF GLANDS

Freshly collected glands have been found to be the best for the induced breeding purpose. But when we need a large number of glands to take up breeding on a commercial scale, it is not always possible to sacrifice so many matured fish for the required quantity of glands. Such limitations dictate large-scale collection and preservation of glands from fish markets. There are several methods under use for the preservation of pituitary glands, the most popular being the preservation in absolute alcohol and after an interval of 24 hours they are dried, weighed and transferred to dark coloured phials containing fresh absolute alcohol.

Alcohol dehydrates and defattens the glands. Details about the place and date of collection, the age and weight of the donor fish, etc., should be labelled on the phials for ready reference. The phials are then kept at room temperature or in a refrigerator. When needed the stored glands are put on filter paper which allows the alcohol to evaporate and are then weighed accurately. However, better results have been achieved from glands preserved in acetone. Immediately after collection the glands are kept in fresh acetone and placed in a refrigerator. After two days the glands are taken out, weighed and replaced in phials with fresh aceton. Such phials are labelled and placed in a refrigerator until use. The glands can also be kept frozen. Fresh glands are frozen immediately after collection and kept in a refrigerator, deep freezer or in insulated cans containing dry ice.

PRESERVATION OF PITUITARY EXTRACT

Pituitary extract is normally prepared just before administration as such extracts cannot be kept long. However, there are certain simple methods for the effective preservation of pituitary extracts. The advantage of extract preservation is that the preserved material remains in the ready-to-use form which is very convenient, especially in villages where most of the basic facilities like precision balance, tissue homogenizer, distilled water, centrifuge, etc., for extract preparation are not available. Besides, extraction from a large number of glands also ensures uniform hormone potency per unit volume of extract. In such cases it is always desirable to ascertain the potency of such extract through several breeding trials before initiating a large-scale breeding programme.

Fish pituitary extract is prepared in distilled water-glycerine media at a concentration of 40 mg of gland for every ml of media. A known quantity of glands is taken and macerated in a tissue homogenizer. Distilled water equal to one-third of the total volume of extract is added to the fully macerated glands and thoroughly mixed. Pure glycerine, twice the volume of the distilled water, is then added. Thus the ratio of distilled water to glycerine is maintained at 1:2. The entire suspension is again thoroughly mixed and filtered through filter paper to remove tissue fragments if any. Prepared extracts can either be ampouled in ampoules of various capacities or may be kept in small phials in a refrigerator. Such extracts should be consumed within one breeding season.

Brood Stock Maintenance and their Selection for Spawning

The two major inputs of induced breeding programmes through hypophysation are the pituitary glands and the properly matured spawners. Success of hypophysation also depends on the condition of the spawner and hence proper attention must be paid to raise quality brood stock in adequate numbers. Preferably 2–3 years old healthy male and female carps should be selected and reared in well prepared ponds of 0.2 to 0.5 ha with minimum water depth of about 1.5 m.

The stocking density should be kept at a relatively lower level ranging between 1 500–2 000 kg/ha. Normal pond management schedules are to be followed strictly involving weed clearance, removal of predatory and weed fishes, pond fertilization and application of supplementary feed, fish health care and monitoring of pond environment.

Details about pond management are given in subsequent sections of this manual. Supplementary feed consisting of 1:1 oil cake and bran mixture should be applied daily at the rate of 1–3 per cent body weight on underwater feeding plates. The addition of 15–20 per cent fish meal, vitamin and mineral mixture to the conventional feed gives better results. For grass carp, aquatic weeds such as Hydrilla, Najas, duck weeds, etc., or green animal fodder such as napier grass, hybrid napier, barseem, etc., are to be provided at the rate of 20–25 per cent of their body weight on a daily basis. The fish should be periodically netted and examined carefully to find out the stage of maturity and state of health. This rearing period normally lasts for 4–5 months. Proper care during this period ensures availability of well matured quality spawners for induced breeding programmes. It is estimated that for a target production of about 10 million spawn (6 million of Indian major carps and 4 million of silver carp and grass carp) about 750 kg of brood stock (300 kg of Indian major carps and 450 kg of silver carp and grass carp) comprising both males and females in a ratio of 1:1 by weight and 2:1 by number are required.

Usually after the onset of the monsoon when there is an accumulation of fresh rain water in the pond and a fall in atmospheric temperature, the breeding programme is taken up. The southwest monsoon period is the normal breeding season for these Asiatic carps in south Asian countries and usually extends from April to September. In some places the monsoon is early and hence the breeding season starts from April onwards. By seining the pond, spawners are caught and carefully examined for selection. Matured males ooze a milky fluid (milt), if the abdomen is slightly pressed near the vent. They are also characterized by the roughness of their pectoral fins. Matured females have a soft bulging abdomen with slightly swollen and reddish vent.

A catheter is found to be quite helpful especially in the case of silver carp and grass carp in selecting the matured female breeders by examining the condition of the eggs. By inserting the catheter in the genital opening of a female spawner, some eggs are taken out and examined at the pond site in a petridish. Uniform size eggs of pale blue colour in silver carp and brown or copper colour in grass carp indicate proper maturation stage. Cool rainy days when the water temperature ranges between 25°C to 30°C are considered to be ideal for induced breeding. Ripe and healthy males and females of desired species are selected from the brood stock ponds, their individual weights are recorded using hand nets and a spring balance and the females are kept ready for the first injection of the pituitary gland.

Induced Breeding Operation

After the selection of brood fish the injectable dosage of pituitary extract is calculated in terms of milligram of pituitary gland per kg body weight of the recipient fish. Females are given two injections at an interval of 4–6 hours while males are given only one injection at the time of the second injection to the females. Considerable variations are noticed in the effective dosage of pituitary extract which depends mostly on the potency of the pituitary gland, gonadal maturity of the recipients and the prevailing climatic conditions.

It has been experienced that a lower dosage is effective when extract is prepared from fresh glands while a higher dosage is required when commercially supplied glands are used for the purpose. The first and second dose in the case of females of Indian major carps may be given at the rate of 2–4 mg/kg and 5–10 mg/kg body weight respectively.

The males are given only one injection at the rate of 2–4 mg/kg body weight at the time of the second injection to the females. Silver carp and grass carp females should be given at the rate of 3–4 mg/kg body weight during the initial injection and 8–10 mg/kg body weight during the final injection. Males receive only one injection at the rate of 3–4 mg/kg body weight. However, as stated the dose of the pituitary may be slightly increased or decreased depending on the local climatic conditions, potency of the gland and the response of the spawners. After deciding on the dosage, the quantity of glands required for injecting the selected brood fish is calculated. Both ready-to-use bottled or ampouled extract or freshly prepared extract can be used.

For the preparation of fresh extract the required quantity of glands should be taken out, blotted, dried and weighed accurately. The glands are then macerated in a tissue homogenizer with a small quantity of distilled water and further diluted so that each ml of the extract should be eqivalent to 20–40 mg of pituitary gland.

The extract is thereafter centrifuged to get rid of tissue fragments and only the supernatant solution is utilized for the injection. The spawners should be grouped into several sets. Each set should consist of both female and male spawners in the ratio of 1:2 and approximately 1:1 in weight. The required number of breeding hapas at the rate of one hapa for each set should be fixed in the pond. A breeding hapa is a rectangular cloth container (2.5 x 1.5 x 1.0 m) closed from all sides except an opening on one side with tying arrangements, through which spawners are introduced and taken out.

These hapas should be fixed in the shallow waters of ponds, canals, lakes and reservoirs with the help of bamboo poles in such a way that two-thirds of it are submerged in the water. Modern facilities such as breeding tanks of metal, cement, fibre glass, etc., or plastic pools with continuous supply of water having controlled temperature ensure greater efficiency and operational ease.

Intramuscular or intraperitoneal injections are administered. Intramuscular injections are commonly given in the caudal peduncle region avoiding the lateral line. In the case of intraperitoneal injection the needle is pushed with ease at the innerside base of the pectoral fins.

Fig. Injecting a Dose of Breeding Hormone

For intramuscular injection, the needle is inserted under the scale initially parallel to the body of the fish and finally pierced into the muscle at an angle of 45°. The most convenient hypodermic syringe used for the purpose is of 2 ml capacity having 20 divisions. The size of the needle for the purpose is also important which depends on the size of spawner to be injected. The BHD needle No.22 is conveniently used for 1–3 kg of carp breeders and No.19 for larger ones. Needle No.24 can be used for small size spawners.

The induced breeding work is generally taken up on cool and cloudy days when the water temperature is around 25–30°C. It is always convenient to apply the first injection between 16.00–17.00 hours and the second injection after 4–6 h of the first injection *i.e.* between 20–23 hours. In the case of mrigal it is desirable to keep this interval of only 4 h. After the first injection to the female spawners, both males and females of the set are released in the breeding hapa or the breeding enclosure. At the time of the second injection both males and females of the set are taken out, injected as per prescribed doses and released back in the breeding hapa.

Table. Doses (mg of pituitary extract/kg body weight of spawners) and injection achedules for hypophysation

Injection	Time of injection (h)	Female IMC	Spawners* GC/SC	Male IMC	spawners* GC/SC
1st	16.00–17.00	2–4	3–4	-	-
2nd	20.00–23.00	5–10	8–10	2–4	3–4

Breeding normally takes place within 3–6 h after the second injection. Gonadotropins induce the hydration process thereby increasing the body weight of the spawners and thus serving as an indicator for the success or failure of the breeding programme.

A 3 per cent increase in body weight of female spawners between the two subsequent injections indicates better breeding success. The eggs are released by the females in the early morning hours and are fertilized naturally inside the hapa by the milt released by males.

The brood fishes are removed from the hapas and the eggs which are non-adhesive and semibuoyant swell like small pearls of 3.5 – 5.5 mm in diameter. The total quantity of good eggs laid is estimated from the total volume of eggs and percentage of fertilization.

Fertilized and viable eggs are transparent in colour while dead ones appear opaque under naked eye. Percentage of fertilization is scored from several egg samples examined in a petridish or watch glass. Silver carp and grass carp normally do not release eggs inside a hapa or a breeding enclosure even after being injected with hormone and hence these fishes have to be stripped and fertilized artificially. The females are examined 3–4 h after the second injection to see their readiness for stripping.

Keeping the ventral side up and by giving a slight pressure at the genital opening, if the eggs are seen oozing out, the fish is considered to be ready for stripping. Otherwise they are released back and examined again after an interval of 1/2 – 1 h. Usually, the dry method of stripping is adopted where the spawners are wiped with a towel and then the female spawners are stripped and the eggs are collected in dry enamel basins and immediately fertilized with stripped milt from the male spawners.

At this stage the eggs and milt are mixed thoroughly for 1–2 minutes with the help of a clean feather and subsequently the eggs are washed 3–4 times with water. The fertilized eggs are then kept in breeding hapas for a few minutes for proper swelling and hardening. It has been observed that in silver carp males the quantity of milt is insufficient and hence extra males should also be injected to ensure maximum fertilization of stripped eggs.

Table. Quantity of eggs obtained from cultivated carp species

Species of carp	Approximate number of eggs/kg body weight
Catla	125 000 – 200 000
Rohu	250 000 – 300 000
Mrigal	150 000 – 200 000
Silver carp	100 000 – 150 000
Grass carp	Around 100 000
Common carp	150 000 – 250 000

INCUBATION OF EGGS AND HATCHING

The eggs are measured by a graduated enamel or plastic mug of 1–2 litre capacity and collected in plastic buckets. From the plastic buckets eggs are collected with the help of a 1 litre mug and spread uniformly at the rate of 3–4 litres of eggs in double-walled hatching hapas fixed in ponds free from algal bloom and predatory fish species. These double-walled hapas are open from the upper side. The outer hapa is made of thick cloth or very fine meshed nylon cloth while the inner one is made of round meshed mosquito netting cotton/nylon cloth.

Table. Dimension of breeding and hatching hapas

Type of hapa	Dimension (m)			Specifications
	Length	Width	Depth	
Breeding hapa	2.5	1.25	1.0	closed from all sides except at the opening with tying arrange-ment. Thick cotton/ nylon cloth.
Hatching hapa				
Outer	1.8	1.0	1.0	Upper side completely open. Thick meshed nylon/cotton cloth.
Inner	1.5	0.8	0.5	Upper side completely open. Round mosquito netting of cotton/nylon cloth.

The number of eggs to be spread in each hapa depends on the size of the eggs of the species concerned. The following table will be helpful in deciding the amount of eggs to be incubated in a hapa.

Table. Quantity of ®eggs of cultivated carp species to be incubated in each hapa

Species	No. of eggs/1 (Approx.)	Amount of eggs in 1/hapa
Catla	22 000 – 25 000	4.0
Rohu	28 000 – 30 000	3.0
Mrigal	26 000 – 30 000	3.0
Silver carp	22 000 – 25 000	4.0
Grass carp	22 000 – 25 000	4.0

Hatching time is temperature dependent. Usually hathing takes about 15–18 h at temperature range of 26–31°c. At lower temperature the hatching time is considerably larger. The hatchlings pass out through the mesh of the inner mosquito netting hapa to the outer hapa. When hatching is completed, the inner hapa with egg shells is removed and the hatchlings are left undisturbed in the outer hapa for three days till the yolk sac is completely absorbed and the spawn become ready for stocking in nursery ponds.

Common carp and other unwanted fish when present in the pond have been reported to cause severe damage to carp eggs in breeding hapas The use of 1/4 inch mesh size drag net as a barrier to prevent common carp from destroying fertilized eggs in breeding/hatching hapas may be a suitable way to solve the problem of those fish farmers who have only one pond and utilize it for composite fish culture

The hatching technique has, however, several drawbacks and large-scale mortality and loss of developing eggs and hatchlings may occur due to natural hazards such as a sudden rise of water temperature, development of algal bloom, depletion of dissolved oxygen, presence of predatory crustaceans, etc. With a view to improving the hatching technique and reducing mortality of hatchlings, a glass jar hatchery has been designed by the Central Inland Fisheries Research Institute (CIFRI) and found to be very useful in terms of percentage survival of hatchlings.

Water hardened eggs are incubated in vertical hatching jars where the flow of water is so regulated during the incubation that the eggs are gently stirred without being spilled over. In each jar of 6.35 1 capacity, 50 000 eggs can be kept for hatching. Normally the rate of flow of water is kept at 600–800 ml/min for Indian major carps and 800 – 1 000 ml/min for Chinese carps.

It normally takes 12–15 h for the developing eggs to hatch out in Indian conditions. Various modifications of this hatchery system are now available and extensively used. Chinese hatchery system consisting of cisterns with diagonally pointed nozzles as water inlets and outlet with filtering screen and valve are also becoming popular. It requires a large volume of water with sufficient pressure to create a circular water current in the hatching cistern. 700 000 to 1 200 000 fertilized eggs can be used per cubic meter of water. Spawn are collected through drainage outlet.

POST-SPAWNING CARE OF BROOD FISH

It should always be remembered that spent carps are potential breeders for the next breeding season and hence they should be saved and properly cared for. Before releasing them back in the pond they should be given prophylactic antibiotic treatment. Streptomycin sulphate and penicillin at the rate of 25 mg/kg fish and 20 000 I.U./kg fish respectively in the form of injection has been found to be very effective in preventing post spawning bacterial infections and subsequent mortality. Before releasing them back to ponds they should also be given a dip treatment in potassium permanganate solution to prevent any fungal attack. In the case of silver carp and grass carp females, where stripping is the normal practice, recovery from shock and severe stress is difficult under Indian condition and hence they should not be released back into the broodstock pond. However, if the stripping is easy and fast, both the males and females can be released after giving the similar prophylactic treatment. Use of anaesthetics during stripping minimises shock and stress and brings ease in stripping operation.

Multiple Breeding

Under natural conditions, Asiatic major carps breed only once a year. However, in recent years it has been possible to breed them twice in a year. They are induced to breed in the early part of the season, well cared and well fed for the rest of the season and during the end of the breeding season they are again induced to breed by the same techniques. The interval between the two breeding operations may vary from 30 to 60 days.

PRODUCTION OF COMMON CARP SEED

Common carp is the only fish cultivated under composite fish culture which naturally breeds in ponds throughout the year in Indian conditions with two peaks of spawning, one during January to March and the other during July/August. The females deposit sticky eggs on leafy vegetation in the pond which are immediately fertilized by the males. Although they breed naturally in the ponds, the survival of spawn is always poor and hence they should be induced to breed under controlled conditions as per the following successive steps.

Segregation and Care of Mature Fish

Healthy and matured male and female brood fish should be segregated and kept in separate ponds usually by April and October. A mature male easily oozes milt when the abdomen is gently pressed. The female on the other hand has a bulging abdomen with a papilla-like outgrowth with a median slit in the vent region. Segregated brood fish should be fed daily at the rate of 3 per cent of their body weight.

Although they breed several times during the year, breeding should be taken up during mid-January to March and again during July-August.

Breeding Technique

Fully mature male and female brood fish are selected for breeding and kept either in breeding hapas or cement cisterns. Breeding hapas should be fixed in the shallower region of the pond with the support of bamboo poles.

A set of spawners consisting of one female and two smaller males more or less equal to the weight of the female are released in each breeding hapa. Sufficient quantity (double the weight of the female fish) of fresh aquatic weeds such as Hydrilla, Najas, Eichhornia (water hyacinth), etc., are also introduced in the hapa and uniformly spread.

Fish usually spawn within 10–12 hours. Spawned breeders are then taken out and given prophylactic antibiotic treatment and released back to the pond.

The difference in weight of the female before and after spawning gives the estimate of eggs released.

Each gram of ovary contains about 700 eggs An allowance of 12–15 per cent should be given for faecal droppings. By examining several samples of eggs, the percentage of fertilization can also be estimated. Fertilized eggs are dirty pale in colour and more or less transparent, whereas unfertilized eggs are opaque and whitish in colour.

Fig. Hatching Hapas in a Pond

The weeds with attached eggs should be transferred to the hatching hapas fixed in the pond. About 1 kg of weed with attached eggs should be kept in each hapa. The incubation period depends upon the water temperature and varies from 36–72 hours. At a temperature of about 28–31°C the hatching takes place in about 45–50 hours.

The newly hatched out larvae are 4–5.5 mm in length with a prominent yolk sac. The newly hatched out larvae adhere to the leaves of the weeds and remain in this condition for some time. The yolk is absorbed within 2–4 days after hatching depending on the water temperature.

The weeds are removed very carefully from the hatching hapas and the spawn are removed during the early morning hours. Collected spawns are sieved through a coarse mosquito netting cloth to remove debris, measured with a seive cup and transferred to nursery ponds.

However, this early stage of fish seed is not suitable for stocking in all types of ponds. The spawn is nursed for 2 or 3 weeks up to fry stage in nursery ponds and then the fry (2–3 cm) are transferred to rearing ponds where they are reared for three more months up to fingerling (8–12 cm) stage. This is the fingerling stage of the fish seed which should be used for stocking the composite fish culture ponds.

FEED

Undrainable ponds have the ability to continuously supply natural fish food for the cultivated carp species. But the quantum of the natural food usually available in the pond is not sufficient to support the dense fish population cultivated under semi-intensive and/or intensive fish culture systems.

As such, natural feed is always supplemented with some artificial feed to achieve optimum production. A brief account of the natural food available in undrainable ponds and the supplementary feed used in fish culture in undrainable ponds is presented below.

NATURAL FOOD

Some of the cultivable fish species such as trout, salmon, eel, etc., are exclusively fed on artificial food. On the other hand, carps require natural food and many feel that at least 50 per cent of the food ingested by them should be the natural food items.

Hence the availability of natural feed is one of the major factors contributing to fish production in undrainable ponds. Natural feed, being balanced, not only provides the essential nutrients such as proteins, carbohydrates and fats, but also takes care of the much needed vitamins and minerals to the cultured fish which may not be present at the desired levels in artificial feed unless otherwise fortified.

Natural feed, in addition, possess some of the essential amino acids and fatty acids required for growth while most of the artificial feed may be deficient.

Availability of Natural Food for Fish in Ponds

The availability of natural food to fish in ponds depends on the quality and the quantity of the standing crop which in turn is determined by the extent of exposure of the pond to fish culture, stocking density, species stocked, the size of the fish reared and on fertilization programmes.

Table. Natural food preferences of the Asiatic carps at different stages of their life cycle

Species	*Stages of life cycle*			
	Larvae	*Fry*	*Fingerlings*	*Adult*
Catla (Catla catla)	Protozoans, rotifers unicellular algae, etc.	Protozoans, rotifers and crustaceans.	Crustaceans, algae, rotifers and some vegetable debris	Crustaceans, algae, rotifers, plant matters, etc.
Rohu (Labeo rohita)	- do -	Protozoans, rotifers, crustaceans, unicellular algae.	Vegetable debris, phytoplankton crustaceans, detritus, etc.	Vegetable debris, microscopic plants, detritus and mud.
Mrigal (Cirrhinus mrigal)	- do -	Crustaceans, rotifers, planktonic algae.	Vegetable debris, unicellular algae detritus and mud.	Blue-green and filamentous algae, diatoms, pieces of macrophytes, decayed vegetable matters, mud & detritus.
Grass carp (Ctenopharyn godon idella)	Protozoans, rotifers, copepod nauplii.	Protozoans, rotifers, crustaceans, microzooben thos, detritus, microalgae, plant fragments.	Detritus and aquatic plants.	Aquatic plants such as wolffia, lemna, spirodela, hydrilla, najas, ceratophyllum, chara, etc.
Silver carp (Hypophthalm ichthys molitrix)	Unicellular planktonic organisms, nauplii and rotifers.	Copepods, cladocerans and phytoplankt on.	Falagellata, dinoflagellata, myxophyceae, bacillariophycea , etc.	Mainly phytoplankton.
Common carp (Cyprinus carpio) Var. Communis	Protozoans, rotifers, cereodaphn ia, moina, nauplii, etc.	Rotifers, cyclops, cereodaphni a, moina, nauplii, euglena, oscillatoria, etc.	Diaptomus, cyclops, moina, cereodaphnia, ostracods, insects including chironomid larvae.	Decayed vegetable matter, worms, molluscs, chironomids, ephemerids and trichopterans.

The sources from which the nutritive fauna develops in the ponds are numerous, the main among them being the portion of the ponds that never dried, the water which has been used to refill the pond, the bottom soil with organisms in hibernation or their encysted stages, wind-borne encysted organisms (copepods, cladocera, rotifers, etc.), eggs laid by insects, etc. In the presence of sufficient food and favourable environmental conditions, these fish food organisms multiply at a faster rate.

Pond fertilization helps in increasing the amount of natural food in the pond through the supply of the necessary nutrients which are either lacking or are insufficient in the pond ecosystem. This helps the growth of primary producers-the phytoplankton and macrophytes which form the food of fish and herbivorous zooplankters. Organic manure containing practically all necessary nutrients required for biological production, encourages bacterial growth which in turn favour better production of zooplankton and increases the effectiveness of many inorganic fertilizers by providing necessary organic matter base.

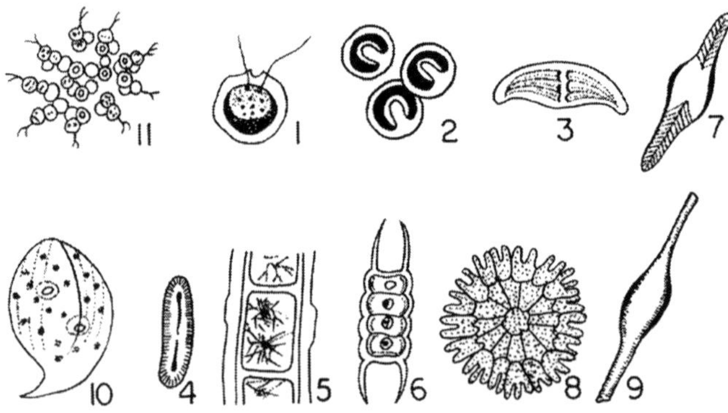

1. Chlomydononos 2. chlorella 3. closterium 4. pinnularia 5. Zygnema 6. Sconodesmus 7. Noviculs 8. Pediostrum 9. Frogilaria 10. Phacus 11. Eudorina.

Fig. Natural Fish Food Organisms (Phytoplankton)

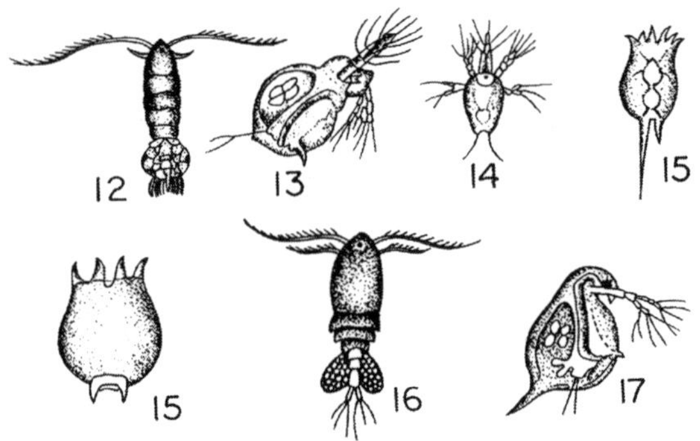

12. Diaptomus 13. Moina 14. Noupllus 15. Keratolla 16. Brochionus 17. Cyclops 18. Daphnia.

Fig. Natural Fish Food Organisms (Zooplankton)

Some of the fish food organisms such as rotifers and cladocerans can be cultured on a mass scale in earthen enclosures, plastic pools, tanks, etc and may be inoculated into the nursery ponds. Cow dung and oil cake are applied initially at the rate of 250–350 ppm and 50 ppm respectively and subsequently after every four days at the rate of half the initial dose.

After the treatment, seeding is done with 2–5 ml of Moina sp., collected from nearby ponds. Moina thus cultured may be used for seeding nursery ponds at the rate of 30–50 ml of Moina/ha. Chemical analysis of plankton show that on an average, crude protein constitutes 44 per cent to more than 57 per cent of the dry organic matter. Plankton has relatively small amounts of fat averaging to about 5–7 per cent.

SUPPLEMENTARY FEED

The fish production rate may be increased significantly by merely supplementing the natural food with artificial feed which can support more fish with increased individual weights, resulting in a more profitable operation. All the carp species including the predominently plankton feeders like catla and silver carp and macrophyte feeder grass carp accept supplemental feed.

Conventional Feeds

The conventional supplementary feed is usually a mixture of brans and oil cakes in 1:1 ratio by weight. In India, oil cakes such as mustard oil cake or groundnut oil cake and rice or wheat bran are widely applied depending on their local availability. In Bangladesh, the most common fish feed is the mixture of mustard oil cake and rice or wheat bran. In Nepal, farmers are advised to feed a mixture having maize, wheat or rice bran and mustard oil cake. In certain regions, finely chopped vegetable matter or grass are also mixed. The same feed is applied in nursery, rearing and stocking ponds. Aquatic weeds or sometimes green animal fodder are given to grass carp. Smaller aquatic weeds such as wolffia, lemna, spirodela, etc., are provided in the early stages while large macrophytes and green animal fodder to the bigger fish.

BALANCED SUPPLEMENTARY FEED

Using locally available feed materials and mixing with vitamin premix, essential minerals and trace elements, a balanced supplementary feed can be compounded without any significant increase in its cost which will give better results than the conventional one. However, the background knowledge of the nutritional requirement of carps becomes essential for formulation of suitable balanced supplementary feed.

The quantity and quality of nutrients required by carps for attaining optimum growth vary with the species, size and stages of the life cycle. Essential nutrients such as protein, fat, carbohydrate, vitamins and minerals are required as raw materials for the formation of body tissues, production of energy and also to regulate the vital physiological processes.

Protein

Protein requirements may be looked at the gross protein and specific amino acid requirement levels. Protein requirement is influenced by several factors like water quality, natural food availability in ponds, dietary protein quality, the amount of non-protein energy in the diet, stocking density, etc.

Table. Protein requirements of certain carps

Species	Crude protein level in diet for optimal growth (g/kg)	Reference
Common carp	450 – 480	
Rohu	450	
Mrigal	450	
Grass carp	410 – 431	Dabrowski (1977)

Though dietary protein levels have been shown as optimal for fry and fingerlings of Indian major and common carps, quality of the protein in terms of its amino acid composition is important or else growth would suffer even if the dietary protein level is high. Plant proteins are deficient in certain essential amino acids like methionine. Their quality can be improved by the addition of animal proteins such as fish meal, bone mea', blood meal, etc.).

Table. Essential Amino Acid requirements of common carp (Cyprinus carpio)

Amino acid	% of protein	% of diet	Total protein in the diet (%)
Arginine	4.2	1.6	38.5
Histadine	2.1	0.8	38.5
Isoleucine	2.3	0.9	38.5
Leucine	3.4	1.3	38.5
Lysine	5.7	2.2	38.5
Methionine ±	3.1	1.2	38.5
Phenylalanine ±±	6.5	2.5	38.5
Threonine	3.9	1.5	38.5
Tryptophan	0.8	0.3	38.5
Valine	3.6	1.4	38.5

Note:

\+ In the absence of cystine

++ In the absence of tyrosine

Carbohydrates

Carbohydrate requirement of carp species is highly variable ranging from 10–45 per cent. Common carp utilizes 25 per cent carbohydrates effectively as energy source, while for mrigal fingerlings it is 28 per cent in synthetic diets.

Although higher levels of carbohydrate may be utilized by carps, diets containing over 40 per cent dextrin results in retarded growth and lowered feed efficiency due to lower digestibility. The most likely symptom of over supply of carbohydrates in diet is excessive deposition of fat in the liver and carcass. However, the protein requirements of carps can be brought down to some extent by raising the level of dietary carbohydrates.

Lipids

The polyunsaturated fatty acids (PUFA) is considered to be the most important class of lipids as far as lipids are concerned. Carps can derive their lipid requirement from natural feed available in the pond since these compounds are readily available in planktonic and other biotic communities. Lipids are also considered to be the most important sparing compounds. By adding 5 per cent of soyabean oil the optimum protein requirement of young mirror carp can be brought down to 33 per cent from 38 per cent. The addition increases the dietary metabolized energy from 2.8 to 3.1 Kcal/g.

Vitamins

Studies on vitamin requirements of fish are very limited.

Table. Dietary vitamin requirements of the common carp (Cyprinus carpio) and related deficiency symptoms

Vitamin	Requirement (mg/kg diet)	Major vitamin deficiencysymptoms
Thiamin	Na	Nervousness and fading of body colour.
Riboflavin	7.0	Hemorrhages on skin, fin, mortality
Pyridoxine	5–6	Nervous disorders
Pantothenic acid	30–50	Poor growth, anaemia, skin hemorrhages, exophthalmia
Nidcotinic acid	28	Hemorrhages on skin, mortality
Biotin	1	Poor growth
Folic acid	N	None detected
Vitamin B_{12}	N	None detected
Choline	4 000	Fatty liver
Inositol	440	Skin lesions
Ascorbic acid	Na	Impaired collagen formation
Vitamin A	10 000 IU	Faded colour, exophthalmia, hemorrhages on fin and skin
Vitamin D	N	None detected
Vitamin E	200–300	Muscular dystrophy, mortali-ty
Vitamin K	N	None detected

Note:

N = No dietary requirement demonstrated under variousenvironmental condition.

Na = Not available

Minerals and Trace Elements

Like higher vertebrates, carps also have dietary requirements of minerals such as calcium, iron, magnesium and phosphorus and trace elements such as cobalt, iodine, zinc, copper, manganese, sulpher, fluorine, molybdenum, etc. For common carp the minimum requirement of phosphorus in the diet is 0.6–0.7 per cent and that of calcium is about 0.028 per cent. 1 per cent dicalcium-phosphate is recommended in the feed for adult fish in polyculture system in ponds. Trace elements are growth stimulants and are required in traces.

Common Feedstuffs: A large number of feed stuffs are presently being used as supplementary feed for carps in undrainable pond culture systems. Some of them are widely available and extensively used. These may be broadly classified into two groups: the feeds of plant origin and the feedstuffs of animal origin. Cakes of oil seeds such as groundnut, mustard, linseed, coconut, etc., are a most useful and widely used feedstuff of plant origin with high fat and protein contents. Brans of rice, wheat and other grains are equally popular and used in combination with oil cakes.

Such meal as soya waste after oil extraction is excellent feed for carps. Broken cereals such as rice, wheat, maize, etc., are good but expensive feed materials. Leafy feeds are suitable for grass carp. Tender leaves of various aquatic and terrestrial plants (cassava, maioc, colocasia, banana, sweet potatoes, maize, etc.) and green animal fodder such as berseem, napier, paranapier, elephant grass, etc., are also used. Miscellaneous items such as kitchen wastes, household scraps, residues of bakery, beer brewing or rice-wine industry wastes can be profitably used as fish feed.

Dried fish meal (fish flour) is the most common and cheapest source of animal protein and widely used in livestock and fish feeds. Slaughterhouse offals, prawn head meal, bone meal, silkworm pupae and items like snails, oligochaete worms, etc., are also widely used depending on their availability and price.

Table. Proximate composition of some of the common fish feed stuff

	As percentage of dry matter									
Common name	**DM**	**CP**	**EE**	**CF**	**Ash**	**NFE**	**Ca**	**P**	**Methioine & czstine**	**Lysine**
A. Plant product										
Groundnut oil cake	94.0	40.1	12.2	14.0	7.8	25.9	-	-	0.52	1.44
Groundnut oil meal	89.7	37.3	0.3	6.2	3.0	35.7	0.22	0.75	0.48	1.34
Coconut oil cake	92.3	18.1	8.9	16.4	4.6	52.0	0.21	0.58	0.34	0.45
Soyabean cake	84.8	47.5	6.4	5.1	6.4	34.6	0.13	0.69	1.42	2.90
Soyabean oil meal	88.7	52.8	1.5	6.6	7.6	46.7	-	-	1.58	3.22

Cotton seed oil cake	87.9	26.4	5.7	24.2	6.6	37.1	-	-	0.74	1.08
Sunflower oil cake	91.0	34.2	14.3	13.2	6.6	31.8	0.30	1.30	1.36	1.19
Sunflower oil meal	90.0	42.7	4.0	16.1	7.7	29.5	-	-	1.70	1.49
Linseed oil cake	-	30.5	6.6	9.5	10.2	43.2	0.37	0.96	1.34	1.07
Sesame oil cake	90.0	32.2	14.4	20.3	11.1	22.0	-	-	1.64	0.93
Ground maize	89.6	5.1	8.7	3.9	1.1	81.2	-	-	0.10	0.12
Wheat bran	90.7	13.9	8.3	13.1	4.6	60.1	-	-	0.42	0.53
Rice bran	91.3	13.7	5.4	20.0	18.1	48.8	-	-	0.52	0.56
Rice polish	91.6	12.4	16.7	12.0	14.1	44.9	-	-	0.73	0.78
Millet	88.4	12.0	4.8	11.3	5.0	66.9	0.57	3.21	0.36	0.43
Black gram bran	88.8	7.0	3.6	24.0	8.9	56.5	-	-	0.12	0.51
B. Animal products										
Blood meal	89.5	88.5	1.2	0.4	6.0	3.9	0.28	0.28	1.95	7.08
Bone meal	75.0	36.0	4.0	3.0	49.0	8.0	22.0	10.0	0.25	1.69
Fish meal	86.0	55.6	12.0	2.9	21.3	8.2	-	-	-	-
Prawn meal	89.4	31.2	11.7	17.6	39.5	0.0	-	-	-	-
Silk worm pupae	20.0	54.2	30.3	3.9	5.2	6.4	0.1	1.1	-	-
Fresh cattle manure	17.9	8.4	3.1	22.5	18.8	47.2	-	-	-	-

DM-Dry matter;
CP-Crude protein;
EE-Ether extract;
CF-Crude fibre;
NFE-Nitrogen free extract;
CA-Calcium;
P-Total phosphorus.

Usually the crude protein level of the supplementary feed is fixed at about 5 to 10 per cent below the dietry protein requirement of the fish to be fed. Vitamins, minerals and trace elements are added as required.

Table. Values of digestible nutrients in carps for some common feedstuffs

Feedstuff	Digestible nutrients (%)
Coconut oil cake	67.5 – 69.8
Ground nuts	79.3
Rice bran	79.4
Maize (Corn)	77.9

Maize (fresh)	74.9 – 75.1
Rye	75.9
Sweet potato	25.8
Radish leaves	8.2
Fresh silkworm pupae	34.3

FORMULATION OF FEED

Easy availability, low cost, high digestibility and high nutrient contents are the major considerations in selecting the fish feed ingredients for feed formulation. Feed constitute the major operating cost in undrainable pond fish culture and therefore, our ultimate objective is to supply essential nutrients at the minimum possible cost. Formulated feeds may be either a complete feed with optimum level of all the essential nutrients and energy to provide complete nutrition or a supplementary feed-a diet basically to supplement energy and a portion of protein and other essential nutrients. In undrainable pond culture systems where natural feed are made available by pond fertilization, feed is required only to supplement the natural feed. The initial step involves surveying market prices of the locally available feedstuffs and tabulation of data as mentioned below as an example.

Table. Data tabulation example for selection of feedstuff

Feedstuff content	Market price protein	Protein selection	Cost/kg	Grade for (US \$/kg) (US \$)
Groundnut oil cake	0.15	38.2	0.39	II
Mustard oil cake	0.21	40	0.52	III
Sesame oil cake	0.11	32.2	0.34	I

Thus, out of the three listed above one can easily select the feedstuff most suitable for his operation. Similar methods may be adopted to find the best possible feed for the supply of specific major nutrients. Their amino acid profile is also to be considered for such selection. Using the locally available feedstuff, a diet with desired level of protein can easily be formulated by using the square method. The same method is also used for adjusting energy levels in a feed. The required protein level of 30 per cent, for example, is put in the centre of the square. The two selected feedstuffs with their percentage of protein content are put on the left hand corners of the square.

Sesame oil cake (Protein 32.3%)		30—10 = 20
	Desired feed protein level(30%)	
Rice bran (Protein 10%)		32.2—30 = 2.3Total 22.3

The value of desired protein level of the proposed feed is substracted from each of the feedstuffs in turn and the results are placed at the opposite corner ignoring the resultant positive or negative signs.

The two resultant Fig.s on the right hand side of the square are then added together (20 + 2.3 = 22.3). Now to obtain 30 per cent crude protein level in the proposed feed, the following formula is followed.

- Sesame seed cake $= \frac{20}{22.3} \times 100 = 89.6\%$
- Rice bran in the feed $= \frac{2.3}{22.3} \times 100 = 10.3\%$

Thus, to obtain 30 per cent crude protein level in 100 kg of feed we need 89.6 kg of sesame seed cake and 10.3 kg of rice bran to be mixed together.

The same method can also be used to obtain a desired dietary energy level. It has been experienced that if the minimum dietary requirements for amino acid like arginine, lysine, methionine and tryptophan are met, the requirements of 6 other essential amino acids usually also get satisfied. Vitamins, minerals and trace elements are added in feed according to the requirements of the species of carps under culture.

Pelletization

Considerable wastage is expected when supplementary feed mixtures rapidly separate into their component ingredients during the feeding process.

Fig. Fish Feed in Dough Form

However, by pelletization of supplementary feed mixture, such wastage can be minimised and further improvement in the feed efficiency can be achieved. Feed in pellet forms are more readily acceptable and give better results in comparison with dust feed During pelletization, the soft and dusty feed is converted into hard, water-stable pellets by the process of heating and compression. Even in undrainable ponds use of supplementary feed in pelleted form promise increased production through increased efficiency and minimum wastage.

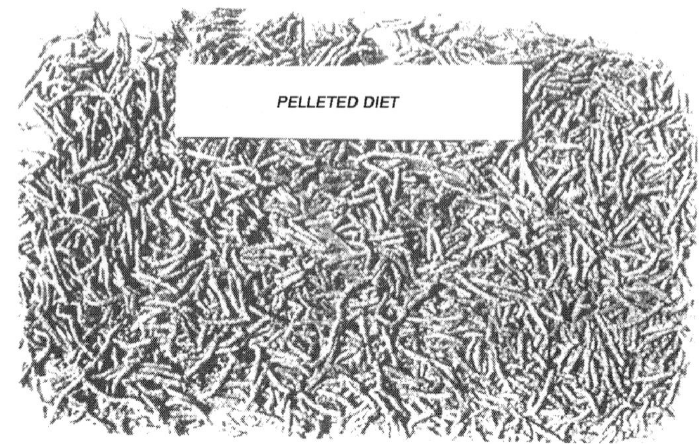

Fig. Fish Feed in Pelleted Form

A generalised but practical account of nutrient specifications of commercial warm water aquacult.

Table. Nutrients specifications of commercial aquaculture feeds (Warm water omnivorous species) (Adapted from ADCP, 1983)

Nutrients	Fry and fingerlings	Juveniles and adults	Brood Fish
Protein (% min)	30	25	30
Lipids (% min)	8	5	5
Ca (% min)	0.8	0.5	0.8
Ca (% max)	1.5	1.8	1.5
P (% min)	0.6	0.5	0.6
P (% max)	1.0	1.0	1.0
Lysine (% min)	2.0	1.6	1.8
Digestible Energy (KcaL/100 g min)	310	280	280
Vitamins (Supplement), (per 100 kg)			
A (i.u.)	600 000	500 000	600 000
D (i.u.)	100 000	100 000	100 000
E (i.u.)	6 000	5 000	6 000
K (g)	1.2	1.0	1.0
C (g)	24.0	20.0	24.0
Thiamine (g)	2.4	2.0	2.4
Riboflavin (g)	2.4	2.0	2.4
Pantothenic acid (g)	6.0	5.0	6.0
Niacin (g)	12.0	10.0	12.0
Pyridoxine (g)	2.4	2.0	2.4

Biotin (g)	0.024	0.020	0.024
Folic Acid (g)	0.6	0.5	0.6
Choline (g)	54.0	50.0	54.0
B-12 (mg)	2.4	2.0	2.4
Minerals (Supplement), (per 100 kg feed)			
Iron (g)	5.0	5.0	5.0
Copper (g)	0.3	0.3	0.3
Manganese (g)	2.0	2.0	2.0
Zinc (g)	3.0	3.0	3.0
Iodine (mg)	10.0	10.0	10.0
Cobalt (mg)	1.0	1.0	1.0
Selenium (mg)	10.0	10.0	10.0

Based upon the nutrient specifications, a number of test diets for carp fry, fingerling and brood fish are under extensive trials to determine which would be the preferred formulations in terms of efficiency and cost.

The conventional rice-bran and oil cake mixture lacks animal protein, minerals and vitamins and rapidly separates into its component ingredients during the feeding process. Considerable improvement is possible if this conventional rice-bran and oil cake mixture is simply fortified with 15–25 per cent fish meal, 0.1 per cent mineral mixture, 0.1 per cent vitamin mixture and pelletized.

Although mineral and vitamin mixtures are commercially available as common additive of animal feed, fish meal at a reasonable price may not be easily available in rural areas.

FERTILIZERS

Considerable quantities of nutrient elements are regularly removed from the pond ecosystem through the harvested fish crops and thus for retaining the pond fertility, the required amount of nutrients need to be replenished. These nutrients are broadly divided into two groups.

The first group of nutrients are nitrogen, phosphorus, potassium, carbon and calcium, while the second group of nutrients which are needed in very minute quantities constitute mainly copper, zinc, iron, manganese, cobalt, boron, molybdenum, etc.

It is the first group of nutrients which are more concerned with pond fertility in terms of primary production, consumed in more quantity and thus need to be compensated from outside in the form of fertilizers. In other words, the main objective of adding fertilizers in fish ponds is to maintain a sustained production of natural fish food during the entire culture period. Fertilizers are also classified into two categories: inorganic fertilizers or mineral fertilizers and organic fertilizers or manures of plant and animal origin.

Organic Manures

Organic manures have been in use in fish culture in India and the Far East countries for a long time. They are available in a variety of forms such as dung of cattle, sheep, pig and goat, poultry droppings; de-oiled cakes of mahua, mustard, castor, linseed, neem, etc. They also come in the form of farmyard manure, compost, green manures, sewage, etc. Of these, cow dung is the most widely used manure in undrainable pond culture system. Most of the organic manures are by-products of local agriculture, animal husbandry and village based agro-industrial activities and hence their procurement is relatively easy at low cost. They are composite in nature and provide practically all the nutrients, including organic carbon, required for biological production.

Several organic manures are immediately assimilated by the aquatic fauna and especially by the zooplankton or even by some species of cultured carps. By improving the quality of the pond bottom mud they encourage bacterial growth which in turn favours better production of zooplankton and also through inducing increased bacterial decomposition help in releasing mineral constituents of the soil into the water. It also increases the effectiveness of many inorganic fertilizers by providing the necessary organic matter base. Though the presence of the major nutrient elements in these manures is rather at a lower level and often vary quantitatively, their effect is sustained over a longer period. However, they are required in large quantities, thereby making the procurement, transport and application somewhat troublesome and costly though the manure itself is cheap. Also, unless proper care is exercised in its use, depletion of dissolved oxygen, in the pond water is likely to occur with consequent loss of fish by asphyxiation. However, better yields of fish are obtained through a judicious manuring schedule.

Inorganic Fertilizers

Commercially produced inorganic compounds containing major nutrients-nitrogen, phosphorus and potassium are known as inorganic or chemical fertilizers. They contain a high and fixed percentage of one or more major nutrients depending on the class (nitrogenous, phosphatic, potassic or mixed) of fertilizer. Due to their high solubility in water, the nutrients become readily available soon after their application. Some fertilizers are also available in liquid form which offer several advantages over the conventional granular or powderedform of fertilizers.

Nitrogenous Fertilizers

Nitrogenous fertilizers usually contain nitrogen as the principal element and are commercially available as ammonium sulphate, ammonium nitrate, urea, etc. Most of the nitrogenous fertilizers deplete reserves of bases and make soil acid. Therefore, the form of nitrogenous fertilizers may be selected on the basis of acidity, neutrality or alkalinity of the soil type. Nitrogenous fertilizers are particularly essential for newly constructed ponds which are poor in nitrogen and do not have sufficient organic matter in its bottom, whereas older ponds having a good layer of colloidal mud are capable of producing nitrogen by itself. Further, the efficacy of nitrogenous fertilizers is inhibited by phosphorous deficit. It is best to maintain the P/N ratio at 1/4.

Phosphatic Fertilizers

Phosphatic fertilizers are by far the most effective and favourable for fish culture. It is all the more important because almost all fish ponds exhibit phosphorus deficiency. The most commonly used phosphatic fertilizers are the orthophosphates and are grouped roughly according to their solubility in water. Superphosphates are the most soluble in water, dicalcium phosphate is partially soluble and rock phosphorus is almost insoluble in water. Amongst the phosphatic fertilizers, single superphosphate is extensively used and is easily available.

The more concentrated triple superphosphate is also in use which has P_2O_5 (Phosphorus pentaoxide) equivalent up to 45 per cent with 85 per cent solubility and thus involved relatively lower transport cost. Generally, the phosphatic fertilizers are held in soil and liberated gradually with the result that its action is extended to subsequent years of its application, mostly depending on the nature of the pond bottom.

Potassic Fertilizers

Although potassium ranks as a major nutrient like nitrogen and phosphorus, its importance in pond fertilization is less pronounced since it is available in a required quantity in natural waters. Muriate of potash (Kcl) and sulphate of potash (K_2SO_4) are the two commonly used fertilizers as a source of potassium. The favourable action of potassic fertilizers can be seen in ponds with low alkalinity, with peaty bottoms. In general, for ponds in which phytoplankton production is rather slow, potassic fertilizers may be tried. It also improves the hygienic conditions of fish ponds, particularly the rearing ponds.

Calcium

Though calcium is not considered as a nutrient to be used as fertilizer, it is another integral part of the ecosystem and is usually applied to get the benefit of added fertilizers used in a pond. In ponds where the water is poor in calcium (less than 8 mg Cao/1), the freshwater flora, molluscs and crustaceans are either rare or absent which in turn diminishes the nutritive value of the water. Calcium present in required quantities also neutralises the harmful action of excessive magnesium, sodium and potassium salts. It is usually applied in the form of lime, which is widely available as ground lime stone ($CaCo_3$), slaked lime ($Ca(OH)_2$) and quick lime (Cao).

Procurement of organic and inorganic fertilizers is relatively easier than other essential inputs like feed and seed. Organic manures are locally available and in most cases they are available within the community. However, due to extensive adoption of intensive crop farming there is a growing demand for animal manure or compost in agriculture. Instead of procuring the whole lot of required manures at a time and storing them for application over extended periods, it is always convenient and desirable to procure materials in small quantities and apply them as and when required. While storing the manure, it should be covered to protect it from direct sunlight. Inorganic fertilizers being extensively used as an agricultural input, the listed fertilizers are easily available in the local markets. Prolonged storage, high humidity, etc., cause deterioration in the quality of inorganic fertilizers and hence only a specified quantity of materials required for 2-3 months should be procured at a time. Selection of fertilizers depends mainly on their nutrient content, cost and suitability for the specific soil condition.

6

A Corporate Strategy for "Fish for all" In India

Marine fish landings have levelled off since the mid 1980's. Aquaculture has stepped in to bridge the gap between demand and supply. But can aquaculture provide fish for all? Do the fish eating population in the developing countries have the purchasing power to create a demand base for the supply side to build-up and achieve an economic and sustainable optimum?

Fishing is non-agricultural according to WTO. Fisheries in India is an occupation of the least cared for segment of the populace but practised by almost 6 million population, full time by 3 million fishers, 1.4 million part time fishers and 2.1 million occasional fishers. The fisheries sector contributes about 1.5 per cent of the total gross domestic product at current prices indicating the abysmal levels of personal income of the fishers themselves.

It is common knowledge that with liberalisation the terms of trade and gains from trade would substantially improve and would help create a market for goods and services that enjoy comparative advantage in production, processing and marketing. But markets are a function of effective demand and in that process each country has to introspect on fish as food or fish for the market. Number of factors influences the supply and demand for low value food fish. Does a market exist for aquaculture of low value food fish. Is there a scope for fish for all in India?

Therefore, fish for all requires structural changes in demand, policies and technology affecting fish prices, producer and consumer behaviour. This chapter addresses some of these issues and concludes with some suggestions for improving poverty reduction and fish for all.

THE FISH MARKET

Global consumption of fish has doubled since 1973, and the developing world has been responsible for 90 per cent of this growth. Whereas the growth of fish as food in the richer countries has tapered off, in the poorer countries it has grown rapidly. China dominates aggregate consumption of fish products. It accounted for about 36 per cent of global consumption in 1997, compared with only 11 per cent in 1973. India and Southeast Asia together accounted for another 17 per cent in 1997, with total consumption doubling since 1973.

The changing profile of fish consumption around the world comes as no surprise, partly because countries with rapid population and income growth, and urbanisation tend to have the greatest increases in consumption of animal products, including fish products.

Recent studies also indicate that the prices for most food commodities will fall as a result of scale economies resulting from globalisation. But fish prices are least likely to decline or are most likely to rise clearly indicating that the demand for fish outpaces its supply. The economics of commercial aquaculture cannot support fresh fish production for the masses. The supply of various fresh fishes in the market that cater to the palette of the poor cannot be supported by aquaculture as the returns on investment are far from encouraging.

MARKET PROFILE, STRUCTURE, CONDUCT AND PERFORMANCE

The domestic market for fish In India is governed not only by the purchasing power of the consumers but also by their tastes and preferences. About 30 per cent of the population in India is vegetarian. According to ESN Nutrition country profile for India, FAO has reported that fish and seafood provide 2 per cent of the dietary energy supply while cereals supply 62 per cent. The per capita consumption of fish is estimated to be 5 kilograms per year for the whole population and it is 8 kilograms for the non-vegetarian population of the country as against the world average of 16 kilograms. It may be noted that the cited study puts the rate of growth of fish consumption in India and the South East Asia as having doubled over a period of 1973-1997. This may be true when viewed in conjunction with South East Asia but looked at independently, the growth rate of fish consumption in India was only 2.3 per cent over 1985-1997.

This is basically because the Indian domestic market for fish is inelastic both in terms of income and price. The cross price elasticity of fish in India is also inelastic. This is because for the size of the country and its population, fish commands practically only a niche market in India.

While the people of the states of Kerala, Bengal and Goa are passionate about their fish, the fish eating population in other states are just sporadic in their consumption of fish. The regional tastes and preferences of fish eating population of the country and the frequency of fish consumption also exert substantial influence on the market.

The monthly per capita consumption of fish varies from a negligible quantity (<0.1 kg/ month) in Haryana, Himachal Pradesh and Jammu and Kashmir to a high of 3.79 kg/ month in Lakshadweep. Even in a fish eating country like China the per capita consumption of aquatic products ranges from 1 kg in the western provinces to 40 kg in the eastern provinces.

Table. Total Consumption of Fish as Food 1973-1997

Region Country	Total Consumption (Kgs/ Capita/Year) (Actual)			Projected	Annual Growth Rate (%)	Projected Growth Rate (%)
	1973	**1985**	**1997**	**2020**	**1985-1997**	**1997-2020**
China	5.5	8.1	16.5	35.9	10.4	1.3
South East Asia	17.6	19.8	23.0	25.8	1.3	0.5
India	3.6	3.7	4.7	5.8	2.3	0.9
Other South Asia	6.2	5.4	6.0	6.1	0.9	0.1
Developed world	22.6	24.3	21.7	21.5	-1.0	0.00
Developing world	7.3	9.0	14.0	16.2	3.8	0.60

The geographical mismatch between production centres and markets also compound the problems of fish production and marketing in India. Andhra Pradesh has established freshwater fish production facilities and its market is West Bengal, a good 1000 kilometers away. The Kolleru lake area in West Godavari and Krishna districts are the heartland of freshwater aquaculture.

The indirect benefit of this development is the growth in employment via fish seed production and supply, ice making, packing and transportation sectors. The structural imbalance has left the sector unstable. A glut in freshwater fish in the West Bengal market leaves the Andhra Pradesh production centres gasping for breath as there is no local market for these fishes. The break even price appears to hover around ₹. 25/Kilogram, below which the producers take a break from production. Such is the volatility of the market for freshwater fishes.

Confirmed markets for select fishes in select regions like freshwater carps in West Bengal, seer fishes, pomfrets, threadfin breams, sardines and mackerels for Kerala, Goa and Tamil Nadu apparently offer less and less scope for production of such fishes by way of aquaculture. The exportability of a fish and the quantity landed bear a direct relationship to its price in the local market.

STRATEGIES FOR THE FUTURE

A two pronged strategy could be thought of in trying to resolve the problem of providing food fish to the poor in India.

Based on the world average rate of 16 Kgs. of fish, 3.7 million tones will be required for providing fish to 70 per cent or 231 million of the Indian population. If the objective were to meet the protein dietary requirement of the fish eating Indian, at a rate of 0.5 Kg of fish per capita per week and 26 Kgs/ year a production of 6.0 million tones for 231 million population would be required.

Million tones of freshwater fishes consisting of carps and catfish and 1 million ton of marine sardines and anchovies are the low valued species that are available for human consumption. As decided in the Second International Symposium on Sustainable Aquaculture in Oslo, Norway in 1997, it is possible to make a conjecture that one protein crop for local consumption and the next for the export market be followed makes good reading but may not take off in real sense of the concept.

With the projected demand far exceeding supply and the added pressure of demand for fish meal production for aquaculture feed production and the additional responsibility of providing nutrition to the vegetarian population, it is necessary to recast the goal of attaining fish for all in India as aquatic food for all.

Seaweed is considered to be medicinal food of the 21st century and it alone contributes nearly 25 per cent, *i.e.*, 10 million tones to the overall world aquaculture production. Other aquatic plants such as Salicornia, Spirulina, Duck weed, etc., have enormous potential with several nutritive qualities. When demand picks up through product development for human diet it may even exceed fish production at a cheaper and fast rate.

With enormous availability of resources in terms of ocean wealth, freshwater and brackishwater areas supplemented by reservoirs and tanks, the prospects for enhancing production of low value fishes does not seem to be very difficult.

Then the problem is one of markets. If markets for products of multi-national companies led by Kentucky Fried Chicken, McDonalds and Pizzas of all sorts can make deep inroads into the food habits of the consuming public in urban India and Coke and Pepsi in both urban and conservative rural India, it is only a matter of time before some corporates could come up with the idea of marketing fish as a value added product for different segments of the Indian market. NDDB's Amul has shown how this can be done.

The marketing strategy to promote fish consumption by effecting a change in the inherent and traditional attributes that qualify for a local market needs to be examined. This strategy can possibly be made by targeting the urban ready to eat packaged fish products market on the lines of multi national products market that has revolutionised and overhauled the concept of tradition in the values based Indian soft drink market of yore. Value addition, product differentiation and market positioning will be required to generate and sustain a market that would take care of the product distribution. If it can be done in milk, it can be done for fish in India.

The case for this argument is further strengthened by the fact the estimates of per capita calorie consumption in urban India were higher than for rural India at 2156 Kcalories per day compared to 2149. This is surprising given the perception that the rural population tends to consume more calories because of the greater intensity of work in rural areas. Studying the National Sample Survey data of the 55th round, Chandrasekhar and Ghosh have further argued that increasing urbanisation of rural areas has meant that urban lifestyles have penetrated into rural areas and have influenced the narrowing down of rural-urban differences in food consumption. This explains the calorie convergence as well. According to the National Sample Survey, the proportion of household expenditure on items other than food has been increasing. Conversely, it implies that household expenditure has fallen from 60 per cent in 1977-78 to about 47 per cent in 1999-2000 in urban areas. With rising incomes, people's diet are becoming more diversified. Correspondingly, substantial increases have taken place in the share of other foods such as fruits, vegetables, meat, eggs, fish and milk in food expenditure.

Corporatisation of fish farming through fisheries cooperatives, buy back arrangements, satellite farming and creation of a market for value added low value fishes and sustaining it through modern marketing strategies seems to the only answer to fish for all in India. We have bend the rules like Beckham!!

THE POLICY GAPS

Fisheries has always been given a slip shod treatment by successive budgets. Despite proving itself time and again in terms of revenue generated from export earnings, fisheries has repeatedly got only a miniscule percentage of successive budgets allotments.

Table: Matrix of Change in Output Values in Agriculture, Livestock and Fisheries (Per cent) (1985-86=100) (1981-82 prices)

Sectors	**1986-87**	**1987-88**	**1988-89**	**1989-90**	**1990-91**
Agriculture	98.02	96.83	115.78	116.71	122.00
Livestock	104.54	106.98	111.60	116.10	120.83
Fisheries	102.90	108.85	118.09	132.82	139.16
Inland Fisheries	103.41	109.39	114.51	124.27	134.88
Marine Fisheries	102.04	107.96	139.13	148.78	146.33
Sector	**1991-92**	**1992-93**	**1993-94**	**1994-95**	**1995-96**
Agriculture	118.27	124.43	127.97	135.38	130.53
Livestock	125.01	131.25	138.23	143.76	149.00
Fisheries	145.73	155.57	168.02	178.63	190.84
Inland Fesheries	143.78	146.34	165.65	168.17	185.00
Marine Fesheries	148.98	171.02	167.55	196.12	200.61

Basic principles of economic development advocate the development of a sector through forward linkages, *i.e.*, creation of infrastructural facilities and support systems that would facilitate the growth of the identified sector. One of the much touted reforms in India is the opening up of the country to foreign direct investment (FDI). The food processing sector has attracted a portion of this investment but lack of innovative policy guidelines and projects have been instrumental in keeping the fish out of the poor man's palette. Political risk, commercial risk, policy risk and regulatory risks have been responsible for keeping the foreign direct investment into India at a low level. But the biggest problem in attracting FDI is the problem of mindset and the historical concept that FDI must piggyback on technology.

VALUE CHAIN OF FISH AND FISHERY PRODUCTS

The chain consists of a series of activities that create and build value. Value chain analysis describes the activities that take place in fishery businesses and relates them to an analysis of the competitive strength of the business. An introductory note brings the idea of supply chain and value chain of fish and fishery products. Moreover, emphasis has made to understand the nodes along with the value chain and its stakeholders. Drivers and governors of change on the demand composed of several key factors, such as demographics, consumer preferences, buyer specifications, regulatory change and market access. Principal concerns of demographics are ethnicity, race, geographic distribution, extent of travel, literacy rate and retailer promotions. Convenience, year round availability, variety and nutritional content, food safety, greenness and special fair trade and trade arrangements are the main concerns of consumer preferences.

INTRODUCTION

Moreover, buyer specifications consist with several other factors, such as volume, presentation, certification, private standards, labelling, price point and service, technology, management information systems, category management, supply chain management, transport and handling advances. Market conditions and procurement practices (factor prices for production and shipping, producer preferences, technology, regulatory change, demographics) are the key concerns on change in supply. Value chains analysis provides opportunities to identify strategic windows for each and every node of the chain. Moreover, results of the value chain analysis facilitate the maximum utilisation of resources while achieving the sustainability in resource use.

The benefits of the world, especially the human's gain from fishery are diverse and may be enumerated in several ways. Most commonly, benefits are computed as commodity output — the weight or number of fish produced. Commodity output may be further split between the animals harvested by capture (fishing for wild animals) or culture (produced as captive animals) — commonly called the capture fisheries and the culture fisheries, respectively. Benefits are also commonly measured as wholesale or retail economic value of the commodity output.

Such benefits are easily calculated for commercial fisheries because the products are usually sold, but for sport or recreational fisheries, the quality of the fishing experience is very important, so measures of catch in weight, number or economic value only partially measure the benefits provided to fishermen or to society. Even in commercial or subsistence fisheries, substantial benefits may be associated with cultural or religious aspects beyond the national boundaries. Although such benefits are difficult to measure, they may be very important to the communities and they pass it from generation to generation as their identity. Beyond the direct benefits derived from harvested fish or the fishing experience, benefits are also derived by individuals and society from simply knowing that a particular natural resource exists. Society and individuals receive intangible benefits from preserving species and habitats, especially those in danger of extinction. Such benefits are often significant, but, like the benefits from recreational fishing, they are also exceedingly difficult to quantify in economic terms.

FISH SUPPLY CHAIN

Supply chains for most of the fish species start from oceans and end up with consumer markets far from thousands of miles. A supply chain is a network of retailers, distributors, transporters, storage facilities and suppliers that participate in the production, delivery and sale of a product to the consumer. The supply chain is typically made up of multiple companies who coordinate activities to set themselves apart from the competition.

A supply chain has three key parts, these are:

1. Supply focuses on the raw materials supplied to manufacturing units, including how, when and from what location.

2. Manufacturing focuses on converting these raw materials into semi-finished or finished products.
3. Distribution focuses on ensuring these products reach the consumers through an organised network of distributors, warehouses and retailers.

WHAT DOES FISHERY VALUE CHAIN MEAN

Value chains for capture and culture fisheries differ from fish to fish and from country to country, and frequently within regions. Value chains of economically important species, such as tuna, salmon, skipjack, shrimp, tilapia, etc., composed of several nodes and products that pass through longer chains to meet the consumer. In contrast, some of the species are not economically important, but socially important, such as Hilsa for Bangladesh, Mackerel for Thailand, etc., consists with shorter value chains. Value chain describes a high-level model of how fishery businesses receive raw materials as input (captures and culture fisheries), add value to the raw materials through various processes and sell finished products to customers.

Moreover, fishery value chain can be defined as interlinked value-adding activities that convert inputs into outputs which, in turn, add to the bottom line and help to create competitive advantage. A value chain typically consists of inbound distribution or logistics, manufacturing operations, outbound distribution or logistics, marketing and selling, and after-sales service. These activities are supported by purchasing or procurement, research and development, human resource development and corporate infrastructure.

VALUE CHAIN ANALYSIS

Value chain analysis looks at every step, a fisheries business goes through, from raw materials to the eventual end user. The goal is to deliver maximum value for the least possible total cost. The value chain framework has been used as a powerful analysis tool for industry's strategic planning for nearly two decades now. The value chain framework shows that the value chain of an industry or a company may be useful in identifying and understanding crucial aspects to achieve competitive strengths and core competencies in the marketplace.

The model also reveals how the value chain activities are tied together to ultimately create value for the consumer. Analysts conducting the value chain analysis should break down the key activities of the company according to the activities entailed in the framework, and assess the potential for adding value through the means of cost advantage or differentiation. Finally, it is important to determine strategies that focus on those activities that would enable the industry or a company to attain sustainable competitive advantage.

The nature of value chain activities differs greatly in accordance with the types of species and companies. The value chains of companies have undergone many changes in the last two decades due to advancements in technology facilitating change at a very rapid pace in the business environment. Outsourcing will cause major changes in organisations and their value chains, with significant managerial implications.

Value chain analysis is an innovative, sector-based approach to competitiveness focuses on getting more value from goods and services produced for export. Value chain analysis can help fish export of developing countries to be competitive in the international market.

Goal of value chain is to offer the customer a level of value that exceeds the cost of the activities, thereby resulting profit margin. Cost advantage can be pursued by reconfiguring the value chains. Reconfiguration or structural changes of value chain refers to activities such as new production processes, new distribution channels or a different sales approach. Moreover, differentiation of value chains stems from uniqueness. Differentiation advantage may be achieved either by changing individual value chain activities to increase uniqueness in the final product or reconfiguring the value chain.

DRIVERS AND GOVERNORS OF CHANGE ON FISH DEMAND

Several factors are affecting on the demand function of fish and fishery products. Price, income, income distribution, substitutes, tastes, fashion, advertising and expectations of the consumers make the changes along the demand curve. Moreover, demographic characters that leads to change the position of the demand curve, upward or downward shifting of the curve.

DEMOGRAPHICS

Population growth rate and age distribution are key important factors affecting the demand function of fish and fishery products. Many developing nations having positive population growth rates generate larger youth population, and their food consumption habits and preferences directly affect the food demand function. The opposite side of this coin are developed nations with slow or negative population growth rates.

Thus, food consumption pattern and food preferences of large elderly population have greater impact on global food fish supply chains. For example, world's largest fish consumer, Japan, has experienced very low population growth.

As a result, Japan has aging population where twenty five per cent of the total population are over 65 years. Japanese diet is based on fish and rice, and ageing people demand more traditional fish cantered diets.

ETHNICITY AND RACE

Ethnicity and race are other important determinants of the demand function. Socio-cultural values, religious concerns, and attitudes make difference among the marketplaces. Especially, countries in the East place high demand on wide variety of fish and fishery products compared to other parts of the world. Moreover, countries with larger Muslim population place high demand on meat products than fish Food habits and religious concerns have a great impact on species selection, for example, sea cucumber and shark fins are luxury fish products for Hong Kong and China markets however; in other markets they have no value.

GEOGRAPHIC DISTRIBUTION

Geographic distribution is a major phenomenon to decide on fish demand. Communities around the world have their own methods to harvest, handle, store and prepare the fish. Available fish species in their own destinations lead to develop unique methods of harvest and consumption. Many tropical countries are blessed with multispecies fishery, and food habits of the communities are based on multiple fish species, and preparation styles differ from location to location.

EXTENT OF TRAVEL

Extent of travel, passing national boundaries and exposure to different cultures is challenging experience to the traditional demand curves on fish and fishery products.

Especially, today's concern on global village lead to change the traditional face of the fish markets all over the world. Consumers exposed to different cultures and societies are demanding different products compared to people with less exposure. Markets should be composed of fish and fishery products from different destinations to cater for new world consumers.

LITERACY

Literacy rates and education level leads to knowledgeable society, which is more concerned on food safety and quality. Health, food safety and hygiene are the key concerns in developed country compared with developing nations. In addition, consumers are placing growing concerns on sustainability, depletion of fishery resources, social responsibility and climate change. Moreover, consumers in developed country markets are willing to pay extra premiums for fish and fishery products from sustainable base.

RETAILER PROMOTION

Retailer promotion is another important determinant of demand function. Developed country markets are composed of giant retail chains and there is high competition among retailers. Their expenditure on promotional campaigns is high and getting the advantages of economies of scale compared with small-scale retailers in developing countries. In contrast, developing country markets are less competitive and individual retailers are prominent. Mobile fish retailers and vendors play a great role in supplying fish to rural destinations of Asia, Africa and Latin America.

Moreover, individual retailers are using to establish strong social networks to market their products. Word of mouth is their cost- effective promotional tool and they bring fish and fishery products to the door step of the fresh fish concerned consumers.

CONSUMER PREFERENCES

Price, quality, convenience, year round availability, variety, nutritional concerns, safety and hygiene are principal determinants of consumer demand on fish. Food habits and food consumption behaviour directly affects consumers concern on price and quality. World's biggest fish consumer, Japan, concerns more on fresh fish and they fetch highest price. Raw fish is centred for their diet and in general, they shop daily for fresh fish. On the other hand, Western markets consume cooked forms and their concerns are more on quality and food safety.

Weekend shopping behaviour is popular in Western destinations and these places more attention on convenience. Quality standards add extra cost to the production process and quality requirements differ from market to market. Thus, European Union (EU) market is based on EU directives food safety and sanitation, and US market is based on United States Food and Drug Administration (USFDA) requirements, whereas Japanese market is based on Food and Sanitation Law. Quality concern markets are willing to pay extra for the maintenance of quality standards.

CONVENIENCE

Convenience plays important role in fish and fishery marketing. Especially, busy mothers and house wives are reluctant to buy fish due to its time-consuming initial preparatory work. There is high demand for clean, cut and ready to cook or ready to eat forms of fish and consumers are willing to pay extra premiums. Moreover, the availability of different value-added meat products make meat more popular compared with fish. Fish and fish- based meals are popularising all over the world due to health concerns. Product development can play a greater role in this endeavour.

YEAR ROUND AVAILABILITY

Aquaculture makes fish available year round compared with capture fisheries. Especially, regular supplies to the market are essential to have loyal group of consumers. Seasonality is common with many fish species and which makes consumers to search substitutes. Many developing country fish suppliers are supplying seasonal species to the markets; this lead consumer preferences to change from time to time. Value addition will help to bring the different forms of fish products to the marketplace while reducing post-harvest losses. Post-harvest losses in developing county markets are as high as 30–40 per cent of the harvest.

VARIETY AND NUTRITIONAL CONTENT

Fish and fishery products already acquire the minds of health concerned people worldwide. Fish is rich in Omega 3 fatty acid which makes it more popular in modern markets. Year round availability of different species as well as different value-added forms will lead to fulfil the needs and wants of today's consumers. Aquaculture provides promising answers to the variety of products available in the market year round basis. Moreover, value addition helps to reduce post-harvest losses and bring the regional specialties over the national boundaries.

SAFETY

Today's consumers are more concerned with food safety than ever before and high-value markets such as EU, Japan and the United States have strickt regulations to enforce this and to ensure quality and safety.

Developing country markets are also placing increasing attention on food safety and sanitation measures, not only for exported products in order to comply with the regulatory requirements in the importing countries but also as their own citizens to a greater degree than before demand safe and wholesome food in general, and fish products in particular. Rising levels of economic wellbeing, improved market information, education and awareness programmes will help to minimize the gap between demand and supply of certified food fish and products.

GREENNESS

Sustainability is the main concern of the green or environmental friendliness. Moreover, states and policymakers are facing severe issues of rising levels of food crisis. Consumer and fisher awareness on sustainability will help to reduce the threats on fish stocks and make it available for future generations. Consumers of high-value markets place more attention on products from sustainable resource base and they are ready to pay extra for the conservation measures. Eco-labels, organic labels and Marine Stewardship Council (MSC) label are generating consumer awareness. Health concern consumers are paying more attention to chemical and antibiotics free stuff. Consumer's willingness to pay premium prices on chemical-free, sustainable products encourages producers to think twice on their way of production.

FAIR TRADE

Fair trade labels spell the social responsible behaviour of the company. Rarely fish and fishery produce processing companies hold the fair trade label. Only the Icelandic fishing community holds the fair trade label for their wild salmon products. Millions of small-scale subsistence fishers depend directly or indirectly on this industry.

Therefore, it is worthwhile to pay attention to apply fair trade label to sustainable fishing communities across the world. Consumers of high-value markets are willing to pay premium prices for fair trade products and this is encouraging producers of developing nations. Moreover, this facilitates the fish processors to provide better packages to their employees and help to protect the resource base.

BUYER SPECIFICATION

Volume

Buyer specifications are very important to the marketing of fresh products. Buyers are twofold, individual buyer and institutional buyers, thus volume of trade differs according to the type of buyers. Mainly seasonality, economic status, cultural aspects and purchasing power of the consumers affects the trade volume.

Presentation

Generally products presentation style appeals and attracts consumers, and this is especially important for fish and fishery products. Unfavourable odour and its easy perishability make fish unattractive to consumers. Good packaging materials will improve the handling and shelf life of the products. Clean cut ready to cook or eat fishery products attracts more consumers than the raw whole fish. Food habits and food culture have direct impacts on the consumer preferences.

Labelling

Food labelling is intended to provide information on product composition and safety. Country of origin labelling, meaning all fish and shellfish has to carry labels stating the origin and the means of production (farmed or wild). Recently the EU adopted regulations requiring labelling of all fisheries and aquaculture products.

This labelling regulation is intended to strengthen traceability – the ability to trace fishery products from sea to market and allow consumers to choose their seafood according to specific criteria that might be of concern to them. All fisheries products on sale at retailers will have to be labelled with the following information: the commercial name of the species, the production method (wild or farmed) and the area where the fish was caught.

Private Standards

Mandatory public (regulatory) standards carry with them, private standards a legal obligation for compliance and there are responses to a perceived market failure. They are often implemented in the presence of negative externalities, to ensure the provision of public goods, or to mitigate information asymmetry. Private standards for food safety and food quality can be distinguished on two dimensions: the source or scope of the standard and the economic function of the standard. Private standards emerge from a variety of sources and include proprietary standards established by firms, third-party standards established by independent standard-setting bodies and other non-governmental organisations, and voluntary consensus standards established by industry bodies or coalitions of firms.

Private standards can also be distinguished by the economic functions they perform, including product differentiation, supply chain management, and liability reduction or protection of a firm's (industry's) reputation. Private standards can enhance product differentiation if the standard is communicated to consumers through labelling or the presence of a logo on the final consumer product, both of which act as quality signals. Alternatively, the primary purpose of a private standard could be to enhance supply chain management by improving information flows and reducing transaction costs in the supply chain. Finally, private standards may serve primarily to reduce liability as a component of a due diligence defence in the event of a food safety problem.

If effective, private standards can reduce transaction costs by facilitating longer-term supply chain relationships and in doing so lowering both the search costs of finding reliable suppliers and the monitoring costs of ensuring the quality of supplies. For this reason, a credible system of verification (often by a third-party certification body) is necessary for most private standard systems, both proprietary and consensus. While ostensibly voluntary, private standards can be *de facto* mandatory if a majority of the market adopts the standard as a requirement.

Certification

Certification and labelling of certified products aim to identify products that follow certain minimum standards or regulations, such as standards for quality, organic production, fair trade, or sustainability. A variety of seafood certification schemes have been developed over the past decade, all claiming that the fish that they certify have been sustainably caught or farmed and it is the best option for consumers to purchase.

Following are the guides and advisory lists of some certifying organisations:

- Marine conservation society, fish online web site and *good fish guide* (United Kingdom and Northeast Atlantic)
- The Monterey bay aquarium seafood watch
- Greenpeace: International seafood red list
- Australian marine conservation society: produces Australia's *Sustainable seafood guide*, a consumer guide, advising consumers the species which are in danger of being fished out
- Royal forest and bird protection society of New Zealand, *Best fish guide*
- *The Blue ocean institute seafood guide*, based in New York.
- Oceans alive: best and worst seafood choices
- Audubon society's national seafood wallet card (United States)
- Monterey fish market seafood advisory list (West coast, United States)
- *Canada's Seafood Guide* (Sea choice), initiative of sustainable seafood Canada
- The Environmental Justice Foundation (EJF):*Consumer guide to prawns*

Price Point and Service

As for the boats, with today's enforcement, most species are becoming regulated industries and so the dock will have licensed receivers who are responsible for ensuring the legality of the fish catch. Usually a handling company made up of experienced unloading crews who will travel up and down the coast to meet a boat, will unload a catch and assist the captain in grading the catch. Grading is critical because quality is a major selling point in the seafood world.

Thus, many boats stick with the same un-loaders and call to meet them at a dock. The handling of the seafood is a critical quality component. Especially, the trained crew members are handling the catch properly and it usually receives the higher sales price which translates into a better than average return for the catch. Most of the time catch boats are captained by the owner, but larger vessels are owned by a company or an individual (who often owns multiple boats), and have a paid captain and crew.

Most boat owners pay the captain and crew a commission based on product quality and amount delivered. Most seafood raw materials are harvested from a boat and depending on whether it is a day trip (out and back the same day) or an overnight (some trips take ten to fourteen days), the fish can have some processing prior to landing site. The fishermen want to bring the fish to the dock in its most simple and stable form. Usually the guts are removed on the boat and often the head as well. This allows availability of more space in the boat hold. The fish will be sold at the dock, often an auction house that will sell the catch in loads to the highest bidder of the day.

Once the market price of the fish is established, the dealers at the dock will then sell the product to various fish processing centres and factories. First, price of seafood is at the docks where in general, price setting mechanism is based on demand and supply. Moreover, most of the fish are off loaded and they are practising minimal handling and post harvesting techniques. The second is the amount of premium (or commission) that the dealer adds as their charges for the operation and decide the market price.

Technology

This includes marketing information systems, category management methods, progress in supply chain management, transport and handling advances.

Marketing Information Systems

Marketing information systems, often based on simple mobile phone and local-centre web access, help poorer groups to make smarter decisions. Although market intelligence systems are widespread globally, they mostly serve to large companies in developed countries. Flexible local networks connecting producers, traders, Non-governmental Organisations (NGOs), the public sector and consumers help them to quickly find and use the information they need. Artisanal fishers have rapidly caught on to using mobile phones to find out the best prices for their catch. "One stop shops" in Bangladesh, and similar networks in Laos, Cambodia, and Vietnam, also offer fishers inexpensive local access to market information. Small-scale fishers around the world are the losers of market ignorance. Middlemen and traders are the winners with high-profit margins. In general small-scale fisher's story ultimately ends with poverty.

Category Management Methods

The fish products and supplies category includes almost everything to do with fish. The fish products and supplies category are extremely diverse. To begin with, it will come as no surprise that it includes leading global players, supplying a variety of both fresh and processed fish and fishery products to customers around the world, while respecting strict industry-specific standards for sustainability.

Progress in Supply Chain Management

The supply chain for fish and fishery products can involve a large number of stakeholders between the fisherman/fish farmer and the final consumer. Most seafood is traded internationally; particularly the high-valued species most commonly associated with illegal, unreported and unregulated fishing. There are four possible routes that fish caught by a foreign fleet may make its way to the consuming nation: first, it may be exported directly after harvest; second, it may be exported after only primary processing occurs within the foreign harvesting nation; third, it may be exported after both primary and secondary processing occur within the foreign harvesting nation; forth, it may be exported after harvest to a third country processor that will then re-export the product to the consuming nation. A relatively new feature of the global supply chain is the emergence of a third country processor – a country to which nations export unprocessed products simply to become processed, only to have those products re-exported. The principal countries serving this role are China and Thailand. A growing and significant amount of fish is exported to China post-harvest, processed, then re-exported around the globe.

Transport and Handling Advances

Reliable temperature maintenance is the key important feature in fish and fishery product transport. People who are involved in the handling and transporting of perishable commodities are responsible for their part in the cool chain. Breaks in the cool chain can result in irreversible damage to the quality of foods. In the transport of perishable products into remote regions ideal procedures may not always be possible and so in these instances early planning will allow products to be delivered as efficiently as possible. Distributors and transporters need to be able to manage frozen, chilled and odour-producing foods, as well as ethylene-producing and ethylene-sensitive products. Many developing countries are lacking such facilities and post-harvest losses are very high. A large portion of the harvest is discarded without marketing. In one hand, this is threat to the resources base and on the other hand it leads to poverty.

This means important decisions related to storage facilities, truck design and capacity as well as supply patterns that will be required to meet food safety regulations. Maintaining the cool chain is essential to minimize product deterioration and maximum shelf life of the product. Many potential problems in the supply chain can be avoided or effectively managed by understanding the critical handling issues and carefully planning each load.

Regulatory Change

Official Standards and Associated Certification

Standards and certifications aim to protect consumers, environment, sustainable resource utilisation, fishers and trade relations. Common forms are regulations (fishing gear and effort controls, close seasons, catch controls, protection of vulnerable and endangered species, etc.), voluntary standards (MSC label, Eco-labels, Organic labels, etc.), and code of conduct. Developing countries have been generally reluctant to participate in labelling activities. They have highlighted the embedded protectionist elements to some of these initiatives.

Labelling (Nutrition, Country of Origin Labelling, Allergens)

As food markets evolve with new technologies, increased product differentiation and more affluent consumers, there is heightened focus on food safety and quality. Regulatory systems have responded with new product and production standards, approval processes, risk-assessment processes and labelling requirements while, at the same time, a plethora of private food safety and quality standards have emerged alongside these regulatory developments. EU adopted regulations requiring labelling of all fisheries and aquaculture products.

This labelling regulation is intended to strengthen traceability – the ability to trace fisheries products from sea to market and allow consumers to choose their seafood according to specific criteria that might be of concern to them. All fisheries products on sale at retailers have to be labelled with the following information: the commercial name of the species, the production method (wild or farmed) and the area where the fish was caught.

Environmental labelling in fisheries includes;

- Country of Origin (mandatory)
- Product certification and catch documentation

- EU requirements to mark or label commercial destination, production method and area of fish capture
- "Dolphin-safe" and "Turtle-friendly" labels on tuna and shrimp designed to minimize by-catch
- Organic labels
- Nordic Technical Working Group on Fisheries Eco-Labelling Criteria
- Marine Aquarium Council certification
- Global Aquaculture Alliance codes of practice and certification
- ISO 14000 series on environmental management performance
- MSC label on sustainable fisheries

Environmental Protection

Marine fisheries and some of the inland fisheries are common-pool resources, and many of these resources are overexploited. At the same time, capture fisheries and aquaculture operations can impinge on public goods provided by marine ecosystems, such as marine biodiversity and unique habitat. The common-pool and public goods dimensions of the marine environment justify regulation, but the issues frequently transcend national boundaries. Individual countries have few alternatives to protect the marine environment beyond their own jurisdictions.

International agreements, treaties and policies help to conserve the remaining stocks of threatened species.

The law that applies to the high seas is founded on the United Nations Convention on the Law of the Sea (UNCLOS), which came into force in 1994. An important element of UNCLOS was the undertaking of all signatory countries to promote sustainable fishing. Since the adoption of UNCLOS, a number of agreements have been developed to deal specifically with how to bring about sustainable fishing on the high seas.

One of them is the agreement on straddling stocks and highly migratory fish stocks. The UN system also has a key role to play in combating destructive fishing practices, which damage fragile habitats, in particular seamounts and cold-water corals

The following agreements have been adopted by Food and Agriculture Organisation (FAO), agreement on compliance with conservation and management measures and Code of Conduct for Responsible Fisheries. The international cooperation on marine conservation provides an incentive for countries to use trade policy as an indirect means to protect the marine environment.

Large share of the available fish and fishery products are being traded, trade restrictions can potentially lead to better resource protection and better fishing practices.

Labour and Animal Rights

Ethical consumerism is the intentional purchase of products and services that the customer considers to be made ethically. This may mean with minimal harm to or exploitation of humans, animals and/or the natural environment. Fair trade, MSC labelling and other related initiatives play a great role in protection of both labour and animal rights. Global supply chains place more concern on compliance with fundamental workers' rights as codified in national labour legislation and the core International Labour Organisation (ILO) Conventions.

These rights include prevention of forced and child labour, freedom of association, non-discrimination and equal remuneration for equal work. Child labour is not permitted in stores or distribution centres. Consumers of high-value markets acknowledge the human rights of the workers and willing to pay premium prices for the suppliers facilitate the community development. Fair trade helps suppliers to grow their businesses in a responsible and sustainable way. Some of the leading retail chains operating in United States and Europe are Tesco, Ahold, and, etc., are in the process of implementing the Business Social Compliance Initiative (BSCI) programme with corporate brand suppliers in high-risk countries.

Many initiatives aim to improve living conditions for animals, while, at the same time, delivering safe and quality products. Retail chains aim to offer sustainable seafood in their stores by selling seafood which is harvested in a sustainable way. Thus, they actively work with the industry, NGOs and governments to monitor and improve long-term viability of fish stocks. Many governments and different supply chains work towards developing a more sustainable approach to seafood with the World Wildlife Fund (WWF), New England Aquarium and Shedd Aquarium among others. European companies have strong relationships with the WWF and work with the MSC, which runs a sustainable fisheries certification programme.

MARKET ACCESS

Quarantine restrictions and other non-tariff trade barriers are considered mainly in market access of fish and fishery products. Developing countries, export mainly raw products and only limited quantities of processed products. The former are in turn processed in industrialised countries and these exporting countries are not extracting full benefits from their aquatic resources. Despite the availability of technology, many projects in value-adding for export were collapsed. Careful consideration was not given to the various facets of their feasibility, including quality assurance, marketing, distribution and trade barriers, before embarking on a value-adding fish process.

Value-added fish and fishery products require substantial investment in marketing and publicity to disseminate the brand image of the product. This is not within the capabilities of many developing countries where the fish exporting industry is fragmented at the same time trade associations and support institutions are not well organised.

At present, most developing countries process value-added products packed under the label of the importer that has a known brand and distribution channels. Exports of fishery products are still subject to many trade barriers. Tariffs play important roles in strategic business decisions on whether to export unprocessed fish products, which normally have zero tariffs in the importing country, or finished (consumer ready) processed/semi-processed products, which are burdened with prohibitive tariffs.

Largest fish markets, EU, United States and Japan with stagnant domestic supplies and growing consumption are forced to rely on imports to cover a growing share of domestic demand. Import tariffs in developed countries are so low and, albeit with a few exceptions for many value-added products, do not represent any significant barrier to trade. As a result, developing countries have been able to gain increased access to developed country markets without being hampered by prohibitive custom duties. In fact, today's most important barrier to increase exports, beyond the physical availability of product, is the lack of ability to adhere to quality- and safety-related import requirements, rather than import tariffs.

The World Trade Organisation agreements most important for fish trade, in addition to the member country's individual commitments on import tariffs, are the ones concerning subsidies, antidumping, technical barriers to trade, sanitary and phytosanitary measures and resolution of disputes.

DISTRIBUTION AND RETAILING

Energy, transport and labour are key points of factor costs in distribution and retailing. Factor costs act as major barrier in fish and fishery product marketing in developing nations. Poor infrastructure, logistics and weak policy hinders the success of the fish industry. Moreover, post-harvest losses are as high as 40 per cent in many developing country markets and this hinders the value addition process.

ECONOMIC GROWTH TRENDS

Gross Domestic Product, disposable income, levels and use of consumer credit and inequality of wealth are the major components affecting the fish supply chain. Developed countries constitute the main outlets for fish and fishery products. Japan, the largest single market for fish and fishery products and its high level of per capita fish consumption places year round demand. United

States play an important role as a second largest single country market with growing potentials. Japan's declining fish consumption followed by low demand on high-valued species changes the trade flows to other growing markets. Especially, growing economies and expanding upper middle class in Asia places high demand on fish and fishery products. In developing countries, fish plays a major role in the diet of poorer communities as a principal source of protein.

DRIVERS AND GOVERNORS OF CHANGE ON THE FISH SUPPLY

Fish and fishery products supply chain is a network of food fish-related business enterprises through which fish and fishery products move from production through consumption, including pre-production and post consumption activities.

The term "Value-added" is used to characterise fish and fishery products that are converted from raw fish through processes that give the resulting product an "incremental value" in the market place. An "incremental value" is realised from either higher price or expanded market.

Moreover, value-added is also used to characterise fish and fishery products that have incremental value in the marketplace by differentiating them from similar products based on product attributes such as: geographical location (Mediterranean tuna, Norway salmon, Thailand Black Tiger shrimp, etc.); environmental stewardship (MSC label, Eco-labelling, fair trade); food safety (HACCP, Free from antibiotics and heavy metals, etc.); or functionality. Value and values are also used to characterise the nature of certain business relationships among interacting fish and fishery business enterprises, rather than any attribute of the product itself. This collection of relationships is known as a supply chain and these relationships are expressly based in an articulated set of values, they are becoming known as values-based supply chains or value chains.

PRODUCT/ MARKET CONDITIONS

Supply side of the fish and fishery products affects different factors like: market demand, prices, season, climatic conditions, population dynamics, economic status, fuel prices, trade policy, legal environment, and, etc. Perishable nature of fish requires special attention on handling, grading and packaging, and the market price reflects the quality of fish. Fifty per cent of fish supplies come from developing countries where market infrastructure facilities are minimal. Huge post-harvest losses and poor infrastructure contributes to the inferior quality of fish and its export earnings. Most fish suppliers in developing countries act as raw material suppliers of industrial nations, which allow them to earn little profit from their valuable natural resources.

PROCUREMENT PRACTICES

Value chain integration, compliance with private standards, preferred supplier arrangements and new terms of sale are most important considerations for the suppliers. In general, ten important considerations for responsible fish trade include legality, objective assessment, communication, promotion, continuous improvement, engagement prohibition, research, traceability, ethics and environment.

Factor Prices and Availability for Production and Shipping

Infrastructure development has been a major factor in reducing trade costs and there by facilitate trade expansions. Expansion or improvement in quality of infrastructure services lowers marginal costs, raising the minimum efficient scale of production, transportation, or marketing. Lower costs and greater economies of scale raise the potential for increased or new sales in export and domestic markets as an efforts to take advantage of economies of scale in production, procurement, or marketing lead firms to look beyond national borders for both trade and investment opportunities. Promoting efficient financial intermediation, coordinating regional public goods, reducing macroeconomic vulnerability to shocks, and strengthening security ties offer government's similar incentives to design, develop, and manage regional infrastructure cooperation and integration. In this context, infrastructure is one of the "three Is," along with incentives and institutions, which are key determinants of overall growth, magnitude and productivity of capital inflows to liberalising economies.

Producer Preference

Fishers have to bare overall investment on boat, fishing gear and especially price levels and their variability and production risk Data confirms that approximately 75 per cent of fish species with commercial value have been overexploited and some are close to extinction. 52 per cent of commercial stocks are fully exploited, *i.e.*, they are at or near their maximum sustainability production levels. In addition, 25 per cent are in very bad condition, 17 per cent are overexploited and 7 per cent are depleted. However, 1 per cent is recovering from depletion.

In general, producer preferences receive less priority in capture fish production. Moreover, choices of producers and available facilities greatly affect the aquaculture production. In practice, there are differences in fish supply chains among different countries and regions that correspond to socio-economic, environmental conditions and cultural differences. Differences also exist in relation to fish species and products, and harvesting techniques (industrial production, artisanal production, aquaculture or capture). The length of the supply chain can also vary depending on the product and country of origin and final destination of a product (whether for domestic consumption of export). Fish and fishery products supply chains can also vary in complexity from one company to another, depending on the level of integration of the different links and the ownership of the entire production process.

Technology

The application of modern fisheries technology starts from culture and ends to export of the product. Post-harvest fisheries technology involves processing, preservation, handling, harvesting, marketing, etc. Developing countries, where tropical weather and under developed infrastructure contribute to the problem, losses are sometimes staggering proportions. Losses occur in all operations from harvesting through handling, storage, processing and marketing. Many developing country producers were marginalised from global supply chains due to their poor maintenance of quality standards. In general, low-tech developing country suppliers earn less for their resources; whereas industrial nations earn extra premiums, by marketing information systems, supply chain management, quality assurance regimes, transport, handling, post-harvest and production technologies.

Regulatory Change

Regulatory change is the capacity to deal with market access requirements, standards, dealing with local and national restrictions on land use, inputs, labour contracting and management know-how.

Demographics

Availability of seasonal labour, existence of a local market for seconds and an urban market for export quality product are important features of demographics on supply chain. Non- availability or less numbers in fisheries labour forces open the doors for migratory labour. Philippine crews in Japanese and Taiwanese vessels, Cambodian labour in Thai vessels are common feature. Multi ethnic and multi cultural labour management is essential for today's fish production systems.

THE PRODUCTION OF FISH MEAL AND OIL

The world's fish catch is of the order of 75 million tons per year, but only about 1 per cent of man's food is fish, although 10 per cent of his animal protein intake is fish protein. The fraction of the annual catch used for reduction to fish meal and oil is about one third.

The fishmeal and oil industry, which started in northern Europe and North America at the beginning of the 19th century, was based mainly on surplus catches of herring from seasonal coastal fisheries. This was essentially an oil production activity; the oil finding industrial uses in leather tanning and in the production of soap and glycerol and other non-food products. The residue was originally used as fertilizer, but since the turn of this century it has been dried and ground into fish meal for animal feeding. In fact, one definition of fish meal is that it is a solid product, ground, that has been obtained by removing most of the water and some or all of the oil from fish or fish waste. Its main use is in the diets of poultry, pigs and fish which need higher quality protein than does other farm stock, such as cattle and sheep.

Some doubts have been expressed that the world fish catch can be increased substantially; a figure around 100 million tons being regarded as a reasonable maximum. The first aim should be to produce fish for direct human consumption and there will be considerable pressure to reserve the extra production for human feeding. Only where it is uneconomic or impracticable should the catch be reduced to fish meal and oil. Ninety per cent, however, of the fish that are currently reduced to fish meal and oil, the so-called industrial fish (menhaden, sand-eel, sardine, anchoveta, pout, etc.) are presently unmarketable in large quantities as human food. Much of the increased catch will be previously unexploited resources of unknown and perhaps unpalatable species and will thus be available for reduction. Apart from unpalatability, the reasons why this portion of the catch cannot be used for direct consumption include the facts that the fish are too small or break down or turn rancid too quickly for economic storage and subsequent heading, gutting, cleaning and processing. Turning high quality fish into fish meal and oil should not be encouraged. It is obviously more efficient, however, in a protein-hungry world to harvest the unacceptable species for feeding to animals, subsequently consumed by man, than to leave them unharvested in the sea.

Small oily fish are the mainstay of the fishmeal and oil industry. Even in frozen storage these fish turn rancid rapidly unless special and expensive precautions are taken. With present knowledge they can be used best by reducing them to fish meal for animal feeding and using the oil for direct human consumption in products such as margarine. There is a good demand for high quality fish meal and oil and production can be highly remunerative if suitable raw material is available. The industry can also utilise the offal - from filleting, gutting and other fish processing operations - which often poses disposal problems.

The most efficient course would be to feed the powdered products resulting from reduction directly to humans. This introduces the technology of fish protein concentrates (FPC). Direct feeding reduces the losses of cycling through poultry or pigs, which may take 3 kg of fish to produce 1 kg of edible chicken or pork, and also the losses involved in preparing fish for direct consumption. A fillet may contain only half the protein of the original fish after heading, gutting, filleting and skinning.

The production of FPC is within the capacity of the fishmeal and oil industry. There are problems as the hygienic requirements must naturally conform with those for human food.

The fish must be fresh and sound and the plant must be easy to clean and sterilise after use. These are technological problems and although the solutions are expensive, the industry already possesses the design and organisational expertise. Two types of FPC have been and are being produced: a type A, with a fat content of less than 0.5 per cent and a type B, with a fat content of less than 10 per cent. The major problems of using FPC are social rather than technological; these are the difficulty and expense of incorporating new powdered products in the diet.

FPC type B tastes fishy after production and "fishmealy" or rancid after storage, because most of the flavour is in the oil fraction. FPC type A is flavourless, but the removal of the oil, by solvent extraction, is expensive. In some areas, the rancid flavours are accepted as they are similar to those of traditional products. FPC must also be milled finely as it has little water holding capacity and would taste gritty when incorporated in food; this process is expensive. It is hoped that technological solutions to these problems will be developed and that FPC for human feeding can be made available at competitive prices.

Meanwhile, the search for socially acceptable methods of incorporating it in food must go on. For example, type A can be chemically refined to impart functional capacities (water holding, jelling) to the powder. This raises the cost, but it is nevertheless cheaper than meat and can be used profitably as a meat extender, for instance, in sausages. From the above, it can be seen that the production of FPC is an enterprise which should be embarked upon only when a ready market for the products has been established.

The industry can make a valuable contribution to human nutrition both directly and indirectly. Wherever there is an abundance of fish that, for one reason or another, cannot be used for direct human consumption, the establishment of a fishmeal industry should be strongly encouraged and assisted, not least as a start to rational utilisation. However, the uninitiated should beware of trying to start an industry without proper planning and with inexperienced staff or inadequate equipment.

The purpose of this document is to explain the complexity of the industry and to provide information on the planning and operation of a fishmeal and oil industry. The production of meal and oil is a sophisticated process requiring considerable skill and experience. The products will meet commercial and international standards only if they are manufactured under hygienic conditions in properly operated and controlled plants.

RAW MATERIAL

RESOURCES

Fish used for reduction to meal and oil may be divided into three categories:

- Fish caught for the sole purpose of fishmeal production (for example by Chile, Peru, Norway, Denmark, South Africa and the USA);
- By-catches from another fishery (by most fish-producing countries);
- Fish offcuts and offal from the consumption industry. (The UK and Germany use these materials to produce white fish meal; South Africa makes rock lobster meal from the carapaces and other parts which are not utilised).

A fishmeal industry requires a regular supply of raw material. When planning fishmeal factories, it is necessary to know the type of fish species available, the length of fishing season, the location of the fish, the catchability of the fish by different fishing gear and, if possible, the attainable catches per year for a continuous period.

COMPOSITION OF THE FISH

Practically all fish species as well as most other marine animal life may, in principle, be converted into fish meal. A wide variety of fish species is used for the production of fish meal and oil in different countries.

The composition and quality of the raw material are predominant factors in determining the properties and yield of the products. A separation of fatty substances (lipids) from the other constituents of fatty marine animals is one of the major operations in the manufacture of fish meal and oil.

- *Gadoids (the cod-like fishes):* Comprise a number of fish species which can be classified as lean. It is characteristic of these species that most of their fat is located in the liver. Fish meal made from these lean species of fish is called white fish meal.
- *Clupeids (the herrings):* Provide the largest single source of raw material for production of fish meal and oil. They may be classified as fatty although the fat content may vary from 2 per cent to 30 per cent, depending on species and season. The fat is not, as in lean fish, concentrated in the liver, but is generally distributed throughout the body.

Table. Composition of Whole Fish; Average Values Over a Number of Years (in %)

Fish Species	Protein	Fat	Ash	Water
Gadoids				
Blue whiting. North Sea	17.0	5.0	4.0	75.0
Sprat. Atlantic	16.0	11.0	2.0	71.0
Hake. South Africa	17.0	2,0	3.0	79.0
Norway pout	16.0	5.5	3.0	73.0
Clupeids				
Anchoveta	18.0	6.0	2.5	78.0
Herring. spring	18.0	8.0	2.0	72.0
Herring. winter	18.2	11.0	2.0	70.0
Pilchard. South Africa	18.0	9.0	3.0	69.0
Anchovy. South Africa	17.0	10.0	3.0	70.0
Scombroids				
Mackerel, spring, North Sea	18.0	5.5	1.6	75.0
Mackerel, autumn, North Sea	15.0	27.0	1.4	56.5
Horse mackerel, North Sea	16.0	17.0	3.8	62.7
Horse mackerel, South Africa	17.0	8.0	4.0	72.0
Elasmobranchs				
Dogfish	19.0	8.9	2.3	70.0
Salmonoids				
Capelin, Norway	14.0	10.0	2.0	75.0

- *Scombroids (the mackerels):* Are also fatty fish species.
- *Elasmobranchs (the sharks and the rays):* Are not specially caught for meal and oil production. Some species, however, provide raw material as trash fish and as offal from processing.
- *Salmonoids (the salmons and other closely related fish):* Are generally not harvested for fishmeal production, but offal from salmon is used. However, there is one species, the capelin, that has become a considerable source of material for meal and oil.
- *Crustaceans:* The carapaces and shells are used, as well as small crustaceans that are unmarketable for direct human consumption.

SAMPLING OF RAW MATERIALS

As the composition of the fish may vary widely during the year, systematic sampling and analysis of seasonal variations provide important information when considering the establishment of a fishmeal industry.

ECONOMIC EVALUATION OF THE RAW MATERIAL

From reliable analyses of the raw material one may estimate the amount of fish meal and oil which may be produced, and hence the value of the raw material. The water content gives basic figures for the cost of drying. There is an interrelationship between fat and water in fish: fat and water are complementary constituents inasmuch as fat replaces water in the flesh due to seasonal variation. For a given quantity of raw material, increasing fat content will lead to improved oil yield, reduced demand on drying energy and increased processing capacity of the plant.

In some countries where the fishing fleet and the fishmeal industry are separate commercial entities, the composition and extent of deterioration of the raw material are often used for evaluating the price. Where the fishing fleet is operated as an integral part of the industry, such evaluation may be used to predict product yield and quality and as a control of production efficiency.

Evaluation requires that representative samples from each catch be submitted for analyses at a control laboratory. Sampling is not straightforward because considerable variations in fish size and quality may exist within the same catch. In purse seines, for example, there appears to be a tendency for the smaller fish to sink to the bottom while the larger fish mass in the upper part of the nets. When the catch is transferred, there is therefore a corresponding segregation of fish; consequently the collector must exercise care to obtain samples representative of the whole catch.

Most conveniently the sampling is done during the unloading of the fishing vessel. An automatic sampling device, installed immediately after the weighing equipment, is recommended, but sampling might be done by hand.

Stratified spot sampling of 4-5 kg samples of fish should be made no less than 30 times during unloading of a vessel containing industrial fish. The sampling container will finally hold about 250 kg fish which has to be ground and thoroughly mixed before further sub-dividing of the sample can take place. The final sample of fish for laboratory examination will be approximately 500 g.

METHODS OF ANALYSIS

The evaluation of raw material requires the carrying out of a number of proximate methods of analysis, mainly to determine protein, fat, water and ash contents, and the determination of volatile basic nitrogen (usually expressed as mg^{-N}/100 g minced fish).

Under practical conditions it is often sufficient to make determinations only of water and volatile basic nitrogen in the samples.

DETERIORATION OF THE RAW FISH

The rapid deterioration of fish is due to the action of bacteria from the surfaces and the digestive tract and to autolytic breakdown caused by enzymatic action in the tissues and in the tract. Bacterial and autolytic deterioration result in breakdown of both the lipid and protein fractions.

AUTOLYTIC DETERIORATION

In a number of fish species used for fishmeal production, particularly small pelagic fish species such as sardines, anchovies and herring, the digestive enzymes may cause extensive autolysis leading to softening of the meat, rupture of the belly wall and formation of considerable amounts of blood water containing both protein and oil. This process is aggravated by the production of large quantities of gastric enzymes at the time of feeding. Such solubilisation causes difficulties in handling and processing and may lead to serious losses of both protein and oil.

Fat deterioration (lipolysis) caused by different fat splitting enzymes (lipases) is a general feature in fatty fish. Fish oils are largely composed of glycerol combined with fatty acids to form glycerides. Splitting of the glycerides of the oil and formation of free fatty acids (FFA) result in reduced quality of the oil with economic consequences.

OXIDATION

Oxidation of lipids (rancidity) and browning of the oil occurs under aerobic (in the presence of oxygen) storage conditions; but in transport vessels and storage bins the condition in the interior of the mass of fish is anaerobic (oxygen is absent).

MICROBIAL SPOILAGE

The anaerobic conditions of bulk storage of whole fish create a complex medium in which microbes can grow, with formation of a variety of chemical spoilage products. Some important end products are the volatile basic nitrogenous compounds (mainly ammonia and trimethylamine) and the amount of total volatile basic nitrogen (TVB-N) is often used as a measure of deterioration. Some volatile bases are formed by the bacterial breakdown of amino acids, in turn derived from protein, but the trimethylamine is formed by bacterial metabolism of trimethylamine oxide. The extensive production of ammonia in a load of deteriorating fish may result in significant losses of protein. In elasmobranchs ammonia is also produced from the urea which is a constituent of their blood and muscle.

The chemical compounds resulting from bacterial activity are numerous and some are not yet well described, but the sulphur containing compounds, which seem to be formed mainly under anaerobic conditions, are significant. Hydrogen sulphide (H_2S) and mercaptans may be produced by decomposed fish in lethal concentrations in the holds of fishing vessels and in closed fish bins. In Denmark, for example, thorough ventilation is compulsory before and during the unloading of fish.

Another feature of bacterial deterioration is the transformation of sulphur from sulphur containing amino acids into compounds which are catalyst inhibitors; that is they inactivate the catalyst used in subsequent hydrogenation of the oil into fat for margarine production.

During meal production, the aqueous phase is particularly vulnerable to bacterial putrefaction. Bacterial breakdown, besides affecting the yield and quality of the end products and the production capacity, also results in the formation of malodorous compounds. Consequently efforts should be made to minimize bacterial spoilage.

PRESERVATION OF THE RAW MATERIAL

The production of fish meal and oil from fresh raw material gives the highest yield and the best quality final products. In many cases, however, it is difficult to avoid partial spoilage as the fish has to be collected from remote areas. The search for economic means of preserving the catch during periods of transport and storage, exceeding about 30 h, has been a continuing challenge to the industry.

As breakdown of fish protein and oil are due to, both autolytic and microbial activity, the preserving method should preferably retard both bacterial growth and autolysis by digestive and tissue enzymes. The storage life of fish can be extended either by physical or chemical means.

Draining

Proper draining of the fish, both aboard and ashore, is a simple and effective method of extending the short-term storage life of fish. Aboard the fishing vessels proper drainage reduces the amount of rubbing together and breakage of the fish during rolling and pitching of the fishing vessel. Moreover, the spreading and rapid growth of bacteria is reduced by restricting the presence of free water containing body slime, gut contents and the bacteria contained therein.

Preservation by Chilling

During storage of ungutted fish in bulk, the rate of breakdown caused by bacteria and by digestive and tissue enzymes doubles with an increase of temperature of approximately 4°C. This breakdown leads to losses of protein and oil and reduces the quality of the fish for processing. At temperature higher than 5°C hydrogen sulphide is produced by bacteria, and its formation rapidly increases with temperature. At 0°C hydrogen sulphide is not formed until storage exceeds 9-10 days.

In tropical and temperate areas where the fish may be caught at high temperatures and far from the plant, chilling is the most effective method of preserving bulk-stored fish. In many cases the cost of chilling can be recovered by the reduced losses of protein and oil. In principle, two methods of chilling may be considered, namely refrigerated or chilled water systems and mixing of ice with fish.

Refrigerated (Chilled) Water Systems

Sea water is readily available, but prolonged storage of fish in sea water is limited by absorption of salt; high salt levels are undesired in fish meal. It is therefore preferable to use diluted sea water or fresh water. The method comprises circulating the refrigerated water through the mass of fish. Merely pumping the water over the fish does not effectively chill the whole mass, as there is hardly any penetration of the water through the bulk of the fish, most of it being diverted around the sides. Advanced systems are based on pumping the chilled water upward through the fish from the bottom of the hold. The method is expensive and hardly practical except for long voyages and storage periods.

Preservation by Ice

Mixing fish and ice in the right proportion for chilling the fish at 0°C is an effective method for preserving raw fish. Fish and ice should be mixed before filling the hold. The melt water is drained off from the bottom leaving the fish dry and compact. The use of ice for preservation is dependent upon the development of rapid, preferably automatic, systems for mixing fish and ice at the high rate necessary in industrial fishing.

In Scandinavia, particularly in Denmark, the following ice mixing (and grading) system has been installed in more than 100 fishing vessels. The Technological Laboratory of the Danish Ministry of Fisheries has participated in the development of a receiving box on deck equipped with a conveyor continuously feeding a rotating drum. This drum grades the fish into two categories: industrial, which includes fish less than 35 mm thick, and food fish, which are comprised of thicker specimens.

The receiving box is equipped to remove the few large fish and other large objects before the catch enters the conveyor and the grader. The box may receive loads of up to 2 t of fish, which are converted to a continuous flow of up to 1 200 kg/min. The food fish pass through the length of the cylinder, while the industrial fish fall through the grader into a trough equipped with a continuous supply of small pieces of ice to chill the fish to 0°C and maintain this temperature until the fish are landed. A conveyor running along the trough takes the mixture of industrial fish and ice to a vertical conveyor that lifts the mixture 2 m above the deck and releases it into a funnel. Wide plastic tubes connect the funnel to the ice scuttle on the deck over the section of the hold that is to be filled with iced industrial fish.

The continuous supply of ice to the trough under the grader is taken from a. store of bulk ice. At the bottom of the store a horizontal conveyor feeds the ice onto a vertical conveyor to the trough. The conveyor speed is adjustable so that the supply of ice can be varied. At landing, there should be little or no surplus ice. Fish at 15°C when caught requires about 23 per cent of its weight in ice to be chilled and maintained at 0°C for four days in an insulated hold.

Chemical Preservation

Chemical preservatives for raw fish immediately act on the bacteria on the surface of the fish, but there is some delay in action on the interior (stomach and intestines) depending upon the rate of penetration of the preservative.

Sodium nitrite, sodium sulphite, ascorbic acid, benzoic acid and many more preservatives have been evaluated, but they are used only to a very limited extent. Sodium nitrite has demonstrated comparatively favourable properties for preservation of species such as herring, as it retards significantly the development of spoilage microbes and reduces the formation of free fatty acids, but unless nitrites are added in strictly controlled small amounts (as is the case in Norway) they may react with other components of the raw material and form nitrosamines which are harmful carcinogenic chemical compounds.

Special measures must be taken when meal is manufactured from fish which has been preserved by nitrite. The use of nitrite must therefore be permitted only under the most careful supervision and should not be encouraged. Formaldehyde is widely used and, under certain circumstances, also exerts a beneficial firming effect on the raw material so that it is rendered more amenable to pressing, after cooking, for removal of oil. Formaldehyde combines with protein by a mechanism akin to tanning and the reactive amino acid lysine is involved. The use of small amounts, however, (for example 0.05 per cent formalin based on the weight of the fish) has no detectable deleterious effect on protein quality.

THE PROCESS

To understand the principles of fishmeal and oil manufacture, it is necessary to consider the raw material as composed of three major fractions: solids (fat-free dry matter), oil and water. The purpose of the process is to separate these fractions from each other as completely as possible, with the least possible expense and under conditions rendering the best possible products.

Fish can be reduced to meal and oil in a number of ways. Common to all methods of practical importance are the following processing steps:

- Heating, which coagulates the protein, ruptures the fat depots and liberates oil and physico-chemically bound water;
- Pressing (or occasional centrifugation), which removes a large fraction of the liquids from the mass;
- Separation of the liquid into oil and water (stickwater). This step may be omitted if the oil content of the fish is less than 3 per cent;
- Evaporation of the stickwater into a concentrate (fish solubles);
- Drying of the solid material (presscake) plus added solubles, which removes sufficient water from the wet material to form a stable meal,
- Grinding the dried material to the desired particle size.

This chapter deals in some detail with the most generally practised method of large-scale production. A more cursory description is given of small-scale processing and plants designed to handle small and irregular landings of fish or to yield products with special properties. Although the basic principles of the process may appear few and simple, a variety of elements is required to make a smooth running and profitable factory. There are also different types of equipment that will do the same job but in different ways. The number of options have increased considerably during the last years, particularly in the fields of energy saving, automation and environmental protection. The prospective manufacturer should therefore devote ample time and attention for consultations with the most competent suppliers of machinery and complete factories, before making his final decisions on layout and equipment.

Here are some factors that need special consideration at the planning stage. The most important prerequisite for a profitable fishmeal project is an ample and regular supply of raw material at an acceptable price. Length of season, that is how many days per year the plant may be in operation, is of the utmost importance for the profitability of the venture. Furthermore, the longer the season, the greater the weight that should be placed on measures to reduce the variable costs, and the more that should be spent on investments to save labour and energy and to ensure higher yields and quality of the products.

Another important point relates to the size of plant needed for the amounts of raw material in question. Capacities given by the equipment manufacturer, particularly for the cooker and press installation, may serve only as indicators at the preliminary discussions. The yield is an empirical value entirely dependent upon the nature of the raw material to be processed, its size, freshness and texture. If experience is not available for the actual fish species it is, therefore, advisable to run some tests to evaluate the behaviour of the raw material and the performance of the cooking/pressing operation.

The composition of the raw material expressed in terms of dry matter, protein and fat, will determine what yield of products may be expected. The fat content is of special importance at the planning stage, because it will decide whether it will pay to install equipment for the recovery of oil, besides telling what yield of oil may be expected. For all practical purposes, one may reckon that for the processing of fish with less than 3 per cent of fat, one may omit the installation of oil- recovery equipment.

Evaporators for the stickwater, however expensive, may today be considered standard items of equipment for fishmeal plants, because they recover dry matter that will increase the yield of meal by 20 per cent or more, depending upon the freshness and nature of the raw material. Furthermore, they eliminate a serious pollution problem that today appears unacceptable, particularly in the vicinity of densely populated areas. For small factories and irregular operation, omission of evaporators may sometimes be justified, but a final decision on this point should be taken only after careful calculations have been made and the pros and cons thoroughly evaluated.

Location of the plant relative to habitation and closed harbours is another feature of the utmost importance for trouble-free operation. Public regulations protecting the environment against undesirable pollution of air and water should be carefully studied, as these will affect the selection of equipment and factory premises and determine the amount necessary for investment in unproductive installations for odour abatement and cleaning of waste water emissions.

THE PRINCIPAL METHOD OF PROCESSING

The bulk of the world's fish meal and oil is today manufactured by the wet pressing method. The main steps of the process are cooking for coagulation of the protein thereby liberating bound water and oil, separation by pressing of the coagulate yielding a solid phase (presscake) containing 60-80 per cent of the oil-free dry matter (protein, bones) and oil, and a liquid phase (press liquor) containing water and the rest of the solids (oil, dissolved and suspended protein, vitamins and minerals). The main part of the sludge in the press liquor is removed by centrifugation in a decanter and the oil is subsequently removed by centrifuge. The stickwater is concentrated in multi-effect evaporators and the concentrate is thoroughly mixed with the presscake, which is then dehydrated usually by two-stage drying. The dried material is milled and stored in bags or in bulk. The oil is stored in tanks.

As already pointed out, there are alternatives to this layout and also different types of equipment to choose among for some of the unit operations. The most important alternatives will be mentioned in the following descriptions of the various processing steps. The raw material is first unloaded from the fishing vessel by crane, wet fish pump, pneumatic elevator or some sort of mechanical conveyor. The fish is weighed or measured by volume before it is transported to the pits or tanks for the storage of raw material.

Large Fish are Hashed

(A) while smaller fish (for example, those less than 40 cm long) are fed directly at a constant rate by the feeding machine (B) To the indirect steam cooker (C) The coagulated mass is pre-strained in a strainer conveyor (D) In a vibrating screen, before entering the twin screw press (E) The products from the press (presscake and press liquor) are treated as follows. The presscake is disintegrated in the tearing machine (wet mill) (F) To facilitate mixing with stickwater concentrate and drying in an indirect steam dryer or a direct flame dryer (G) The meal passes through a vibrating screen Furnished with a magnet to remove extraneous matter like pieces of wood and metal (for example, fish hooks) before entering the hammer mill (J) The ground meal is automatically weighed out in bags by the scales (K) The bags are closed (*e.g.*, by sewing) and conveyed to the store. Alternatively, the meal is stored in a holding and blending silo before bagging, pelleting or storing in bulk.

To remove most of the sludge, the press liquor passes through a decanter (N). The press liquor then passes through a buffer tank (O) before separation into oil, stickwater and fine sludge in the stickwater centrifuge (P).

The sludge is added to the presscake. The oil passes through a buffer tank (R) before water *f* and sludge impurities are removed (polishing) in the oil separator (S). After polishing, the oil often passes through an inspection tank before storage in the oil tank. The stickwater passes through a buffer tank (T) before concentration in a multi-effect evaporator (U). After the buffer tank (V), the concentrate is mixed thoroughly with decanter-sludge and presscake before drying. In some cases the stickwater concentrate, called condensed fish solubles, is sold separately.

The factory can be deodorised by air suction from all tanks and machinery. The air passes through a scrubber (L) and is then burned in the steam boiler or treated with chlorine, after which a further scrubber removes residual chlorine. Methods of effective deodorisation are still under study.

As stated, large fish have to be hashed into smaller pieces before being passed by the feeder into the cooker. This is to ensure uniform processing and equal temperature in the cooked material. Also, the feeder ensures a steady rate of presentation to the cooker. It consists of a rotor with staggered knives and a frame with a row of stationary knives.

Feeder consists of a hopper from the bottom of which the raw material is carried to the cooker by a screw conveyor. The conveyor's speed may be adapted to the rate of throughput desired by means of a stepless gear. When the hopper is full of raw material, a level control mechanism stops the removal of raw material from the raw fish pits or silos. When the level has sunk to a fixed lower level, another level controller starts the intake flowing again. Today pumps are increasingly used for the transportation of raw material, and these can easily be controlled by the automatic level controller of the hopper.

Here we can follow the streams of the three major fractions of the raw material, solids (fat-free dry matter), oil and water, through the factory. The actual figures will, of course, vary with the composition of the raw material, particularly with the oil content, but the diagram is sufficient to illustrate the general trend. The prospective manufacturer may estimate his expected yield of meal on the basis of the dry matter content of his raw material plus moisture and residual fat in the meal. For instance, if the dry matter content of the raw material is 18 per cent, and moisture and fat together make up 20 per cent of the meal. The expected yield of meal will be (18 x 100)/80 = 22.5 per cent by weight of the raw material. Likewise, the yield of oil will be the fat content of the raw material less the small amount (2.5-3 per cent) remaining in the meal.

Heating ("Cooking")

The purpose of the heating process is to liberate the oil from the fat depots of the fish, and to condition the material for the subsequent treatment in the various processing units of the plant. "Cooking", as this operation has traditionally been called, is therefore a key process of the utmost importance for the whole functioning of the factory.

Until fairly recently, the general view has been that the best results and optimum performance of the plant would be obtained at the highest possible temperature which, at atmospheric pressure, would be 100°C. New experiments, however, have shown that the walls of the fat cells are broken down before the temperature reaches 50°C. The oil is then free, and theoretically it should be possible to separate it from the solid material.

Another important observation from recent investigations is that coagulation of the fish protein is completed at about 75°C and, furthermore, that the process is very rapid. This new experience leads to the conclusion that there is very little, if anything, to be gained by heating the material beyond 75°C or by using a long heating time. The problem is primarily a question of heat transfer and temperature control to ensure a uniform, optimum temperature throughout the whole mass.

Since reduction of heat load on the material, that is the combined effect of temperature and time, tends to improve the quality of the products, we may expect new technological answers to the heating problem, in line with this new knowledge. However, at the present state of technology, we have to accept that optimum conditions for a particular type of raw material must largely be established through practical experience.

The most common practice is to cook the fish in a steam cooker, through which it is conveyed continuously. Heat is generally transferred indirectly from a surrounding jacket and a heated rotary screw conveyor. This is an improvement over the direct steam injection cooker, in which water is condensed in the mass during the process and has to be removed by the press and then evaporated from the press liquor. However, in indirect cookers provision is also made for the admission of live steam directly into the mass as this may sometimes be advantageous.

Cooking is an exacting operation in production and is sometimes difficult to control. Production of cooked material which can be readily pressed is dependent on the quality of the raw material and on the process conditions. A precise time-temperature programme for this process can therefore not be set up and, as mentioned above, a process of trial and error is generally required when fish of unknown history is processed. The most common practice of cooking good raw material, however, is to heat to 95°-100°C within 15 to 20 min.

Most manufacturers operate cookers to ensure rapid heating of the mass to a temperature of about 95°C. The proof of good cooking is good pressability of the mass which leads to proper removal of press liquor and, in particular for fatty fish species, efficient recovery of oil, giving a meal with low fat content which is a criterion of quality. The process must be controlled to ensure sufficient cooking, but overcooking must be avoided as this results in problems with pressing and the presence of large amounts of suspended particles in the stickwater, which makes evaporation difficult.

The cooker is designed as a cylinder having a steam heated jacket throughout and a steam heated rotor, designed as a screw conveyor with hollow flights. The cooker is equipped with covers throughout for inspection and cleaning and with a nozzle system for blowing direct steam into the mass. The cooker may be provided with automatic temperature control equipment, automatic level control for raw material feeding, discharge control equipment (which is required particularly for handling soft raw material) and a trap for collecting heavy foreign matter like stones and scrap iron. Cookers like this are generally available in sizes which can process from 16 t to 1 600 t of raw material per 24 h.

Furthermore, the capacity is influenced by the resistance to heat transfer largely caused by the existence of films and coatings on the heating surfaces. An important way of reducing the tendency to scaling, caused by coagulation of protein on the hot walls, is to use moderate steam temperatures, especially in the early stages of heating.

Another measure is, of course, to introduce and enforce good routines for effective cleaning at regular intervals.

An entirely different type of heating device is the so-called Contherm apparatus, recently tried out in connection with fishmeal and oil manufacture. The results, so far at low rates of throughput, have been quite promising. A vertical cylindrical heat exchanger provided with an agitator keeping the material in rapid movement, thus contributing to effective heat transfer. During rotation, the agitator blades (knives) are pressed against the surrounding heating surface in order to prevent the formation of scale. To reduce the viscosity of the material and to increase the rate of heat transfer, some stickwater should be added to the fish.

Advantages of the Contherm heater are rapid heating with a holding time less than 2 min, effective temperature control, and quick and easy routines for dismantling and cleaning.

Another innovation is the tubular heater (pre-cooker) primarily designed and used for the utilisation of waste heat, either from the evaporators or from the dryers. Because of the relatively low temperatures of these vapours or gases, they are particularly useful for preheating the raw material. The heater consists of a set of tubes coupled together and surrounded by a cylindrical jacket. The raw material is moved through the tubes by pumping, and on its way it is heated by the hot gases circulating around the tubes, in the space between the latter and the jacket.

In practical use, the raw material may reach temperatures in the range of 50° to 60°C before it leaves the pre-heater and enters the conventional indirect steam cooker. Besides representing an important saving of energy this way of operation reduces the problem of scaling on the heating surfaces considerably, implying that the capacity of the heating units may be maintained at a high level for longer periods.

Pre-straining

One result of the heating process is that the oil and a major part of the water is released and to a large extent may be removed from the solids by simple draining. Removal of more liquid is achieved by subsequent treatment of the solid part in presses or centrifuges, or in a combination of the two. To facilitate the functioning of the press, the liquid liberated in the cooker is drained from the coagulated fish pulp in a strainer conveyor or in a vibrating or rotary strainer.

A strainer conveyor set at an incline between the cooker and the press. It is designed on the same principle as that of a screw conveyor except that the lower end (that closer to the cooker) is fitted with an easily replaceable strainer in the shape of a half cylinder. Strainers with different sizes of perforations may be required for various types of fish.

The fundamental principle here is that the cooked material is conveyed to a strainer which is kept vibrating by an electric motor. The liquid phase passes through the strainer holes whereas the solid phase is vibrated along the surface of the strainer to an outlet.

Pressing

To ensure free drainage of liquid in the press, the material should be porous; that is, there should be many open channels in its mass for the passage of liquid. Cooked material from small and autolysed fish will, as a rule, contain large quantities of fine particles (sludge) that tend to clog up these channels. In such cases, the porosity of the presscake may be improved by increasing the diameter of the holes of the pre-strainer. A greater part of the fines will then follow the liquid phase and not hamper the function of the press. To take advantage of this measure, the capacity of the decanters (desludging centrifuges) should be sufficient to handle the increased volume of sludge in the liquid.

The purpose of the press is to squeeze out as much liquid as possible from the solid phase. This is important not only to improve the oil yield and the quality of the meal, but also to reduce the moisture content of the presscake as far as possible, thereby reducing the fuel consumption of the dryers and increasing their capacity.

Two types of continuous press are used in the fishmeal industry; these are provided with either one or two screws. Both work on the principle of helical screw conveyors rotating in a tightly fitting cage, which is provided with perforations for the drainage of press liquid. The screws are made with a taper, thus ensuring that the volume between the flights is gradually reduced. This means that the material, during passage along the press, is subjected to increasing pressures and, as a consequence, additional amounts of liquid are expressed. The performance of the press is largely determined by the profile and the compression ratio of the screws, that is, the ratio between the flight volumes of the inlet and outlet flights. Whether standard screws based on fish of average nature and quality, or screws with a special profile and compression ration should be used, is a question for careful consideration and discussion with the press manufacturer.

Occasionally difficulties are experienced, particularly when processing soft and autolysed fish. The press "slips", meaning that the screws rotate in the material without conveying it forward. This problem may be minimized by incorporating special devices in the single screw press; but the most efficient measure is to use two screws mounted side by side and rotating them in opposite directions.

Pressing is carried out in a press chamber consisting of two hollow interlocked cylinders. The cylinder wall is made of heavily supported strainer plates made from stainless steel. The two press screws have tapered shafts and the screw pitch varies so that the pitch, and thus the flight distance, is greatest at the thin end of the shafts. The screws rotate in opposite senses. The material is fed in at the end where the shafts are thinner, and is carried towards the end where they are thicker. As can be seen, the space for the material gradually reduces and, to compensate, liquid is pressed out through the strainer plates surrounding the screws.

The performance of the press may be regulated in two ways: one may adjust the level of cooked material in the hopper above the press, a high level resulting in higher pressure and consequently a more complete filling of the inlet screw flights; the other factor is the rate of revolution of the screws; increased speed means greater throughput and a shorter pressing time. How to adjust these two factors to obtain optimum performance is largely a matter of experience and skill.

Good performance of the press depends upon relatively tight fitting of the screw flights to the surrounding strainer plates. If the distance between the flight tops and the screens becomes too wide, for instance after long wear and tear, both the efficiency and the capacity will suffer; rebuilding and readjustment of the screw flights are then necessary. Another factor that needs continuous surveillance is the performance of the strainer plates. Regular inspection and cleaning is necessary to ensure that the holes are open and allow free escape of liquid. As pointed out earlier.

Temperature is a factor of great importance for the whole cooking and pressing operation. Basic information today indicates that moderate temperatures are preferable from the standpoint of release of oil and denaturation of protein. On the other side, high temperatures reduce the viscosity of the oil and tend to facilitate the flow from the solid phase. With the equipment we just have described, we must again rely on experimental data to establish optimum conditions for a particular raw material.

Processing problems may be encountered under two entirely different conditions. One relates to completely fresh fish that tends to retain more oil and water than desirable. For the time being, there is no solution to this problem except by resorting to one of the two equally deplorable measures; either by reducing the speed of the press and thereby the capacity of the whole plant. Or by storing the fish for a day or two before processing, thus leading to deterioration of quality.

The other situation occurs with soft and autolysed fish. The answer to this problem is to bleed off in the pre-strainer more liquid and fines to be handled by the decanters. Some processors will often resort to the use of coagulating agents like formaldehyde, which help to solidify the material and improve the performance of the press.

This, practice, however, should be restricted as far as possible because formaldehyde reacts with the essential amino acid lysine, and thereby reduces the nutritional quality of the protein. Calcium chloride ($CaCl_2$) has also been used as a hardener, but this practice was abandoned because it raised the chloride content of the meal to unacceptable levels, particularly in cases where stickwater is incorporated and whole meal produced.

Centrifugation Instead of Pressing

To separate solids from liquid by centrifugation is a standard operation in many industries including the fishmeal and oil industry. With the development of centrifuges that can handle materials with high contents of solids and at high rates of throughput, it 15 now possible to use decanters instead of presses to separate the solids from the liquid in cooked fish. The advantages are several. First, it presents a simplification of the process. Secondly, centrifugation is a better known and more controllable unit operation than pressing and filtration. Thirdly, centrifugation is a much quicker process than pressing and significantly reduces the heat load on the material, a factor of importance for the manufacture of special products.

Perhaps the most important advantage is the ability of the centrifuge to process soft and very fluid material where the press would fail completely. Better hygiene and simpler procedures for washing operations are further features on the plus side.

On the negative side one should note that the centrifuge will discharge the solids with a higher moisture content than the press. This means increased fuel consumption for the drying operation. Furthermore, the centrifuge tends to produce more emulsions and fines, causing problems in the subsequent separation of oil, water and sludge in the liquid phase.

Although the use of decanters for the separation of solids and liquid in cooked fish material for the time being appears relatively unimportant, centrifugation is an interesting area where we may expect new developments. Combinations of press, strainer and centrifuge in various ways also open interesting possibilities which should prove worthwhile investigating.

Separation of Press Liquor

The liquor coming from the press and the pre-strainer consists of water and varying amounts of oil and dry matter. The oil content is related to the proportion of oil in the fish. The content of dry matter, occurring both in dissolved and suspended (finely dispersed) forms, varies with the size and quality of the fish and with the extent of mechanical handling prior to processing.

The quantity of press liquor will also vary with the nature and quality of the raw material, and increases particularly with advancing autolysis of the fish. Under average conditions one may estimate the volume of press liquor at about 70 per cent of the raw material while the remaining 30 per cent makes up the presscake.

The separation of the three fractions of the press liquor, sludge, oil and water, is based on their different specific gravities. If press liquor is left for some time in a tank, it will settle out in three layers: sludge at the bottom, water in between and oil at the top.

In the early days of fish oil production, this method of settling under the influence of gravity alone was standard procedure. It had many drawbacks such as poor yield, impure fractions and, above all, it was extremely slow. With centrifugation we get several thousand times greater forces at our disposal, and the separation process may now be accomplished in seconds when compared with the hours required for the settling method.

An important prerequisite for efficient separation is high temperature, implying that the press liquor should be reheated to 90°-95°C before entering the centrifuges. This applies to sludge removal as well as to separation of oil and water.

The suspended solids are first to be removed. This is done in a horizontal centrifuge, a so- called decanter or desludger. It consists of a partly cylindrical and partly conical rotor drum (bowl) and, inside this, a screw conveyor of the same shape. The press liquor is fed into the rotor where, by centrifugal force, it is thrown towards the bowl's periphery. The denser solids are rapidly precipitated along the inside rotor surface. The screw conveyor rotates with the bowl, but at a rate some 30 to 50 rpm faster than the speed of rotation of the drum; the deposited solids are thus scraped off continuously. Before being discharged, they are lifted out of the liquid phase and pass through a drying or dewatering zone.

The performance of the decanter may be controlled in two ways. It is possible to adjust the thickness of the liquid layer (a thick layer represents a longer zone and allows more time for clarification of the liquid) and, associated with this, there will be a correspondingly shorter zone of sludge and less time for dewatering the solids. The reverse will, of course, be the case with a thin liquid layer.

The other regulating parameter is the speed of the screw conveyor relative to that of the bowl. The higher the content of solids in the liquid the faster the conveyor should rotate in relation to the bowl in order to remove the precipitate. In addition to these parameters one may naturally influence performance by regulating the feed. Optimum conditions are dependent both on quantity and nature, specially particle size, of the solids in the liquid. Decanters are available in various sizes.

For smaller plants, the investment in a decanter may not be economically justified. In such cases a vibrating strainer, although less efficient, may be a cheaper but entirely satisfactory solution. Separation of stickwater from oil takes place in vertical disc centrifuges, either of the nozzle type, which discharge the stickwater and remaining sludge continuously, or of the self cleaning type, which is often preferred.

In the latter, the stickwater is continuously discharged, whereas the sludge is collected in the bowl and periodically ejected according to a timed programme which depends on the quantity and the nature of the sludge. The stickwater with a dry matter content of 6-9 per cent is concentrated in evaporators. The sludge in most cases can be pumped to the presscake.

The main component of the bowl is a stack of conical discs lying on top of each other at distances of 0.5 to 2 mm apart. The discs have a number of distribution holes to provide passages for the liquid from the bottom of the disc stack. The decanter liquid is fed from a control tube (1). The oil moves along the discs towards the centre and discharges through the holes in the nut (3). The stickwater moves towards the periphery and discharges behind the separating plate through the regulation ring (4). This is inter-changeable to adjust the separation. The sludge separates along the bowl periphery and is discharged through the bowl slot into the frame chute at regular intervals (2). Centrifuges are available with rates of throughput ranging from 500 to 25 000 litres/h.

Oil Polishing

Oil polishing, carried out in special separators, is the final refining step done at the factory before the oil is pumped into storage. Polishing is facilitated by using hot water, which extracts impurities from the oil and thus ensures stability during storage.

The efficiency of separation depends upon both design and mode of operation of the centrifuges. The speed of separation depends upon the motility of the particles and upon the centrifugal force of the separator. Motility depends upon material properties, such as viscosity and specific gravity, which in turn depend upon temperature. Accordingly, good temperature control is required; the temperature of the feed should be maintained at about 95°C, but not less than 90°C. The centrifugal force is proportional to the angular velocity squared and to the radius of the centrifuge bowl, while the stress on the material of construction is proportional to the angular velocity squared and to the square of the radius. Centrifuges are designed to operate at high speeds and are, therefore, generally constructed with small radii. Centrifuges operating at about 5,000 rpm, yielding a centrifugal force of 5,000 x g (natural gravity), are generally used in the fishmeal industry.

Evaporation of Stickwater

When decanters and separators have removed the major part of oil and suspended solids from the press liquid, we are left with the so-called stickwater. For all practical purposes, one may estimate the amount of stickwater at about 65 per cent of the raw material.

Besides water, stickwater will contain the following components:

- Dissolved protein
- Minerals
- Undissolved (suspended) protein
- Vitamins
- Residual oil
- Amines/ammonia

The content of residual oil will depend upon the efficiency of the separating process and should be as low as possible, certainly well below 1 per cent. The other components, usually put together and called stickwater dry matter, amount to 5-6 per cent for fresh fish, and correspond to nearly 20 per cent of the yield of meal. After transportation and storage, specially of small fish caught during the feeding season and at high temperatures, the percentage of stickwater solids may rise to even higher values.

To recover the stickwater solids, one has to remove large quantities of water by evaporation and subsequent drying. This requires heat, and the question of heat economy and fuel consumption becomes, therefore, of paramount importance. The usage of heat may be influenced in various ways.

At the planning stage, one should carefully consider what type of evaporating plant to select, and particularly evaluate to what extent it is economically feasible to make use of waste heat, for instance that represented by the vapours in the exhaust gases from the dryer. Furthermore, there is the question of the number of evaporation stages, increasing numbers resulting in significant reductions in steam requirement. Typical figures for steam consumption are 0.6 to 0.65 kg, 0.4 to 0.45 kg and 0.2 to 0.35 kg steam per kilogramme water evaporated in double, triple and quadruple effect evaporators, respectively.

On the other hand, the costs of construction rise with increase in the number of evaporator units. Generally, large catches of fish and long periods of operation speak in favour of cutting variable costs by investing in a greater number of evaporation stages. Other factors to be considered are, of course, local prices of fuel, electric energy and capital. For general guidance, it may be mentioned that double effects are used for rates of throughput of 30 to 150 t, triple ones for 200 to 400 t and quadruple for 500 t and more of raw fish per 24h.

Selection of the operating conditions will also greatly affect the heat economy of the whole factory. Because multiple effect evaporation is a more economical way of removing water than one stage drying, it is specially important to achieve a high concentration of dry matter in the final stickwater concentrate before it is discharged from the evaporating plant and conveyed to the dryers for drying together with the presscake.

The factor which largely determines how far you may concentrate the stickwater without running into trouble is the viscosity which rises steeply during the last stage of concentration.

As increasing temperatures tend to make the concentrated stickwater less viscous, one may take advantage of this fact by completing the evaporation in the unit with the highest temperature. Another factor that can contribute greatly to the viscosity of the concentrate is the content of suspended solids (sludge), and great care should therefore be taken to keep this as low as possible, both by preventive measures and by efficient removal in decanters or sieves. Although evaporation at high temperatures offers certain advantages, there are quality considerations that pull in the opposite direction. Some of the vitamins and amino acids are particularly sensitive to heat, and heating for any length of time above 130°C should be discouraged, as this may lead to considerable losses of vitamin B_{12} and of the important amino acids, cystine, lysine and tryptophan. There are also other changes which take place under the influence of heat, such as degradation of the protein and evaporation of volatile components. Furthermore, there is the problem of discolouration.

The significance of these changes should, of course, be carefully considered with special view to the marketing and end use of the products, before making the final decisions on equipment and operating conditions. Quality criteria will naturally centre around the nutritional value of the products but, with a view to a possible development towards products for human consumption, greater weight should be placed on sensory or organoleptic properties, like flavour and odour.

This system works according to the I-II-III-IV mode of operation, that is, the stickwater flows in parallel with the flow of steam. It is fed continuously to stage I and progressively concentrated during the subsequent passage through stages II, III and IV. Live steam from the boiler plant is supplied to the pre-heater and to the heat exchanger of the first stage, while the vapour emanating from this stage is used for heating in the second. Vapour from the second stage is used in stage III, and so on to stage IV. Vapour from the last stage is normally condensed in a condensing tower, but it may also be used, for instance, to preheat raw material.

The conventional mode of operation is to feed dilute solution to the first stage operated above atmospheric pressure and to withdraw concentrate from the last, which is operated under reduced pressure. Some factories, however, prefer to feed dilute solution to the second stage and withdraw concentrate from the first. This subjects the concentrate to the highest available temperature in the system (generally above 100°C),

Which has the following advantages:

- Reduction of viscosity of concentrate,
- Effective decomposition and removal of nitrogenous contaminants, for example nitrites and dimethyl nitrosamine, and oxides of sulphur if present, and
- Destruction of any pathogenic bacteria, including Salmonella, that might have infected the material in earlier stages. In some factories these effects are attained by treating the concentrated stickwater in separate heated pressure tanks.

During evaporation, solids are deposited on the hot surfaces impeding heat transfer and blocking the tubes. These deposits must be removed regularly, generally during shut-down periods (for example at weekends). Such removal necessitates chemical and mechanical treatments. Chemical treatment should be carried out when required, usually once a week. Mild steel evaporators may be cleaned with about 14 per cent caustic soda solutions, recirculated at about 80°C for 5 h and left standing overnight. The apparatus is then emptied and thoroughly rinsed with water before the factory resumes normal operation. Mechanical scale removal in mild steel evaporators may be necessary several times a year.

The weekly cleaning of stainless steel evaporators is usually done with stronger cleansing agents. Two hours' treatment with caustic soda will dissolve protein deposits, and a subsequent one hour's treatment with 5 per cent nitric acid at 60°C will remove more firmly bound material. Mechanical cleaning of stainless steel evaporators should be avoided if possible but, if it should prove necessary, it should be carried out with great care to avoid scratches or other damage to the surface, which would result in loss of an important property of stainless steel, that is its smoothness. The smoother the surface the less firmly does the scale adhere to the surface. Monthly cleaning (caustic soda) on the steam side of the evaporators is also advisable.

Oil separation from partly concentrated stickwater is practised by some manufacturers. The density of stickwater is higher in the concentrated than in the diluted state. This greater difference between the density of oil and concentrated stickwater produces an increase in the centrifugal potential and thus facilitates extra oil removal. Consequently, oil separation from the concentrate may lead to slightly leaner "whole" fish meal and will also increase the yield of oil. Oil separation seems to be more efficient after the second evaporation step than after later effects because of the lower viscosity of the concentrate at this stage.

The separated oil tends to be rather dark and of less value than oil separated before concentration. High contents of sulphur are particularly harmful because some sulphur-containing compounds act as catalyst poisons during the hydrogenation process of the edible fats industry. "Concentrate oil" should, therefore, preferably be stored and sold separately.

Stickwater concentrate may be sold separately under the name "fish solubles". Because of the character of the product, however, the market is limited and is usually located not too far from the place of production. The most common way of utilising stickwater concentrate is to mix it with the presscake and to dry the mixture to so-called "whole meal". The dry matter content of the concentrate is determined by the viscosity/dry matter relationship for the actual raw material, and may vary between 30 per cent and 50 per cent.

The commonly used evaporators operate with vertical tubes partly filled with boiling liquid, gradually giving off water vapour while moving upward in the tubes and into the chamber, separating liquid and vapours. The volume of liquid is quite large and it takes, therefore, a long time before the desired concentration has been reached, and concentrate starts flowing to the dryers. This time lag between pressing and concentrating is particularly undesirable and causes problems in factories with the intermittent supplies of raw material. In such cases, the falling film evaporator becomes of special interest because it operates with a short holding time and small liquid volume.

Here the stickwater enters at the top of the tubes, which are heated from the outside by steam or hot gases. On its way down, water evaporates and the liquid becomes more and more concentrated, and finally ends up at the bottom as concentrate. The falling film evaporator also offers advantages in connection with energy saving systems using vapour recompression. So far, it has found limited use in the fish-meal industry largely because it requires special skill and attention from the operator. Because of its many advantages, however, the falling film evaporator is definitely a new alternative to consider for future plants.

Drying

The purpose of the drying process is to convert the wet and unstable mixture of presscake, decanter sludge and concentration into a dry and stable fish meal. In practice, this means drying to a moisture content below 12 per cent, which generally may be considered low enough to check microbial activity. This drying is done by heating the material to a temperature where the rate of evaporation of the water is considered satisfactory. Increasing the temperature will speed up the drying process. There are, however, certain critical limits t observe in order to avoid reduction of quality, especially of the protein.

With the equipment and conditions normally used in the fishmeal industry, the temperature of the drying material should not exceed 90°C in order not to impair nutrituional value. A prerequisite for optimum drying conditions is that the material should be divided into relatively small pieces or particles so as to facilitate the escape of water vapour from below the surface into the air. The presscake is, therefore, passed through a wet mill where it is disintegrated by fast moving hammer heads mounted on a rotor. The presscake is beaten against a screen in the bottom provided with sharp edged, square holes.

To avoid sticking and lump formation during one stage drying of presscake to which stickwater concentrate is added, thorough mixing is necessary. This may be achieved by heating the concentrate to a high temperature (about 100°C) before mixing. Such heating also serves to destroy bacteria, including *Salmonella*, if present. Mixing is generally performed in the screw conveyors, the concentrate preferably being added before disintegration of the presscake in the wet mill. In two stage drying the concentrate is added to the presscake between the dryers.

The type of dryer to be chosen will depend on several factors, i.e.:

- The nature of the material to be dried,
- Fuel economy,
- Plant layout,
- Plant capacity,
- Odour considerations.

The two main principles of drying are direct heat drying and indirect steam drying. The direct rotary dryer, also called "flame dryer" or "direct hot air dryer", is used in the production of some 75 per cent of fish meal in world trade. Heat for vaporisation is provided by a current of flue gases diluted with secondary air, in direct contact with the fish material being dried. The direct action of the drying medium is both the strength and the weakness of the system. It represents the most efficient mode of heat and mass transfer but, unless operated properly, it may constitute a source of contamination of the product.

Flue gas contaminants may range from products of incomplete combustion, for example particles of soot, to oxides of sulphur and nitrogen which are capable of reacting with nutritional components (such as protein and oil) in the meal. Manufacturers should therefore avoid the use of the crudest types of fuel, which may contain up to 1 per cent by weight, or more, of sulphur and nitrogen. The temperature of combustion must be high enough to ensure complete fuel combustion; inlet air temperatures of 500° to 600°C are considered safe levels.

The direct rotary dryer is operated "in parallel" with respect to flow of air and fish material. Consequently, in addition to being the supplier of heat and the carrier of water vapour, the movement of the air also contributes to the transport of meal through the dryer. Accordingly, the air velocity must be adjusted so that the fish material is given sufficient dwell time in the dryer for proper drying. The drying time required, dependent upon process parameters and type of raw material, is established by careful adjustment for air flow coupled with measurement of fishmeal moisture during the start-up period.

The average dwell time in the dryer ranges between 10 and 20 min. By adjustment of the heat input, the evaporative capacity of the dryer can be varied. This is of importance to fishmeal manufacturers who have to face large fluctuations in quantity and quality of the raw material. Air temperature is a most important control parameter, since it affects the rate of evaporation. The temperature of the inlet air may range within wide limits without apparent damage to the meal. The reason for this is that the fish itself gets cooled through evaporation and normally does not exceed about 80°C, even though the air temperature may be several hundred degrees.

Adding stickwater concentrate to ground presscake, now almost universally practised, requires high concentration and good mixing to avoid problems of wet material sticking to metal surfaces; but these may be overcome by returning an adequate portion of dried material to the dryer inlet. Two stage drying, that is two rotary dryers operated in series, is practised in many instances on grounds of fuel economy and easier control of moisture content, and in these instances, the solubles are added to the partially dried presscake after the first drying stage.

Estimates of moisture content during drying are carried out manually, primarily and very roughly through "feel" of the fish meal to the hand, and by analysis. Fluctuations in moisture content of the end product are counteracted by manipulation of the hot air. Some factories employ indirect automatic moisture control based on continuous temperature measurement in the exit air. The temperature at this point is sensitive to variables in the process parameters of the system (for example flow, moisture content and homogeneity of the feed). Thus, when the exit air temperature drifts away from a fixed value an automatic device adjusts the oil burner and restores the desired condition. This control prevents gross variation in product quality.

Rotating at a peripheral speed of about 1 m/s, the cylindrical compartment is equipped with horizontal and helical flights which provide cascading and good agitation of fish material, a large area of contact between fish and air and, accordingly, means for efficient dehydration. As stated, hot air is produced by mixing flue gases from oil gas or coal combustion with a stream of secondary air.

Because large seasonal catches of fish must be processed within relatively short periods of time, there has been a demand for large size rotary dryers in the industry capable of processing up to 1,000 t of raw material per day.

The indirect steam dryer works on the following principle: the mixture of presscake and stickwater concentrate is fed continuously into one end of the rotary apparatus, and is dried in direct contact with steam heated elements (tubes, discs, coils, etc.), emerging at the other end. A counter-current steam of air is blown through the dryer to facilitate removal of water vapour. The heat is transferred from the steam to the pulp through the heating surface, and rotary agitation of the pulp promotes the heat transfer.

The steam temperature (pressure) is limited by the dimensions and strength of materials of construction (discs, tubes or coils). A maximum steam temperature of 170°C corresponding to 6 atmospheres gauge pressure is most frequently used in steam dryers. Overall heat transfer is slower than in the direct dryer and a drying period of 30 min or longer is required. It consists of a steam heated stationary cylindrical jacket and a steam heated rotor equipped with steam heated double walled discs perpendicular to the rotor which provide good agitation and heat transfer to the fish meal.

The evaporated water is removed by air drawn through the dryer by a centrifugal fan. There is an air dome on the top of the dryer to allow for the passage of air and water vapour. The entire drying process may be watched through inspection windows. The meal discharge is controlled by a gate valve at the discharge opening. These dryers normally use steam at a pressure of 6 kg/cm^2 and are designed to remove up to 2,700 kg water per hour, corresponding to about 300 t of raw fish per 24 h. One of the advantages of disc dryers is their ability to dry stickwater concentrate together with presscake without deposits forming on the heating surfaces.

The main difference between this and the rotary disc dryer is the design of the rotating heating elements. The coils are mounted on a hollow shaft and supplied with steam at a pressure of about 7 kg/cm^2. These dryers are available with heating surface ranging between 20 and 400 m^2 and of handling materials corresponding to as much as 400 t of raw fish per 24 h. The indirect tube dryer is a horizontal rotating cylinder with internal steam heated longitudinal tubes. To transfer heat from the tubes to the pulp and to remove evaporated water, air is drawn through the dryer. The drying process in steam dryers is controlled by adjusting the steam pressure and by varying the rate of discharge of meal; the latter is done by adjusting the level of the material in the dryer.

In indirect dryers the fish meal is at no stage in contact with flue gases. The gentle transport of material through the stationary cylinder of a disc dryer appears to yield a product with a physical structure different from that of the rotary dryer. The particles are longer and less prone to spillage through grated cage floors and, consequently, the meal is more acceptable for mink feeding.

From a nutritional point of view, direct and indirect drying methods seem to yield products of equivalent value, The steam dryer has an important advantage in regard to air pollution. Owing to the small volume of effluent gases (30 per cent or less of that of a direct heated rotary dryer of comparable capacity), odour abatement is much simpler.

The great advantage of the direct dryer is the large drying capacity of each unit making for simpler machinery arrangement and cheaper installation for a given rate of throughput. With respect to heat economy, there is little to be said in favour of one or other type, when the efficiency of the steam dryer and that of the boiler are considered together.

Indirect hot air dryer have started to attract the interest of the fishmeal industry in recent years. They offer the same advantage as the steam dryers in the sense that the gases of combustion do not come into contact with the drying material. The hot air is generated in a heat exchanger where the gases from the combustion chamber move on one side of the heating surface and uncontaminated air on the other. After having transferred the heat to the current of clean air, the flue gases leave the system through the stack. With respect to the dryer itself, the performance is very much the same as that of the direct fired rotary dryer, the main difference being that clean, hot air replaces the current of flue gases with its various contaminants.

MILLING AND STORAGE OF FISH MEAL

MILLING

Before milling, the meal should pass another vibrating sieve and magnet to remove extraneous matter, like pieces of wood, cloth, fish hooks, and nails, which might still be present. The purpose of milling is to facilitate uniform incorporation in feeds. A properly milled meal has an attractive appearance and is readily mixed into feed rations which require homogeneous blending.

Different users require fish meal of different particle sizes. The ideal in milling is to produce small particles averaging around 40 mesh Tyler screen and of as even a size as possible. In practice, however, there is a great variation in particle size, ranging from 10 mesh to over 100 mesh.

Most purchasing specifications require the fish meal to pass through a 10 mesh screen, otherwise it is too coarse for uniform incorporation. Production of excessive fines (particles below 150 mesh) should be avoided, for example by screening before milling and passing only the oversise particles through the mill. Large amounts of fines are undesirable for several reasons. They cause dusting when handled, sift through woven bags resulting in loss of weight and in pollution, cause compacting of bulk meal and tend to clog the nostrils of chickens eating the feed.

There are numerous types of dry mill on the market. In view of the need for high rates of throughput and ready access for cleaning, hammer mills have proved particularly suitable. The coarse meal is disintegrated by the impact of rapidly rotating hammers, pivoted on horizontal or vertical shafts. A grating is usually attached around the rotor which retains the meal until it is fine enough to pass through the perforations.

The rotor consists of a central shaft to which a number of rotor plates are fastened perpendicular to the shaft. Between the rotor plates, hammers are held in position by bolts so that the hammers are removable. Special grinding plates are fixed inside the housing. At the lower part of the housing, there is a screen with round holes. By rotation of the rotor the material is hit by the hammers and the grinding plates and forced through the screens. The ground meal is cooled by air which is also used for transportation of the meal.

ADDITION OF ANTIOXIDANT

Reactive fish meals are "stabilised" by means of antioxidant immediately after manufacture, and may be stored in bulk or shipped as soon as they are cooled. The amount of antioxidant required for avoiding undue heating depends on the degree of reactivity of the oil (lipid unsaturation), and varies with fish species. Considerable excesses of ethoxyquin are, however, added for safety. Thus, South African pilchard meal (iodine value about 180) is "stabilised" with 400 ppm of ethoxyquin though 200 ppm would suffice, and herring meal (iodine value about 120) by 700 ppm of BHT or 200 ppm of ethoxyquin. The antioxidant is added immediately after drying. Anchoveta meal (iodine value about 190) is generally protected by 400 to 750 ppm of ethoxyquin.

Very careful control is necessary because of the small amount of antioxidant that is added to the fish meal and the need for even dispersion. For this reason the antioxidant is added to the meal in the screw conveyor leading from the dryer to the mill so that mixing can occur *en route*. Automatic controls are available for the addition of the antioxidant, complete with alarm bells and other devices to warn the factory personnel if anything is amiss, to avoid any fish meal being bagged without having been adequately treated. For ethoxyquin dosage it is essential to install proper automatic control and all fish meal passing the doser after the sounding of the alarm must be diverted, until the correct dosage has been re-established, and passed through the dosing system again.

In some factories the antioxidant is mixed with a constant amount of stickwater concentrate and this solution is then added to the presscake in the screw conveyor to the dryer. The effectiveness of the antioxidant is similar, whether added before or after drying. It must be stressed that stabilised meal retains a small trace of reactivity and is not completely stable. Nevertheless, the oil quality (energy value) is retained during prolonged storage; and, far more importantly, so is the protein quality of the meal, which otherwise could decrease through reaction with oxidised fish oil.

WEIGHING OUT FISH MEAL INTO BAGS

Meal is frequently stored and transported in bags. The manner of weighing the finished meal varies and the degree of automation generally depends upon the processing capacity of the factory. At some fishmeal plants and particularly plants with a processing capacity of less than approximately 60 t of raw fish per 24 h, the bags are weighed and closed using a platform scale. More advanced and automatic methods are generally used in large plants. Stitchers for the bags range from portable sewing machines to large factory floor units. Self closing, valve bags for automatic bags for automatic filling and weighing machines are also used.

Bags: The bags usually hold 50 kg each, and may be open-ended and stitched, or with valves which are tucked in. Bag material ranges from hessian to multi-layer paper (with or without plastic lining), or sheet or woven plastic (low density polyethylene). The hessian bag, made from woven jute, is much used in tropical and sub-tropical countries. The relatively open fabric enables water vapour and heat to escape readily from the meal.

The open fabric, however, has a number of disadvantages, such as:

- The rapid entry of oxygen from the atmosphere facilitates a high rate of oxidation of residual oil in fish meal not treated with antioxidant. Indeed, the associated heat of reaction may be high enough to cause spontaneous combustion unless the meal is cured (that is allowed to oxidise slowly in single bags or rows of bags) or is protected by means of antioxidant;
- The meal is open to rodent and insect infestation and is readily contaminated through bacterial and fungal attacks;
- Seepage of meal causes loss of product and pollution;
- Under humid conditions the fish meal absorbs much water and may go mouldy and lumpy.

The paper bag (multi-layer, lined with polyethylene) is widely used by the industry. It keeps out insects and microbes and retards penetration of oxygen and water vapour from the atmosphere. As a result serious temperature increase may be avoided and there is negligible uptake of water vapour during storage.

The (solid sheet) plastic bag offers exceptionally good protection. A large variety of plastic materials (low density polyethylene, PVC, etc.) is now available, and bags may be tailored to suit specific requirements (for example, short- or long-term storage, rough handling, etc.). One of the most important criteria for the quality of plastic packing material is its resistance to penetration of water vapour and oxygen.

Table. Passage of Oxygen Through Paper and Plastic Bags

Material	Temperature(°C)	Area(cm^2 x 104)	O_2 Passage NTP (ml/m^2 day atm)
Polythene	27	1.196	1 510
Paper 6-ply	23	1.38	18 360
Paper 5-ply	22	1.28	53 200

Oxidation and spontaneous heating are reduced to minute proportions only in tucked-in valve bags. If the bags are stitched the stitching holes allow sufficient entry of air to sustain some heating until the meal is cured, especially during handling of the bags. On the other hand, reactive meal in valved bags remains uncured and, if not treated with antioxidant, may be a serious source of spontaneous combustion if bulked immediately after removal from the bags.

Drop testing has indicated that polyethylene bags of 0.25 mm are stronger than multilayer paper bags. Nevertheless, transport and handling frequently result in more serious puncturing damage to polyethylene than to multi-layer paper bags. Also, the filled polyethylene bag is less rigid which, with its relatively low coefficient of friction, tends to make stowage more difficult and may more easily result in slipping and displacement during transport.

Palletising: Wooden pallets holding about 1.5 t (30 bags) are often used to facilitate handling and stacking of bags after manufacture. Pallets may be stacked three high with fork lift trucks, after the meal has cooled to room temperature.

COOLING

Whether the freshly prepared fish meal is stabilised with ethoxyquin or not, it must be cooled to room temperature before it is stored in bulk. Bags of stabilised fish meal are left standing for a few days in single or double rows, or on singly-spaced pallets. Unbagged fish meal should be cooled by an air current or continually turned till cool. This can be done either in properly designed silos as, for example, in Norway and Denmark, or by turning the heaps of fish meal by means of bulldozers or conveyors as, for example, in the USA. Unstabilised reactive fish meal should be “cured” for 28 days, that is regularly turned if unbagged, or in small units if bagged, before stacking in bulk. For the first few days the bags should be placed on the floor apart from each other, or in single rows, depending on the initial reactivity of the meal; thereafter they may be stacked in double rows for the remaining 28-day period. Handling and storage on the floor involves a certain risk of Salmonella contamination.

PELLETISING

Pelletised fish meal, mainly produced by large manufacturers, facilitates bulk storage and transport. The flow properties are improved and dusting is reduced. Pellets do not represent any essential space saving compared with bulk stored meal; nor are oxidation and spontaneous heating retarded by pelletising. The bulk density of pellets is the same as that of fish meal (generally 600 to 700 kg/m^3). During handling, however, some of the pellets break and the broken pieces and meal formed in this way occupy the spaces between the pellets and thus increase the bulk density. Pellet diameters vary between 8 mm and 12 mm. Pelleting machines of 120 hp are capable of turning out about 5 t of pellets or more per hour.

The principle of the pellet press:

- Is the press mould (matrix),
- The press rollers,
- The distributor,
- The knife, and
- The pellets.

The rollers press the meal through the holes of the matrix, and the knife cuts the pellets to the desired length. Usually, steam or hot stickwater concentrate is added to facilitate the formation of firm pellets. The pellets are usually made from hot meal emerging from the dryer and are cooled with fresh air in a cooling tower.

STORAGE

Storage methods for fish meal vary, depending upon many factors, including climatic conditions, production capacity, use of antioxidant and transport and marketing arrangements. Factories should have storage capacity for a reasonable buffer stock. In case of difficult marketing and shipping conditions, large storage, capacities, for instance, sufficient to hold 30 days' production, may be required.

Fish meal must be protected from moisture and fishmeal stores must therefore be moisture proof. If necessary, the inner surface of the roof should be insulated or the stores provided with ceilings to avoid condensation and drip at night, with consequent localised mould growth and lumping in the fish meal. Only in arid regions may fish meal be stored out in the open. Fish meal must also be protected from undue self heating, whether it is treated with antioxidant or stored after curing. For this reason, bulk storage units should not exceed about 5 m in width.

Many different stacking arrangements for cooled bags are available from IAFMM. These arrangements are designed to limit the dimensions of the stacks, or to provide channels or "chimneys" through the stacks to carry away the small amount of residual heat generated. In this way, undue internal temperature rise is avoided and moisture migration from warm to cooler areas inhibited. Moisture migration can result in condensation, mould growth and lumping. Mould growth (as distinct from bacterial growth) may lead to spontaneous heating up to about 40°C at which temperature the moulds are destroyed; but at this elevated temperature spontaneous heating through oxidation of the oil may be accelerated, unless the fish meal is properly cured or stabilised with antioxidant.

Shipping stowage recommendations, also available from IAFMM, provide for athwartship twin columns of bags with 15 to 20 cm gaps between each tier, with cross dunnage. Bulk storage: It is estimated that about half of the world's fish meal is stored in bulk in sheds and silos.

Major manufacturers are taking an increasing interest in bulk storage because:

- All handling, from production to loading on transport vessels, becomes simpler, cheaper and results in a considerable saving in manpower used in maintenance, filling, weight control and stowage of bags;
- Transport vessels and international receiving centres are being more and more geared to bulk handling, so that bulk storage in the factory is more compatible with modern overall handling systems.

In general, facilities for bulk storage are either of the open type (access of air through doors and other openings) or of the sealed type (space sealed off from the surroundings, as in special silos). The open type predominates in the fishmeal industry, and the ready availability of oxygen causes lipid oxidation of freshly made reactive meal not treated with antioxidant to proceed relatively rapidly. In order to dissipate the heat of reaction, the meal requires frequent aeration. This is particularly important during the initial storage stage when it is most reactive.

A suitable practice of aeration involves conveying the meal from one storage space to another. If suitable antioxidant, however, is admixed with the meal, the latter is stabilised and considerably less aeration is required; indeed, only that which is necessary to cool the meal to room temperature. In open storage, special care should be given to pest and rodent control to prevent infection, for example by Salmonella.

The facilities in use for bulk storage of fish meal are the same as those employed in granaries, except for some modifications due to the "compacting" properties of the meal. The two most generally used systems are sheds, divided into several compartments, and silos. Storage sheds may be of single or multistoried construction. Owing to the weight and the pressures exerted on the walls, such sheds are usually of single floor construction. Multistorage sheds should preferably be of concrete construction throughout, particularly the floors and outer walls. Silos have found use in the fishmeal industry in recent years, not only because they offer good protection to meal during storage, but also because they increase flexibility in handling. This is perhaps the most important advantage of the silo over other types of storage facility.

Fish meal that is stored in specially designed silos may be kept in motion by continuously extracting it from the bottom and returning it to the top by means of automatic conveyor mechanisms. In this way, the meal is aerated for cooling and curing, and is also blended. It is also prevented from compacting and bridging. Generally, fish meal does not flow readily and tends to compact under pressure, especially at elevated temperature. The silos need special construction because of the relatively poor flow property of fish meal. Cylindrical silos are often preferred, but silos with square or rectangular cross-section are also satisfactory. The ease of discharge depends on the meal's physical properties and in particular on particle size distribution, especially fines content, moisture and fat contents, amount of solubles added, etc., and bridging is best prevented by assuring sufficient ventilation and circulation of meal during storage. The flow properties of fish meal can be improved by reducing the moisture content to 7 per cent or by pelletising.

The point of discharge at the bottom is the most critical part of the silo and is preferably constructed of steel. Depending on the cross-section of the silo, there may be several points of discharge.

The conical discharge section of cylindrical silos should have a slope at least 10° greater than the meal's angle of repose, which is of the order of 45°. Discharge chutes from corners of square silos are generally wedge-shaped, with three sides vertical and the fourth at an angle. A number of silos are normally arranged in one or more rows, which may take the form of a compact block. The multi-row arrangement is general for square silos since one silo will have walls in common with others, a saving in investment.

Blending silos constitute an integral part of the production and storage system. They are generally smaller than storage silos, and emphasis is placed on the efficiency and rate of their discharge and recirculation mechanisms to handle one to three days of peak fishmeal production. During blending, meals of various qualities are homogenised.

This results in an overall quality increase because of:

- Uniformity of the main constituents, protein, fat and water;
- More even grain size, which makes mixing of the meal into animal diets easier, and

- Uniformity of colour, which improves the meal's market appeal.

Fish oil is stored in conventional tanks made from mild steel. The following design features are usually included:

- Separation of residual water from the oil during storage necessitates water drainage at the tank bottom;
- In cold climates, the tanks must be equipped with steam-heated coils to keep the oil fluid during discharge;
- To facilitate good setting oil storage tanks are preferably insulated;
- To prevent contamination by sludge and water, unloading should be from a tube situated some way above the bottom of the tank.

SPECIAL METHODS OF PROCESSING

In previous sections we have described the most common processing methods used in large and medium sized factories. For smaller factories and under special circumstances, simplified or entirely different installations may prove economical.

In the following we shall give a few examples of different approaches, some of which aim at products with special properties.

CENTRIFUGAL METHODS

In these systems, the separation of the coagulated fish pulp is based on centrifugation instead of pressing. In one of these systems (Centrifish, DeLaval pat, Sweden), the fish is cooked in an indirect apparatus heated by flue gases, and the coagulated material separated into an oil-stickwater phase, containing some suspended sludge, and a solid phase in a decanter centrifuge. The liquid phase from the decanter is separated into oil, stickwater and sludge by means of self-cleaning centrifuges. The solids are dehydrated in an indirect tube dryer heated by flue gases.

The compact arrangement, which does not require a steam boiler, has made this system attractive for installation on board the ship. Without evaporation, however, about 20 per cent to 30 per cent of the solids is lost with the stickwater.

PACKAGED FISHMEAL PLANTS

Packaged fishmeal plants of the traditional "press" type have also been developed for shipboard use. The processing capacities of compact plants range from 5 t to about 60 t of raw material per 24 h. Often the equipment is built in units to suit the requirements of the user and to facilitate installation. Such units may be cooker, press and dryer unit, separator and oil unit, evaporator unit, etc. A cooker, press and dryer unit, with the cooker at the top, the press below it and the dryer at the bottom. This unit has a processing capacity of 60 t of raw fish per 24 h.

MEAL PRODUCTION WITHOUT COOKING

A number of methods have been devised where the raw materials are dried without preliminary cooking. These are particularly suitable for lean fish (less than 3 per cent fat) and offal, but may, in some circumstances, also be adapted to treat fatty fish species.

By the Schlotterhose method, lean fish is dried in two stages, using indirect steam dryers. In stage 1, the moisture is generally reduced to about 55 per cent under reduced pressure. The low pressure eases the removal of vaporised water and the relatively low temperature prevents meal from sticking and reduces lump formation. In stage 2, when sticking is less of a problem, drying is completed at atmospheric pressure.

Other methods (for example, Vega) employ two direct rotary dryers operated in series at atmospheric pressure. The feed to the first dryer may consist of a mixture of wet, raw, lean fish and semi-dried material. Due to decreased moisture content through mixing, this compounded feed is less prone to sticking than the wet raw material alone. The semi-dried material is dehydrated to the desirable moisture content in the second rotary dryer.

Dry rendering methods are applicable to some oily raw materials, mainly fish offal. If, however, the raw material contains highly reactive oils, for example from pilchard, there is a risk of inefficient oil removal during pressing.

In one such method (Hartman) the raw material is dehydrated batchwise in a single stage steam dryer to the desired moisture content, whereupon the dried material is treated in a hydraulic press. In order to achieve good pressing, the drying must be properly controlled. If the dried material contains less than 8 per cent of water, there is a risk of inefficient oil removal. There is also a risk of oil darkening by direct contact between oil and meal during the drying process. Such degradation could limit the use of oil or require extra oil refinement and thus decrease profitability.

SIMPLIFIED WET PROCESSING

A simplified version of the traditional wet processing method has been developed in recent years. It is applicable only to lean fish, where equipment for oil recovery serves no purpose. Furthermore, it is appropriate only for plants with low rates of throughput, where capital costs have to be reduced to the lowest possible level.

The process starts with cooking the raw material in a conventional indirect steam cooker. The cooked material is then dried to whole meal in a dryer with rotating heating surfaces. Finally, the meal is milled to the desired particle size, and bagged. Since the evaporation of all the water removed is carried out in one stage, the heat economy is, of course, much inferior to that of the conventional method based on multiple stage evaporation of the stickwater.

This drawback, however, should be more than compensated for by reduced investments in equipment.

SOLVENT EXTRACTION

For certain special purposes, fish meal from oily fish may not be used because of extremely low tolerance to fat of marine origin. In such cases, the fat content of the meal can be further reduced or practically eliminated by extraction with solvents. This treatment introduces an extra cost that has proved difficult to retrieve from the actual markets, represented particularly by the pig-feeding industry. Solvent extraction for the production of an odourless fish meal for human consumption has so far had little success, but new approaches in this field are still being tried.

Dry extraction of meal is carried out in reaction vessels where meal and heated solvent (for example, ethanol, isopropanol or a hydrocarbon) are given sufficient time for adequate oil extraction. Reduction of the oil content from 10 per cent to 1 per cent in menhaden, pilchard or anchovy meal would require about 4 litres of hexane per kilogramme of meal. More thorough extraction is achieved by successive re-extractions, up to five times or more, or by counter current extraction. After extraction, the meal is put through a process of solvent removal, which may be effected by steam stripping followed by hot air ventilation in a dehydrator. The permissible amount of residual solvent in the meal differs with the type of solvent used, the limits for chlorinated hydrocarbons being very low.

The liquid withdrawn from the extractor is fractionated to separate the fish oil, expel the water and recover the solvent. The oil is frequently dark and polymerised and not suitable for refining for human consumption. The recovered solvent requires additional treatment before it may be re-used for extraction. One of the best methods of removing undesirable fishy odours from the solvent is to pass the vapours through a special grade of active carbon. The active carbon can be regenerated by steaming when saturated with these unpleasant odours. Relatively high temperature boiling solvents, such as ethanol, isopropanol and certain hydrocarbons, are usually employed to obtain more thorough extraction of phospholipids and other odorous and flavourous substances, and on grounds of safety. Wet extraction is the term given to the process of extracting oil and water from the wet raw material (fresh fish or presscake). From a technical standpoint, ethylene tetrachloride, which forms an azeotrope with water at 87.7°C, is suitable. At this temperature, water boils off together with the solvent, while the oil is simultaneously removed by extraction. As the tolerance for chlorinated solvents generally is very low, adequate removal of these solvents requires extra processing, details of which depend upon the ultimate use of the product. Because of these objections to chlorinated solvents, alcohols like ethanol and isopropanol present more acceptable alternatives, particularly where products for human consumption are concerned.

ENZYMATIC TREATMENT

Several methods have been developed for producing FPC or dried powder for animal feed by proteolysis of fresh whole fish. These methods are suitable for use on board the trawlers. In one method the fresh fish are pasteurised and put into a reaction vessel with papain (or other enzymes) at 55°C for about 1.5 h. The solubilised material is filtered and the cake dried and microground into a greyish product, which has a slight smell. The filtrate is treated in a separator and the oil withdrawn, while the aqueous phase (about 70 per cent) is dehydrated in a spray dryer. The product is light yellow and has a faint smell.

FISH SILAGE

There has been growing interest in producing liquid protein fodder from ensiled fish. Among the methods of ensilage used are treatments with mineral or organic acids (sulphuric or formic) and fermentation. In all methods the fish is ground and an example of production of acid silage is mixing with 3.5 per cent of formic acid in a holding tank. The mass is hydrolysed to a stable product at a pH of 4. If mineral acids are used, the acidity must be reduced to pH 2 for stability. In micro-biological methods the ground fish is mixed with a source of carbohydrate (for example, 20 per cent molasses) and a lactic acid producing micro-organism. Alcohol and lactic acid contribute to preservation. The silage products are generally dark brown semi-pastes, not unlike concentrated stickwater in appearance. They are convenient ingredients in liquid feeding compounds used locally, but the high water content makes long distance transport uneconomical.

FISH PROTEIN CONCENTRATES (FPC)

The term fish protein concentrate (FPC) usually refers to fish meal intended for human consumption. The term may apply to a variety of products that, broadly speaking, fall into two categories, FPC type A and FPC type B.

Under the term FPC type A we find fish meals that, through special processing techniques, have been made practically odour-free and tasteless. The most common method commercially used so far is based on wet extraction with isopropanol or ethanol. In spite of its high nutritional value, FPC type A has failed to find a market of commercial interest, largely because of poor so-called functional properties, but also because of the relatively high costs of production. Efforts to improve the functional properties of the product, especially by lowering the processing temperatures, are still being made. Whether this will contribute to the opening of an interesting market., remains to be seen. The FPC type B category is comprised of products where measures have not been taken to conceal that they originate from fish. Basically, FPC type B is produced by using the same processing principles as are used for ordinary fish meal, that is mechanical extraction of the oil and removal of water by evaporation and drying.

The main differences from traditional production methods are stricter requirements for fresh raw material and for better hygienic standards being applied to equipment and premises. Methods of handling all the way from catch to product, as well as the quality of the ultimate FPC, should also comply with the regulations of the food control and inspection authorities.

Experience has shown that the bacteriological standard tentatively agreed upon by internationally recognised experts, is difficult to reach by conventional factories, but improved equipment has been developed to facilitate cleaning and inspection. Although FPC type B is being used in relief programmes to improve nutrition in a number of developing countries, no product has so far attained the status of an internationally recognised commercial food commodity. Further development work is needed, firstly to define more precisely the quality criteria of products with the widest possible acceptability and, secondly, to develop technology that combines good performance with sound economics.

POLLUTION ABATEMENT

POLLUTION FROM EMISSION OF MALODOURS

Pollution by malodours from fishmeal factories is not considered hazardous to health, but is disagreeable, arid measures to diminish or eliminate inconveniences are required in most cases, specially if a factory is placed near denser population centres.

The human nose is very sensitive to bad smells and the smell impression is reduced to only half if the concentration of odorous components in a gas is reduced to 10 per cent; in other words, a 99.9 per cent reduction in concentration reduces the smell impression to only one eighth. A substance like trimethylamine may be detected at concentrations of down to 0.0002 ppm, which is the so-called threshold value. It is therefore imperative that the procedures for the abatement of malodours are very effective.

The odour from fresh fish of human consumption quality is generally acceptable, but during storage bacteriological and enzymatic decay result in the formation of highly obnoxious substances, such as trimethylamine, ethylmercaptan and even of poisonous ones such as hydrogensulphide, which have to be removed from the exhausts from the factory by special techniques. It is therefore important that the fish raw material is as fresh as possible before entering the process, preferably by preservation by means of ice and, in this connection, it should be remembered that the velocity of decay roughly doubles for each 4°C increase in temperature. During processing, malodours may be formed, specially by oxidation and pyrolysis in direct fired dryers.

In considering deodorising possibilities special attention should be given to the following factors:

- Freshness-of raw material as mentioned above;
- *Volumes and odour load of gases handled:* Gases with high concentrations of odorous substances result from the cooking, pressing and drying operations and their volumes should be kept to a minimum in order to facilitate treatment, but also in order to increase their value for waste heat recovery. Gases with low concentrations of odorous substances (and those which contain less disagreeable ones), but with rather large volumes, may result from conveyors, milling, meal cooling and room ventilation;
- *Centralisation of exhausts:* It is very important to collect the gases with high loads of odour in as few exhaust points as possible, preferably only one or two, in order to facilitate treatment. Special attention should also be given to diffuse exhausts at ground level which, for instance, may occur during unloading of raw fish;
- *Method of drying:* Effluent gases from direct rotary dryers can be difficult to handle because in some circumstances (poor fish, wet milling too finely, etc.) they are prone to form aerosols; and the vapours are emitted in larger amounts than from indirect dryers. In addition, if temperature is not carefully controlled, scorching of the fines of fish meal could occur, and this would greatly increase the problem of abating the odours;
- *Location of the fishmeal factory:* Factories in remote areas may operate without deodorising, while in some areas regulations may be strict. Clearly then, the solution in one area may not necessarily be the solution in another area;
- *Meteorological conditions:* Prevailing wind directions in connection with the pattern of wind velocity is important when considering the possibilities of efficient dilution in the atmosphere of gases with low odour content by exhaust from chimneys of reasonable height. Winds of low velocity carrying odours into populated areas will almost certainly result in many complaints.

In industry, several methods are practised to minimize odours that would otherwise escape to areas around the factories; it is virtually impossible to abate odours present within the factories.

Scrubbing of effluent gases in properly designed, water-film type scrubbing towers leads to a marked reduction in odour. As cooling condenses most of the water and other condensable vapours, it cuts down the gas volume by some 40 per cent and eliminates the characteristic white vapour from the stack. The vapours are admitted at the bottom and the cooling water (fresh or sea water) at the top of the tower. In order to product a large contact area between gas and cooling water, the tower is filled with packing material such as corrugated plates.

Vapour emissions may also be reduced by means of indirect scrubbing towers, that is the gases are not brought in direct contact with the cold water. The main advantage of this method is the conservation of water, as it may be recooled and re-used. The vapours escaping from the scrubber may be burnt in the steam boiler, or the odoriferous gases may be oxidised by chemical treatment with chlorine or other oxidising reagents.

High temperature combustion. Heating the gases to 750°C for about one second effectively destroys the content of malodorous components. This observation is the basis of the most widely used method of deodorisation today. All equipment from which heavily loaded gases may evolve, such as cookers, presses, dryers, tanks and centrifuges, are completely encapsulated and kept at a small under pressure by means of a ducting system, leading to a water scrubber followed by a fan, which in turn delivers the uncondensed gases to the boiler plant, where they are used for combustion in the furnace, the conditions in which comply fully with the above conditions. During starting and stopping of operations the supply of air to the boiler may be surplus to its requirements. The odorous gases will then need to be treated by some other method such as chemical inactivation.

Decades of operation of the system have proved that there is no additional risk of corrosion in boilers when using the washed gases as combustion air. Deodorising by combustion is of course specially applicable to plants operating with steam dryers. The system may also be applied to plants using direct fired dryers, but in these circumstances heat exchangers will normally need to be installed or, alternatively, the system may need to be converted to indirect hot air drying.

Surplus air with a low odour intensity such as from the milling and meal cooling plants, and which could not be fully used in the boiler, may in many cases after treatment in a scrubbing tower be satisfactorily dispersed by a chimney of sufficient height. Chemical inactivation has found some application in the fishmeal industry. The effluent gases leaving the scrubbing towers are brought into contact with strong oxidising agents such as chlorine releasing compounds or permanganate. These are applied in the gaseous or aqueous state. The use of chlorine gas is generally cheaper than other oxidising agents.

In view of the corrosive nature of chlorine in aqueous media, the contacting equipment should be made of stainless steel or reinforced plastics. Moreover, a final scrubbing stage is required, after oxidation, to remove all traces of chlorine from the treated vapours. The escape of chlorine to the atmosphere would be a hazard to health and indeed to life.

An effective deodoriser scrubber for a vapour discharge of about 1 200 m^3/min consists of four superimposed units, each having an internal cross-section of approximately 8.5 m^2, and having 144 corrugated sheets each (3 m long and 1 m wide). The sheets are placed vertically, with the corrugations horizontal (that is on their sides) and spaced about 1.25 cm apart. Water is sprayed downward on the sheets so that the water flows as a downward film and the vapours pass upward in countercurrent, and are chlorinated between the third and top stage of scrubbing. The total sea water consumption is about 4,500 litres/min. Electric power for pumping water and for air movement is of the order of 50 kW. The amount of chlorine used depends on factors such as the quality of the raw fish material and operating temperature.

In another chemical inactivation system the gases are washed with pH adjusted sodium hypochlorite solution in vertical wash towers of acid resisting fibreglass. In all chemical deodorising systems it is imperative that the pH and the proper concentration of active reagent are constantly controlled, possibly automatically, as the system may otherwise be utterly inefficient.

Catalytic combustion is also being attempted in the fishmeal industry. In the presence of platinum, alloys of platinum and metallic oxides, the malodorous components are decomposed at 350°C to 400°C.

The process may be carried out in two different ways:

1. The active material adsorbs the odorous components at normal temperatures and is then heated at intervals to the point of combustion;
2. The gases are continuously heated to the combustion temperature.

Catalytic combustion still needs to be justified by practical experience. Adsorption by active carbon. This method may be used for treatment of gases with low odour intensity. The applicability of the technique will largely depend upon economic factors which are largely determined by the number of possible reactivations of the active carbon charge.

POLLUTION FROM LIQUID EFFLUENTS

For environmental and economic reasons the organic effluent is kept to a minimum in properly managed factories. Unloading by pumping with addition of sea water and fluming will normally not be allowed inside harbours, for which reason dry unloading by elevators or pneumatic unloaders is preferred in such places. Polluted water, originating from cleaning fish holds, pound boards, etc., can be minimized by using high pressure spraying equipment and can be cleaned in strainers followed by grease separators. In cases where fresh water is used for cleaning, the effluent can be pumped to the blood water tank of the factory and thus enter into the normal production. This procedure could also, in many cases, be applied to blood water from the bottom of the fishing boats.

Pollution of fresh water from factory operations occurs from the centrifuges, pumps and specially from the cleaning of equipment. When high pressure spraying is used for the last mentioned purpose, the quantity will be rather small and it can therefore be collected and pumped to the blood water tank for further processing. This in fact means that the stickwater concentrator is the ultimate purifier for the fresh water effluent. Ample capacity, however, is normally at hand and the contaminating dry matter and oil, which would otherwise be a nuisance, are thereby recovered.

Sea water is used in large quantities in the condensers of the stickwater concentrators and in the deodorisers. Contamination in the effluent stems from volatile components in the raw fish, from dust particles from the dryers and meal equipment and from possible carry-over from the concentrators. It appears that minimising of the pollution is directly connected with strict control of raw fish quality and with the efficiency of cyclone and concentrator operations. Even if the sea water effluent represents by far the largest part of the total liquid pollution, it usually causes no problem, as the polluting components are easily decomposed, as their concentration is normally low and as the receiver conditions in the sea are generally favourable. In cases of low depth and poor current flow authorities may demand that a pipeline should be laid out to a certain distance and/or depth.

Spent caustic solutions used for cleaning concentrator calandrias and cookers can be gradually discharged together with the seawater effluent or possibly treated in a municipal effluent plant. Stickwater should, for economic and environmental reasons, never be discharged to the sea or to rivers. The contamination from a 500-t/24 h fishmeal plant that does not utilise stickwater may easily correspond to one million personal equivalents in sewage terms.

INSTRUMENTATION

The industry is conscious of the importance of quality and this has contributed to the increasing use of instrumentation for the automatic control of process machinery and for monitoring and recording performance.

The cooker and the press may be operated at controlled loads by level control of the material in their feed tubes. The temperature of the hot air going into the direct dryer is generally maintained constant by automatic adjustments of the fuel supply. Automatic temperature control, and even automatic fire extinguishers are also available. Stable operation of the ventilation system may be maintained through pressure control of the air in the exit compartment. Pressure deviations may be corrected by manually or automatically adjusting the air shutter in the exhaust tube. Stickwater concentrators may, in practice, be fully automated. The finally extracted concentrate, the solubles, is continuously controlled for constant viscosity and signals of deviations from the setpoint act on the extraction pump, the revolutions of which are steplessly variable. Alterations in the extracted volume will in turn be automatically compensated for in the individual stages of the plant as these are furnished with level controllers acting on the valves and on transfer pumps between the stages. Great efforts are being made to effect continuous measurement of the moisture content in the finished fish meal and, based on this, to arrive at complete automation of the whole operation by use of Programmable Logic Control systems. This development will be followed with great interest.

STEAM PRODUCTION AND POWER PLANT

Steam production is an essential auxiliary process in meal manufacture because of the steam requirements of the main machines, cookers, presses, steam dryers and evaporators. Principally, two different arrangements for steam supply are utilised: the oil-fired steam boiler (the most widely used; at variable loads it delivers steam at constant pressure, and is automatically controlled) and the supply of steam together with electrical power. The joint generation of electricity and heat is advantageous in regions with unsteady, inadequate and expensive electric power.

The principle of this arrangement is to let steam at a pressure of about 40 kg/cm^2, expand in a turbine to about 10 kg/cm^2. The work of expansion is converted by a dynamo into electric power while the low pressure steam is applied as required for heating processes in the factory. Back pressure turbines capable of generating 15 to 60 MW electricity are available. In regions where the electricity supply is ample and regular, the combined production of steam and electricity is normally not advisable due to difficulties in balancing the consumption and supply of the two. For large steam boilers the economic advantages of installing refinements such as economisers, combustion air pre-heating, blow-down heat recovery, and so on, should be considered. Furthermore, the use of alternative fuels such as coal, wood or natural gas may, in several places, prove more economical.

CONSUMPTION OF FUEL, ELECTRIC POWER AND WATER

The following figures for fuel, electric power and water consumption of fishmeal plants are based on data from existing plants with indirect steam drying. The figures are to be considered, as only indicative since they may vary with many factors such as temperature and oil content of the raw fish, the seawater temperature, the number of stages in evaporation plants and several other plant design features.

FUEL OIL CONSUMPTION

The usual type of fishmeal plant with indirect drying requires fuel only for steam production in the boiler. The price of fuel oil varies greatly over the world. Reasonable quotations may, however, often be obtained as fishmeal plants are usually situated near sea ports, and expensive land transportation costs will not be incurred. The high energy prices ruling during the last decade have inspired most factories to check carefully the opportunities which are present for reducing fuel consumption by improving boiler efficiency, insulation of hot surfaces, recuperation of heat in condensates as well as increasing the number of stages in concentration plants.

A new range of equipment has been developed for utilising the heat in the vapours from drying and evaporating activities. These vapours are characterised by high calorific values but at rather low temperatures, and their application to heating raw fish and to preconcentrating stickwater has therefore demanded the design of special types of cookers and evaporators. A considerable number of items of such equipment for waste heat recovery are today working satisfactorily in Scandinavian factories.

Table. Consumption of Fuel Oil

Size of Plant: Raw Material (ton/24 h)	Fuel Oil Consumption Per ton of Raw Material (kg)		
	Presscake Meal	Whole Meal	
	Without Evaporation Plant	With Evaporation Plant	With Additional Waste Recovery Heat
10-60	35	55	-
100-200	34	50	44
250-500	33	48	41
More than 500	30	45	38

ELECTRIC POWER CONSUMPTION

Fair sized fishmeal plants usually receive their power supply as high voltage current from a municipal power works and have power substations of their own.

Table. Electric Power Consumption

Size of Plant: Raw Material (ton/24 h)	kWh Consumption Per ton of Raw Material	
	Without Evaporation Plant	With Evaporation Plant
10- 60	30	35
100- 200	28	33
250- 500	26	31
More than 500	25	30

WATER CONSUMPTION

Fishmeal plants require water for the following purposes:

- As feed water for the boiler;
- For operation of the sludge separators;

- To clean machinery and tanks;
- To clean floors, raw fish pits, etc.;
- For condenser of concentration unit;
- For cooling and deodorising;
- For staff bathroom and canteen.

For purposes (a), (b), (c) and (g) - water has to be fresh.
For purposes (d), (e) and (f) - water could be sea water.

Table. Water Consumption

Size of Plant: Raw Material (ton/24 h)	For Purpose:		
	a-d m3/t	e m3/t	f m3/t
10-60	0.50	9	22
100-200	0.40	7	15
250-500	0.35	7-5	12
More than 500	0.30	5	11

THE PRODUCTS

The two commercially significant products of the Industry are a protein-rich meal and oil.. In 1983 the values of the world production of these products were around US$ 2500 million and US$ 400million, respectively. The meal has a high content of protein which is of high nutritional quality, and is used to supplement other proteins, especially vegetable proteins, in diets for farmed animals.

The oil is used principally for human consumption in margarines and edible oils, following refining and hardening. There is interest currently in the direct human consumption of refined fish oils with a high content of n-3 fatty acids for the prevention and treatment of coronary heart disease.

FISH MEAL

Fishmeal Production

There has been little change in overall world production (around 5 million tons) in the past five years, though there have been changes in certain parts of the world.

The most noteworthy changes have been declining production in Peru and Iceland and increasing production in Chile. Adverse sea temperatures off the coast of Peru (El Niño effect) have reduced fish stocks, resulting in reduced fishmeal production.

About 90 per cent of world fishmeal production is from oily fish species such as mackerel, pilchard, capelin and menhaden. Less than 10 per cent is from white fish offal such as from cod and haddock. Only 1 per cent is produced from other sources such as shellfish and whales. The majority of fish meal is “whole”, that is, only water and some oil are extracted from the fish.

Quality of Fish Meal Related to Raw Material and Conditions of Manufacture and Storage

The quality of the protein in fish, that is the make-up of amino acids in relation to an animal's requirement, and their availability to the animal, are high, particularly in whole fish.

The quality of the protein in skin, connective tissue and bone is lower; consequently, the quality of the protein in offal is somewhat lower than that in whole fish. For example, the proportion of the essential amino acids methionine and lysine in the protein in white fish offal is approximately 10 per cent lower than that in whole oily fish such as anchovy and pilchard.

Table. Fishmeal: World Production (in '000 t)

Country or area	1976	1977	1978	1979	1980	1981	1982	1983	1984
World	49970 1	4571618	4899371	5067071	4959455	5050932	5389253	5229731	5944193
Africa									
Angola	5000b/	3500b/	5000b/	4000b/	5188	5202	5205	5000b/	3000b/
Cape Verde	204	102	23	87	232	143	174	137	165
Cote d'Ivoire	1388	1781	1337	2222	2303	2620	3074	3700	3300b/
Libya	300b/	82	185	147	160	296	261	244	250b/
Mauritania	1742	6400	8000	3150	8849	5862	13525	31064	22372
Mauritius	...	214	270	302	285	309	348	562	558
Morocco	25379	12700b/	21228	17400b/	22600b/	22000b/	17500b/	26900b/	27000b/
Senegal	1855	4377	5681	7896	6646	5037	2741	4630	2244b/
South Africa	211800	176268	190639	174442	154904	155385	142453	172316	118600b/
Tunisia						60b/	400b/	300b/	260b/
Total	247668	205424	205424	209646	201167	196914	185681	244853	177749
America, North									
Bermuda	18700	33400	25190	17000b/	15000b/	1000b/	-	-	-
Canada	59900	56396	74295	68782	66361	76207	63460	61223	63201
Cuba	9300	7300	8900	4900	8486	6020	8297	5685	5996
El Salvador	70	79	42	-	76	806	166	319	-
Greenland	966	1718	1578	1477	1457	1477	1814	1497	592
Mexico	37747	44925	53577	68753	99897	106604	98496	64244	56170
Panama	23142	30947	17584	26041	35200	22080	15070	26084	21860
St Pier Miqu	600	500b/	500b/	482	646	1069	954	809	1165
USA	403700	367900	476700	461700	449800	405635	477119	490131	444693
Total	554125	543165	658366	649135	676923	620898	665376	649992	593677
America, South									

Note: a/ Meals, solubles and similar feedingstuffs or aquatic animal origin; including fish meals from "white fish", oily fish and fish solubles. Whale meal and solubles, crustacean and seal meal and fish silages are also included.

b/ FAO estimates

Freshness of raw material is important in its effect on the quality of the protein in the end product. The importance of minimizing the time between catching fish and processing, and of keeping the fish at low temperatures by icing has already been mentioned as a means of reducing spoilage. As a guide to freshness of raw material the content of total volatile nitrogen in the fish can be measured; it should be less than 80 mg^{-N} per 100 g raw material.

Argentina	21405	23996	20199	33101	28211	22000	21000	17000	12500
Brazil	20200	26261	17987	20230	26398	26566	25069	29100b/	31100b/
Chile	250441	251999	374675	512162	571409	688154	795707	827465	1022727
Colombia	1918	2449	2000b/	2000b/	4500b/	1599	703	651	47
Ecuador	42700	69800	100000	77481	102933	123386	114061	21889	132748
Peru	886372	496954	669658	687953	458125	478277	665499	219325	492000
Uruguay	2191	2900	4921	8635	8255	10492	7257	11787	10869
Venezuela	10800	5887	5791	5285	6133	4206	5502	4639	5107
Total	1236027	880246	1195231	1346847	1205964	1354680	1634798	1131856	1707098
ASIA									
China	...	...	...	...	...	...	...	50000	53000
Hong Kong	1300b/	1300b/	1400b/	1500b/	2000b/	2100b/	2300b/	2400b/	2550b/
India	20400b/	21500b/	17800b/	20400b/	21300b/	27500b/	23000b/	25000b/	24000b/
Indonesia	2385	3961	900	1209	1072	1300	2481	3967	4500
Japan	867580	851766	884264	883670	869799	902089	1006041	1135121	1262649
Korea, Rep.	13395	13560	21822	17715	9616	15221	24860	33035	28228
Malaysia	7800	11935	12159	21120	32973	42661	36290	51823	31493
Other nei	4797	2057	2037	3233	3000	2259	2598	836	679
Pakistan	11000	17300	20100	27700	25600	26300	29600	28300	32655
Singapore	714	1286	1309	3319	1197	2417	2673	3223	3158
Sri Lanka	203	171	204	214	94	147	126	459	157
Thailand	119880	141600	218165	186437	194200	201701	211814	204811	219763b/
Turkey	2500b/	2800	7000	12570	13250	15000	13850	19000	40000b/
Yemen, Dem.	-	1544	1288	626	1315	1378	-	-	-
Total	1051954	1070780	1188448	1179713	1175416	1240073	1355633	1569658	1701069
Europe									
Belgium	3300	3000	2500	2500	1900	1900	1900	1500	1890
Bulgaria	10300	9000	6500	5000	7800	6500	7400	9399	8254
Denmark	349656	316209	278076	336096	357933	337788	319640	321540	318790
Faeroe Islands	28631	27895	24318	19386	19535	20086	16371	24419	24881
Finland	6	7000	10000	10000	6000	4000	4000	2000	1200
France	18223	22971	24990	21993	14039	15963	17509	18392	21502
Germany, Fed. Rep.	53031	48550	44690	40008	36992	38514	36882	35803	36782
Iceland	110531	162667	202165	207860	173009	148436	51062	68077	171974
Ireland	2033	1889	2764	1551	2041	1554	1881	1363	1233
Italy	1215	1030	4830	6650	6300	7565	9092	3291	3554
Norway	464000	464800	331524	327940	297700	299500	284301	346858	286589
Poland	58700	66958	56637	64809	76799	58316	46216	83405	81952
Portugal	7692	8316	8409	11390	11870	19531	28805	14400b/	10000b/
Romania	7500	7800	8000	11294	9533	10942	12401	11653	10480
Spain	38348	37654	34116	339.78	40108	37178	38952	28874	37137
Sweden	15205	10252	9483	8050	11519	13128	11351	11461	11500b/
UK	81000	78000	66000	58600	68300	59735	56437	54200	55000
Yugoslavia	1502	1997	2355	2519	2549	2366	2697	2260	2073
Total	1256867	1275988	1117357	1169624	1143927	1083002	946838	1038895	1084791
Oceania									
Australia	4800	4100	3847	937	451	325	...	...	...
Fiji	130	305	400b/	500b/	357	640	717	960b/	683
New Zealand	-	-	-	-	-	-	-	-	3793
Total	4930	4405	4247	1437	808	965	717	960	4476
USSR									
USSR	645430	591610	503359	510669	555250	554400	600210	605200	673570
Total	645430	591610	503359	510669	555250	554400	600210	605200	673570

Process control in the factory is necessary for the manufacture of high quality fish meal. Excessive temperatures (over 120OC) for prolonged periods in the cooking, evaporating and drying should be avoided since fish proteins are sensitive to excessive heat. It has been shown that the rate of loss in available lysine is less than 1 per cent per hour at temperatures below 120°C; above this temperature the rate increases very rapidly (10 per cent per hour at 140°C). The meal should be allowed to cool gradually with air circulation, that is, controlled "curing" after leaving the dryer. Use of an antioxidant such as ethoxyquin at 700 ppm is desirable for the oily fish species, especially in hot climates, for the purpose of stabilising the oil in the fish meal by preventing oxidation. Rapid oxidation in fish meal can result in overheating in the stored product. Use of antioxidant is required by the International Maritime Organisation if fish meal is to be shipped in a low hazard category. Correct "curing" and/or antioxidant treatment of fish meal will produce a product which can be stored indefinitely under dry conditions without deterioration.

During cooking and drying, any harmful bacteria in fish are killed. Subsequently, contamination of fish meal is possible; good hygiene is necessary at all stages in handling and storage if this is to be avoided.

Salmonella Control

Precautions must particularly be taken against Salmonella contamination. This organism is destroyed in the cooking plus pressing process provided the temperature is raised above 80°C, but poor hygiene beyond this point could result in re-infection of the meal. It must be stressed that although high air temperatures are reached in the dryers, the fish material in the dryer may not reach a sufficiently high temperature for sufficient time to destroy Salmonella.

To minimize the risk, the manufacturers should observe the following precautions:

- The land around the factory should be well kept and regularly maintained to keep down rodents, birds, flies and all insects. Very strict control in this respect is necessary in areas where fish material is processed and fish meal stored.
- Ventilators and other openings in factory and storage buildings should be protected by insect screens and rat wire.
- In order to keep the product dry, storage buildings should have concrete floors and leak-proof walls and roofs and, if necessary, roof insulation to avoid condensation and drip; conveyors should have covers, and
- Walkways to storage areas should be kept clean and foot bath mats charged with a disinfectant. Such as phenolic or quaternary ammonium compounds, should be available for personnel at storage entries.

In summary, it is desirable to keep the wet and dry areas of the plant separate and to reduce to a minimum the passage of personnel and equipment from one section to the other. A proper factory cleaning scheme is necessary. Empty storage bins and unloading areas should be cleaned as soon as possible after use. Process machinery should be cleaned regularly by high pressure jets of hot water and detergent solutions. Stickwater concentrate and decanter sludge must be heated to 93°C or more before adding to the presscake.

For about three quarters of an hour after the start of operations, while the machinery is warming up to normal operating temperature, all presscake produced must be returned to the cooker intake for recooking and repressing in case contamination might have occurred.

Should Salmonella, nevertheless, be detected in fish meal, the contaminated lots must be disinfected, for example in special apparatus in which the meal is heated at about 90°C with live steam for 10 to 15 min and then redried.

Alternatively, biocides such as formic and propionic acids can be used to treat infected fish meal. These are expensive processes, however, and it is far more economical to comply with the outlined precautions. Another way of ridding infected fish meal of Salmonella is to expose it to suitable doses of ionising radiation. This will obviously depend on the availability of irradiation facilities and should, perhaps, be regarded as a method for the future.

The Nutrient Content of Fish Meal

As well as being a rich source of high quality protein, fish meals have a relatively high energy content and are rich in important minerals such as phosphorus, in B vitamins and in essential fatty acids. Fish meals made from offal have a higher content of ash and a lower content of protein. All values are given on an "as received" basis. The protein figures given in Table below represent average values; a range of ±2 per cent to ±3 per cent protein units is possible. This range can be greater for offal meals. It is recommended that the amino acid content of a fish meal be adjusted for protein content, using the figures in Tables a and b; for example, for an offal meal with only 59 per cent protein the lysine content can be calculated as follows:

$$\text{Lysine content} = 4.49 \times 59 \div 65 = 4.08\%$$

Similarly, where protein content is higher than shown in the table, amino acid contents should be adjusted upward. The energy content of fish meals depends upon the protein and oil content. Where these differ from those shown in Table a, they may be adjusted by using the regression equations as follows:

For poultry:

$$\text{ME adjusted} = \text{ME tabulated} + (F_a - F_t) \div 100 \times \text{ME fat} + (P_a - P_t) \div 100 \times \text{ME protein}$$

where F_a and F_t are the actual and tabulated fishmeal fat (oil) contents, and P_a and P_t are the actual and tabulated fishmeal protein contents.

$$\text{ME fish fat} = 27.0 \text{ MJ/kg}$$

$$\text{ME fish protein} = 16.5 \text{ MJ/kg}$$

Worked example: South American fish meal 68 per cent protein, 10 per cent oil

$$\text{ME adjusted} = 13.2 + (10 - 9) \div 100 \times 27.0 + (68 - 65) \div 100 \times 16.5 = 14.0 \text{ MJ kg}$$

Table. a

	Wheat	**Barley**	**Soya 45% protein**	**White Fish Meal a/**	**Herring Type Fish Meals b/**	**S. American Type Fish Meals c/**
Proximate Analysis (%)						
Moisture	12.5	12.5	10.5	10.0	8.0	10.0
Crude protein	10.9	11.1	45.9	65.0	72.0	65.0
Crude fat	1.8	0.9	1.4	5.0	9.0	9.0
Crude ash	1.6	2.5	5.9	20.0	10.0	16.0
Crude fibre	1.8	4.1	5.7	0	0	0
Energy Content						
Poultry						
M.E. MJ/kg	12.5	11.7	9.0	12.1	14.0	13.2
Pigs						
M.E. MJ/kg	14.7	13.2	15.6	15.6	18.5	16.8
Ruminants d/						
M.E. MJ/kg	11.6	11.2	11.7	13.6	16.4	13.1

Note:

a/ Produced from offal and whole fish

b/ Generic term including whole fish of species capelin, mackerel, sprat, sand eels, Norway pout. Herring type meals may have a protein content in the range of 68 per cent to 74 per cent and a fat content in the range of 7 per cent to 12 per cent.

For fish meals of different protein content, the total content of an amino acid can be assumed to be proportional to the protein content, the amino acid make-up of fish protein being similar; *e.g.*, herring type meal 72 per cent protein: lysine 5.56 per cent, methionine 2.16 per cent; herring type meal 68 per cent protein: lysine 5.25 per cent, methionine 2.04 per cent

c/ Fish meals made primarily from whole anchoveta; fish meals made from whole sardine or horse mackerel are similar in nutrient analysis

d/ Rowett Research Institute Feed Evaluation Unit, Aberdeen, UK

For pigs:

$$\text{DE adjusted} = \text{DE tabulated} + (F_a - F_t) \div 100 \times \text{DE fish fat} + (P_a - P_t) \div 100 \times \text{DE fish protein}$$

$$\text{DE fish fat} = 32.0 \text{ MJ/kg}$$

$$\text{DE fish protein} = 23.0 \text{ MJ/kg}$$

Worked example: Offal meal 47 per cent protein, 4 per cent oil

DE adjusted = 15.6 + (5 – 4) ÷ 10 × 32.0 + (47 – 65) ÷ 100 × 23.0 = 11,2 MJ/kg

(Further details of the nutrient analysis of fish meals are available from the IAFMM, Hoval House, Mutton Lane, Potters Bar, Herts EN6 3AR, UK.) The nutrient values given above are based on fish meals of good protein and fat quality.

Table b

	Wheat	Barley	Soya 45%Protein	White Fish Meal	Herring Type Fish Meals	S. American Type Fish Meals
Total Amino Acids a/ (%)						
Lysine	0.31	0.43	2.88	4.49	5.47	5.07
Methionine	0.18	0.20	0.63	1.69	2.16	1.95
Methionine a/						
Cystine	0.34	0.47	1.31	2.29	2.88	2.60
Tryptophan	0.12	0.15	0.58	0.61	0.83	0.78
Histidine	0.24	0.26	1.12	1.31	1.74	1.59
Leucine	0.73	0.83	3.42	4.21	5.40	4.98
Isoleucine	0.41	0.45	2.20	2.41	3.23	3.06
Arginine	0.51	0.63	3.24	4.14	4.21	3.81
Phenylalanine	0.48	0.62	2.20	2.14	2.82	2.75
Tyrosine	0.33	0.40	1.58	1.69	2.25	2.22
Threonine	0.33	0.42	1.89	2.50	3.07	2.82
Valine	0.50	0.65	2.25	2.91	3.90	3.46
Glycine	0.43	0.48	1.89	6.45	4.30	3.68
Serine	0.54	0.55	2.52	3.09	2.75	2.51
Crude protein	9.00	11.90	45.00	65.00	72.00	65.00

Note: a/Amino acids in fish meals and soyabean meal are equally available

Table. C

	Wheat	Barley	Soya 45% Protein	White Fish Meal	Herring Type Fish Meals	S. American Type Fish Meals
Minerals						
Calcium%	0.04	0.06	0.37	8.00	2.00	4.00
Phosphorus % (total)	0.29	0.35	0.55	4.80	1.90	2.60
Phosphorus % (available)	0.12	0.14	0.22	4.80	1.90	2.60
Sodium %	0.01	0.02	0.05	1.30	0.70	0.87
Chloride %	0.01	0.01	0.03	2.00	1.03	1.82
Magnesium %	0.12	0.11	0.30	0.15	0.11	0.25
Potassium %	0.50	0.50	1.90	0.90	1.20	0.70
Selenium ppm (mg/kg)	0.20	0.40	0.60	1.50	2.20	1.40
Iron ppm (mg/kg)	33.00	38.00	36.00	300.00	150.00	246.00
Copper ppm (mg/kg)	5.00	4.00	41.00	7.00	5.00	11.00
Zinc ppm (mg/kg)	29.00	31.00	67.00	100.00	120.00	111.00
Manganese ppm (mg/kg)	38.00	19.00	36.00	10.00	2.00	10.00

Table. D

	Wheat	Barley	Soya 45% Protein	White Fish Meal	Herring Type Fish Meals	S. American Type Fish Meals
			Vitamins			
Choline ppm (mg/kg)	730.00	110.00	2840.00	4400.00	4400.00	4400.00
Panthothenic acid ppm (mg/kg)	13.00	6.60	14.50	15.00	30.60	9.30
Riboflavin ppm (mg/kg)	1.10	1.30	4.00	6.50	7.30	6.60
Nicotinic acid (Niacin) ppm (mg/kg)	58.00	52.00	32.00	50.00	126.00	95.00
Folic acid ppm (mg/kg)	0.40	0.60	3.60	0.50	0.50	0.16
B12 ppm (mg/kg)	0.00	0.00	0.00	0.07	0.25	0.18
Biotin ppm (mg/kg)	0.10	0.14	0.25	0.08	0.42	0.26
Pyridoxine ppm (mg/kg)	4.00	2.90	8.00	3.30	3.70	3.50
			Essential Fatty Acids (%)			
	0.60	0.90	0.40	2.30	4.50	4.50

The Role of Fish Meal in Animal Feeds

Fish meal is used in feeds for poultry, pigs, ruminants, farmed fish and fur producing animals. It increases productivity and improves the efficiency with which feed is converted to animal produce (feed conversion). It is of special value in diets for young animals, for example in broiler starter diets, diets for early weaned pigs, and for farmed fish and fur producing animals.

Fish meal is particularly beneficial in situations which are less than ideal, for example, where feed mixing and quality control of ingredients is poor, where husbandry standards are less than ideal and where disease problems are prevalent.

In diets for very young animals such as early weaned pigs (weaned before four weeks of age), ruminants, fish and fur animals, it is recommended that special quality fish meal is used. It should be made from very fresh raw material and, for ruminants, have a low content of soluble nitrogen. Ruminants can make better use of forage if fish meal is included in their diets, particularly if forage is a major part of their feed.

Fish meal has been shown to be superior to other proteins, specially vegetable proteins in supplying a high quality protein, a large part of which escapes breakdown in the rumen. As well as providing a high quality protein with a near ideal balance of amino acids for farmed fish, antioxidant treated fish meal provides a valuable source of n-3 long chain fatty acids which are essential for fish such as trout, salmon, carp, catfish and eels.

Commercial Value of Fish Meal

Although often traded on a price per unit of protein, the commercial value of fish meal is determined not only on the basis of protein. Its value is affected by fishmeal supply, price of other proteins and, of course, demand. The demand for fish meal and the use to which it is put reflects the special nutritional properties referred to earlier. Many feed formulators calculate a value for fish meal using linear programmes on computers which take into account all its nutrients. In some diets which have a high nutrient concentration, for example starter diets in intensive farming systems, raw materials with a high nutrient concentration are preferred; this is taken into account in computer formulated feeds.

For these diets the higher protein fish meals (65 per cent protein and above) attract a premium. Most feed formulators throughout the world ensure that fish meal inclusion does not fall below a minimum level in certain diets, for example for young poultry, young pigs, fish and breeding stock. The prices of fish meal (65 per cent protein) and soyabean meal (44 per cent protein) in Europe in the past five years. These prices reflect world prices. Although the prices of proteins vary and prediction of future protein prices is difficult, it is anticipated that the price ratio fish meal (65 per cent protein): soyabean meal (44 per cent protein) is likely to be in the range of 1.8 to 2.0. continuing the trend of the past two years.

FISH OIL

Fish oil, previously the main product from raw materials having high oil contents, is now of secondary value. The product, however, is versatile and finds many applications in the food and technical industries and is still of considerable economic importance to producers.

FISH OIL COMPOSITION

The oils contain mainly triglycerides of fatty acids (glycerol combined with three similar or different acid molecules) with variable amounts of phospholipids, glycerol ethers and wax esters.

Table. Prices of Fish Meal and Soyabean Meal a/Yearly Averages of Weekly Quotations

	US$/ton		
Year	Fish Hamb	Soya Rott	Fish Hamb b/ as % of Soya Rott c/
1980	504.4	258.6	197.8
1981	467.5	252.7	184.8
1982	352.9	219.9	161.9
1983	452.6	237.8	193.8
1984	410.1	216.3	189.3d/

Note:

a/ Oil World Weekly, Hamburg

b/ Fish meal, 64-65 per cent any origin, CIF Hamburg (interior price after deduction of a calculated wholesale cost after conversion at current DM/ US$ exchange rate)

c/ Soyabean meal, 44 per cent US, CIF Rotterdam.

d/ Seven monthly figures

Table. Production of Fish Body Oils (in '000 t)

Country	1968	1970	1975	1980	1983a/
Norway	236	180	176	182	213
Japan	40	87	136	223	335
USA	78	93	111	142	167
South Africa	125	79	42	38	38
Denmark	70	51	107	123	81
USSR	57	60	NA	39	56
Peru	292	311	212	78	6
Iceland	16	7	27	82	24
Canada	34	27	NA	12	9
Germany, Fed. Rep.	15	14	NA	10	17
UK	0	0	NA	14	9
Morocco	11b/	5b/	NA	4	5
Chile	34	23	24	111	57
Sweden	4	3	NA	5	3
Faeroe Islands	7	6	NA	7	7
Spain	4	4	NA	7	5
Mexico	1	1	NA	17	12
World	1041	971	1021	1141	1115

Note:

a/ Provisional data derived from miscellaneous sources

b/ Exports

NA: Not available

It is characteristic of the oils that they contain a wide range of long-chain fatty acids with the number of carbon atoms ranging mainly from 14 to 22, and high degree of reactivity (unsaturation) ranging up to six double bonds per molecule.

Fish Oil Properties

The complex nature of fish oil depends upon a number of factors. The fatty acid patterns of the oils vary widely with fish species and, to some extent, with the composition of the plankton and the time of year. These influence the properties of oils both in regard to edible as well as technical applications. The oils contain variable, but small amounts of unsaponifiable components, such as hydrocarbons, fatty alcohols, waxes and ethers, and these also influence the properties of the oils to some extent.

The condition of the fish at the time of processing affects the oil physically, chemically and nutritionally. Fish of poor quality yield a malodorous oil with high contents of free fatty acids (FFA) and sulphur. These latter undesirable properties affect both the economic value and the application of the oil. Some sulphur compounds have an inactivating effect on the nickel catalyst used for hydrogenation (called "poisoning of the catalyst"), thus the catalyst has to be replaced frequently.

In order to manufacture oil of desirable properties, one should observe the following:

- The fish should be as fresh as possible;
- The oil should be cooled before delivery to the storage tank and should be pumped in near the bottom of the tank (not right at the bottom) and removed from the top. The sludge and water should be regularly drained from the bottom to prevent an increase in FFA during storage.

Edible Applications of Fish Oils

Their nutritional and physical properties have made hardened fish oils attractive constituents in diets for man. Hardened fish oil is used almost entirely in margarines and shortenings. Margarines prepared from hardened vegetable oil sometimes recrystallise on storage.

This makes the margarine crumbly and hard. Because fish oils have a widely varied chain length, margarines prepared from them have an excellent plastic consistency. Shortening and bakery margarines have properties different from those of table margarines. The value of hardened fish oillies in its creaming power, particularly in cake making.

Refined fish oils are rich in polyunsaturated fatty acids of the linolenic acid family. Current medical research suggests that these fatty acids might have a unique role to play in prevention of coronary artery disease and the growth of different types of cancers. More clinical studies will have to be undertaken before positive health claims can be made.

Technical Applications of Fish Oils

The highly unsaturated properties make the oils (and particularly their highly unsaturated fractions) suitable for a number of technical applications, particularly as drying oils and varnishes. The saturated fatty acid fraction is a disadvantage for these purposes and must be reduced. Several specialised processes for this reduction are available.

Fish oils are a significant source for the production of fatty acids with a wide spectrum of chain lengths. From these acids are produced several types of metallic soaps, some of which are used in lubricating greases while others are used as waterproofing agents. Small quantities of fatty; acids are used pharmaceutically and medicinally, and for scientific research purposes.

Commercial Value of Fish Oils

The market value of fish oil depends on its chemical analysis. Normally, a basic sales value is established for an oil containing a certain level of free fatty acids (2 per cent to 3 per cent), unsaponifiable matter (3.5 per cent), and water and dirt (0.3 per cent). If these levels are exceeded, the price is reduced accordingly. The price may also be reduced if the oil is dark coloured or malodorous.

Fish Oil Quality

A number of chemical, physical and sensory methods have been developed for the assessment of quality. Analytical work is made difficult due to the labile nature of the unsaturated fatty acids, so oil sampled should be stored at low temperatures in an inert atmosphere before analysis. Saturated oil fractions tend to precipitate during cold seasons in large storage vessels. This necessitates thorough mixing of the oil before sampling.

The test methods employed by the user of fish oil for hardening purposes are often divided into two groups, the first being applied on receipt of a consignment to check the fundamental parameters and the second, more detailed, examination as soon as possible thereafter, but in any case before the oil is used in the refinery. The purpose of this second examination is to determine refining procedures.

The initial testing involves the following:

- *Moisture:* For contractual reasons and because moisture in the oilleads to the formation of rust in storage tanks with consequent accelerated oxidation of the oil catalysed by iron. Thus, high moisture may be a contributory cause of high oxidation levels and a high trace iron content, which can also lead to colour problems in refining. Moisture in the oil is also responsible for the increase of FFA during storage.
- *Dirt:* Usually only visually, unless excessive.
- *Appearance:* Lovibond colour has not been found to be useful, but a golden brown oil is usually easy to refine whereas a dull brown oil gives difficulties. A frothiness can indicate a high phosphorus content and thus a tendency to emulsification problems.
- *FFA:* For contractual reasons and because this is still the most reliable parameter for oil quality and yield assessment.
- *Soap:* To check that the oil is not a blend of neutralised and crude oils.
- *Iodine value (I.V.):* For hydrogen usage and to ensure that the I.V. is in the region expected for the type of oil stated, although these limits are very wide.

The second examination normally includes:

- *Peroxide Value (P.V.) and Anisidine Value (A.V.):* To establish primary and secondary oxidation product levels. These compounds, with others resulting from further decomposition, are responsible for the rancid flavours that develop. Of the two values the A.V. is the more indicative of quality state.
- *Ultra Violet (U.V.) Extinction Values at 233 nm and 269 nm:* These figures quantify the conjugated dienes and trienes, respectively, and are related to oxidation levels, but increases in these values are also obtained when an oil is overheated, resulting in colour fixation.
- *Trace Metals. Iron and Copper:* Both metals are pro-oxidants, that is catalysts for fat oxidation, copper being ten times more active than iron. It is, however, unusual to find high copper levels, but high iron levels occur all too frequently.
- A further problem with iron is that when sulphur is also present a darkening of the oil colour frequently occurs during deodorisation. The trace metal level can be reduced using acids such as phosphoric and citric in the refining.
- *Sulphur:* The effect of sulphur as a catalyst poison is recognised, but the poisoning effect depends on the chemical form in which the sulphur is present, and this is not as yet fully understood. All that can be said is that below 30 ppm in the crude oil (15 ppm in the neutralised oil) sulphur is not a problem, but that a significant poisoning effect is often encountered at higher levels.
- *Phosphorus:* Phosphorus is present in fish oil as phosphatides which are emulsifiers.
- These should be substantially removed from the oil by washing and/or phosphoric acid treatment prior to caustic soda refining so as to improve yields of neutral oil. The phosphorus content must be determined so as to calculate the required amount of phosphoric acid used to denature the phosphatides. The black residue which results from the treatment cakes the insides of solid bowl centrifuges and incomplete "degumming", as the reaction is known, can give separation difficulties when the soapstock is split with sulphuric acid.
- *"Standard" Hydrogenation Test:* This test is the definitive test for the forecasting of plant hydrogenation performance but, as can be seen from the above, it does not give all the information needed by the refiner to produce a high quality oil at optimum cost for that oil. Other catalyst poisons exist, *e.g.*, chlorine, bromine, iodine, which cannot easily be determined in a works laboratory and for this reason

the hydrogenation test should be carried out in addition to the sulphur determination.

The determination of unsaponifiable matter in itself is of no great help apart from a high figure raising doubts about possible mineral oil contamination. Little is known about the quality effects of non-glyceride components of oils or of their degradation products and thus the content in the oil of these chemicals taken as a group is practically without value.

7

Environmental Costs and Sustainability

WASTE AQUATIC TREATMENT BY MICROBES

MICROORGANISMS

Microorganisms are of major important in industrial wastewater treatment, agricultural and aquaculture. They reside in the sediment and other substrates, and in the water of aquaculture facilities, as well as in and on the cultured species.

Microorganisms may have positive or negative effects on the outcome of aquaculture operations. Positive microbial activities include elimination of toxic materials such as ammonia, nitrite, and hydrogen sulfide, degradation of uneaten feed, and nutrition of aquatic animals such as shrimp, fish; production of aqua-farmer.

These and other functions make microorganisms key players in the health and sustainability of aquaculture. Yet, microorganisms are among the least known and understood elements in aquaculture. Like other areas in aquaculture, microorganisms require management and manipulation.

MAJOR MICROBIAL GROUPS

The world of microorganisms is made of bacteria, fungi, algae, protozoa, and viruses. They are group together only because of their small size, and not by their function. If, for example, the same taxonomical rules were applied to larger animals, some fish, shrimp, green plants, birds and mammals would be grouped together. Some microorganisms such as viruses, bacteria, and protozoa are notoriously small, under one mm. Others, like algae and fungi, have large size relatives (such as the brown algae that is among the largest living organisms).

Unlike larger organisms, the morphology of microorganisms is relatively poor and is confined to few shapes and colours. However, their poor morphology is compensated by great physiological versatility.

VIRUSES

Viruses are very small, ranging between 0.01 and 0.03 microns, and only visible by using an electron microscope. They cannot live independently, and only multiply inside the cells of other organisms. However, their demand for a host is fairly specific. For example, it is unlikely that a crustacean virus will attack humans or fish. Viruses are also the simplest of all organisms and are made of nucleic acid (either DNA or RNA), frequently coated with a protein layer.

ALGAE

Algae are photosynthetic organisms (contain chlorophyll) and obtain their energy from the sun and their carbon from carbon dioxide. Their size ranges from one micron to many meters. All organisms that use carbon dioxide for their carbon requirement are called autotrophs. Algae are generally beneficial in aquaculture by supplying oxygen and a natural food base for the cultured animals, such as dinoflagellates that cause the red ties.

FUNGI

Fungi are similar to algae, but they do not contain chlorophyll and require pre-formed organic matter as energy and carbon sources (*e.g.,* sugars, fat, protein, and other carbohydrates). Such organisms are called heterotrophs. Fungi, ranging in size from a few microns to several centimeters, grow either independently by feeding on decaying matter, or in association with plants and animals.

PROTOZOA

Protozoa are heterotrophs, mostly free-living, feeding mainly by devouring smaller microorganisms. Their size ranges between two and 200 micron meters. A large group of

protozoa, the Sporozoa, are parasites. Small numbers of protozoa contain chlorophyll and can switch between autotrophic and heterotrophic modes of feeding, based on light conditions.

BACTERIA

Bacteria range in size from 0.1 to 15 micron, with some giants that may reach half a millimeter. They make up the most metabolically diverse group of living organisms. Although some are parasitic to animals and plants, the majority of bacteria are free-living, having either a neutral or beneficial relationship with humans and other animals and plants. Their metabolic versatility is incredible: while most are heterotrophs, using either light or chemical energy. One of their most remarkable characteristics is their ability to multiply rapidly, with generation times usually ranging between minutes to hours.

MICROBIAL PROCESS

Bacteria and other microorganisms, most notably fungi, are able to metabolise and transform numerous organic and inorganic compounds. Therefore, man has used them for thousands of years for making yogurt, pickles, bread, cheese, wine, and more recently for waste purification and wastewater purification. Process controlled by microorganisms can occur aerobically (in the presence of oxygen) or anaerobically (with no oxygen present). The starting materials and the end products of such processes vary based on the microorganisms' capabilities (as reflected in their genetic makeup), and the environment in which these processes occur (*e.g.,* availability of oxygen, temperature, salinity, pH, etc.

AEROBIC MICROBIAL PROCESS IN AQUACULTUTRE

Generally, aerobic microbial processes yield compounds which can be beneficial, and are either not toxic or have lox toxicity levels in aquaculture ponds or tanks. Oxidation of organic matter to carbon dioxide, a process which is the main consumer of oxygen in aquaculture ponds or tanks.

Oxidation of ammonia to nitrate via nitrite, which also consumes large quantity of oxygen. xidation of reduced sulfur compounds (such as hydrogen sulfide and elemental sulfur) to sulfate, a process that generally has low oxygen demand in aquaculture. Conversion of carbon dioxide to biomass by autotrophic bacteria (such as the nitrifying bacteria) with a relatively mall amount of biomass produced in aquaculture facilities, when compared to the conversion of carbon dioxide to biomass by algae.

Conversion of carbon dioxide to biomass by algae depending on the availability of light. Excluding feeding, the photosynthetic process in aquaculture is the main input of carbon source and natural food for aquatic animals.

ANAEROBIC MICROBIAL PROCESSES IN AQUACULTURE

Microbial anaerobic processes, if not controlled, can produce compounds that are highly toxic to cultured animals.

These processes include:

Consumption of organic matter, without the utilisation of free oxygen, resulting in products which are usually not fully oxidised (such as alcohols, organic acids). Reduction of nitrate and nitrite, which can yield either nitrogen gas or ammonia. In aquaculture, due to the toxicity of ammonia and nitrite, ammonia production is not welcomed, while nitrogen gas production is beneficial. However, in agriculture, the opposite is true - the conversion of nitrate and nitrite to nitrogen das result in a loss of fertilizers. Reduction of sulfur compounds to hydrogen sulfide as a final product, a compound, which is toxic to most animals at even very low concentrations.

FUNCTION OF ENZYMES

Enzymes are "biological catalysts." "Biological" means the substance in question is produced or is derived from some living organism. "Catalyst" denotes a substance that has the ability to increase the rate of a chemical reaction, and is not changed or destroyed by the chemical reaction that it accelerates.

Generally speaking, catalysts are specific in nature as to the type of reaction they can catalyse. Enzymes, as a subclass of catalysts, are very specific in nature. Each enzyme can act to catalyse only very select chemical reactions and only with very select substances. An enzyme has been described as a "key" which can "unlock" complex compounds. An enzyme, as the key, must have a certain structure or multi-dimensional shape that matches a specific section of the "substrate" (a substrate is the compound or substance which undergoes the change). Once these two components come together, certain chemical bonds within the substrate molecule change much as a lock is released, and just like the key in this illustration, the enzyme is free to execute its duty once again.

Many chemical reactions do proceed but at such a slow rate that their progress would seem to be imperceptible at normally encountered environmental temperature. Consider for example, the oxidation of glucose or other sugars to useable energy by animals and plants. For a living organism to derive heat and other energy from sugar, the sugar must be oxidised (combined with oxygen) or metabolically "burned"

However, in a living system, the oxidation of sugar must meet an additional condition; that oxidation of sugar must proceed essentially at normal body temperature. Obviously, sugar surrounded by sufficient oxygen would not oxidise very rapidly at this temperature. In conjunction with a series of enzymes created by the living organism, however, this reaction does proceed quite rapidly at temperatures up to 100°F (38 °C). Therefore, enzymes allow the living organism to make use of the potential energy contained in sugar and other food substances.

Enzymes or biological catalysts allow reactions that are necessary to sustain life proceed relatively quickly at the normal environmental temperatures. Enzymes often increase the rate of a chemical reaction between 10 and 20 million times what the speed of reaction would be when left uncatalysed (at a given temperature). Nutrients locked in certain organics are complex macromolecules, or in hard-to-digest matrices may be released or predigested by a high degree of heat or concentrated acid treatment. In an alternative manner, specific enzymes can promote the pre-digestion of certain complex nutrients and facilitate the release of highly digestible nutrients in organics during processing without the need of excessive heat or rigourous chemical treatment.

Naming of Enzymes

One researcher reports treating grain, sorghum or barley with the enzyme "gumase" while another reports the same with the enzyme "beta-glucanase" When methodologies are examined, it is discovered that both of these preparations are the same product. Unfortunately, this apparent contradiction in terms happens often.

Enzymes have been named by several methods and this fact has been known to cause confusion in their classification. For example, common or "trivial" names of enzymes, generally contain a prefix representing the name of the substance or substrate upon which they act or affect, followed by the suffix "ase". The "ase" simply denotes or identifies that the substance is an enzyme. Examples of this system of nomenclature includes the enzyme that catalyses the conversion of proteins into their component amino acids, the name of this enzyme is "protease" or "proteinase".

Another example is the enzyme that accelerates the breakdown of the two components of starch into sugars. The components of starch are known as "amylose" and "amylo-pectin", thus, the enzyme helping to break them down is called "amylase". Confusion may exist, however, when older names of enzymes are used. Included in these older terms are ficin, pepsin, bromelin and trypsin, which are older trivial names of individual types of protease preparations, the enzymes that accelerate digestion of proteins. There are also many sub- classes of enzymes. Amylases are a prime example; subclasses of amylase include: alpha-amylase, beta-amylase, and gluco-amylase, to name a few. All these enzymes do is accelerate the digestion of starch and are broadly classified as amylases, but their actions are all slightly different in nature.

To help sort this out, the International Union of Biochemistry in 1961 proposed a system for enzymes' classification and naming which is finding acceptance mainly in this discussion. One example of this system, however, is the term: "alpha 1, 4-glucan glucanohydrolase" which is a name for alpha-amylase.

All these systems of nomenclature may become confusing to someone who has use for only a few types of enzymes or uses them for industrial or agricultural purposes. Therefore, the use of the more widely known terms such as "amylase" and "protease" are more or less universally in these fields. It should be remembered, however, that there are many types of enzymes that fit into these broad categories that may be more or less suitable for specific agriculturally related application. The final selection for a specific application should be made only after consulting a knowledgeable individual well versed in the technical aspects of the particular enzyme requirements and applicable characteristics.

ISOLATED FORM OF ENZYMES

Enzymes have been isolated from every type of living organism. Many of these biological catalysts are significant only from an academic or medical standpoint, but some of the available enzyme from this vast repertoire have been utilised for agricultural and industrial purposes for years. The table below lists several of the industrially on sequential enzymes and their sources in nature. It is significant to note that animals plants and microorganisms all yield industrially important enzymes. Some enzymes of animal or plant origin have been used in agricultural applications; however, those enzymes most broadly used are of microbial origin.

Source of Enzyme

Plant

- Malted grains or tubers Amylase
- Pineapple Bromelin (Protease)
- Fig Tree Ficin (Protease)
- Papaya Papain (Protease)

Animal

- Liver Catalase (Peroxide Breakdown)
- Calf Stomach Rennet/Chymosin (Milk Clotting)
- Hog Stomach Pepsin (Protease)
- Hog Pancreas Pancreatic Enzymes (Several)
- Digestive Tract Trypain (Protease)

Microbial

- Fungi (Molds and Yeast) amylase, beta glucanase, hemicellulase, protease, cellulase, pectinase, lipase, (many types of each), lactase

Bacteria

- Amylase, protease, isomerase, lactase (many types of each), rennet, oxidase, catalase, beta-glucanase, hemicellulase.

One encounters many digestive or hydrolysing enzymes in the digestive tract of human and other animals. These biological catalysts are necessary for the full utilisation of foods ingested.

Microorganisms, many being as small as 1/10,000 th of an inch in length, are much too minute to have complicated digestive systems as animals do. Therefore, these microbes must predigest their potential foods outside of their cell boundaries so that they can absorb the very small nutrient compounds of predigested foods.

In order to predigest the potential food sources outside their cell boundaries, many microbes excrete enzymes out through their enveloping membrane with its supportive cell wall and into the surrounding environment. Hence these "extra-cellular enzymes" must function in the environment outside the protection of the cell's wall and membrane, they must be reasonably stable and have relatively high resistance to chemicals and must function over a relatively broad temperature range. To realise the effects of the enzymes they produce, microorganisms also must produce relatively large quantities of these catalysts. All of these factors contribute to the industrial significance and durability of extra-cellular microbial enzymes.

It should be noted that most of the agriculturally and industrial important enzymes, are those that catalyse the digestion or "hydrolysis" of certain large organic molecules like starch, cellulose, and protein. The enzymes actually attack these complex molecules, accelerating their digestion and yielding simpler substances.

Hence this process of digestion is referred to as hydrolysis, the enzymes that catalyse the process are considered to be "hydrolysing enzymes" or "hydrolases".

The hydrolysing enzymes include:

- Amylases, which catalyse the digestion of starch into small segments of multiple sugars and into individual soluble sugars.
- Proteases, (or proteinase), which split up proteins into their component amino acid building blocks.
- Lipase, which split up animal and vegetable fats and oils into their component part: glycerol and fatty acids.
- Cellulase (of various types) which breaks down the complex molecule of cellulose into more digestible components of single and multiple sugars.
- Beta-glucanase, (or gumase) which digest one type of vegetable gum into sugars and/or dextrins.
- Pectinase which digests pectin and similar carbohydrates of plant origin.

ACTIVITY AND STABILITY OF ENZYMES

Wastes processing levels usually dictate some variation in physical conditions under which the enzyme products must function. In order to utilise enzymes to their optimal potential in catalytic ability, we must be familiar with the basic principles that can affect the activity and stability of these enzymes. Enzymes, being biological compounds and being comprised of a high percentage of protein, are subject to many environmental effects. Although the following principles hold true for most biological enzymes produced for commercial agricultural use: The pH of the environment has a profound affect on enzyme activity and stability.

Activity optimal for pH's of various enzymes vary; however, the optimal pH's for the biological catalysts produced by most commercial strains of microorganisms lies between pH 4.0 and 7.5. This range is from moderately acidic to mildly alkaline in nature. These are the pH levels normally encountered.

Another major affect of enzyme activity and stability is temperature. Hence enzymes are biochemical catalysts, made up at least partially of protein, they are sensitive in varying degrees to heat. Raising temperatures of the environment generally multiplies the degree of activity by the enzyme.

Once an optimum temperature has been reached, however, even higher temperatures cause rapid degradation of the enzyme with concurrent and irreversible loss in activity.

Optimal temperatures generally range from 98 °F to 140 °F (37 °C to 60 °C) for most hydrolytic enzymes. High temperatures (over 150 °F, 66 °C) generally have detrimental effects on the enzymes.

However, there is broad variation in resistance and sensitivity to heat among the enzymes' types. Bacterial enzymes such as those from Bacillus subtilis are less sensitive to heat than are the fungal enzymes of *A oryzae.* Some amylase preparations prepared by the fermentation of Bacillus species can withstand even boiling for short periods and have optimal activities in the 158 °F - 176 °F (70 °C - 80 °C) range.

Our laboratory has determined that approximately 85 per cent of the activity from Bacillus subtilis/licheniformis alpha-amylase survives high heat. A. oryzae amylases, however, showed a greater than 90 per cent loss activity in high heat.

When the enzyme-bearing, dried fermentation products of these two microorganisms are kept dry, they are much more resistant to environmental temperature stress than if they are moistened. In fact, very few stability problems are encountered with most enzymes in typical situations.

Working System of Bacteria and Enzymes to Digest Organic Wastes

The following discussion outlines the biological process. This process is responsible for the digestion of organic waste, no matter where it occurs.

With minor variations, this same process digest waste in:

- Aquaculture,
- Agriculture,
- Composting,
- Livestock,
- Municipal,
- Industrial Wastewater Treatment

BACTERIAL/ENZYME DIGESTION

Bacterial digestion is the process of bacteria, consuming organic matter. Enzymes act to break the organic matter into water soluble nutrients, which the bacteria digest. Using complex chemical reactions, the organic waste is metabolised down to water and carbon dioxide (the final metabolic waste products), providing the bacteria with energy for growth and reproduction.

It may be simply shown by the following equation:

Aerobic Digestion:

$$\text{Organic waste + water} \xrightarrow{\text{Enzyme}} \text{water soluble nutrients + oxygen} \xrightarrow{\text{Bacteria}} \text{water + carbon dioxide}$$

Anaerobic Digestion:

$$\text{Organic waste + Water} \xrightarrow{\text{Enzyme}} \text{Water Soluble Nutrients} \xrightarrow{\text{Bacteria}} \text{Water + Carbon Dioxide}$$

Organic waste is consumed by the bacteria, used as nutrients by the bacteria, and is no longer present to produce odours, sludge, pollution, or unsightly mess.

SELECTED BACTERIA CULTURES

Thousand of different types of bacteria exist everywhere in our world, and most of them carry on bacterial organic digestion in some way. However, some of them are found only in a particular environment, require specialised types of food, and/or have very unique biological roles (niches).

A bacteria is a single cell life of form - each individual cell is a separate, unique organism. Bacteria often grow into colonies that appear as jelly-like masses, but each cell remains as independent.

Bacteria reproduce by a process called cell division. A mature bacteria reproduces by dividing into two cells, each identical to each other and the parent bacteria. Under ideal conditions, bacteria can reproduce very rapidly, producing a new generation every 20 to 30 minutes.

Following this reproduction process, we see that the number of individual bacteria doubles with each generation. The population explodes as the number of organisms increases logarithmically. This population boom begins soon after the bacteria is introduced into a favourable environment, after a short lag time when the bacteria becomes acclimated to the new conditions.

Obviously, this population cannot increase forever. At some point, the food source will be depleted, waste products will accumulate, or some other change in the environment. Will cause the population to level off or decrease (such as a change in pH, temperature, or oxygen content of the environment). Also, introduction of any poisons into the environment may have negative effects on the population, as well as competition from other types of bacteria.

Bacteria can be classified into different types:

- Aerobic types (which require oxygen to live)
- Anaerobic (which can live without oxygen)
- Facultative types can thrive under both aerobic and anaerobic conditions.

For waste digestion, we can identify several beneficial characteristics that we want our chosen bacteria to have.

The "good" bacteria that we will choose must:

- Consume (digest) a wide variety of organic material that are present in wastes.
- Digest waste quickly and completely, without producing significant odours of noxious gas.
- Not cause any disease in man or animals - they must be *non-pathogenic.*
- Grow and reproduce quickly and readily in the environmental conditions found in waste disposal systems.

Certain bacteria belonging to the Bacillus species have these desirable characteristics. They consume organic waste thousands of times faster than the bacteria that are naturally present in the waste. They grow and reproduce easily, are non-pathogenic, and do not produce foul odours or gas as they digest waste. These "good" bacteria are cultured (grown by artificial means) on liquid or dry nutrient medium. These cultured bacteria are then freeze dried to put them in a state of suspension.

They remain alive, ready to swim, eat, and reproduce as soon as they are activated (rehydrated) and put into the proper environment.

The proper environment needed for rapid growth and reproduction of these good bacteria must have these characteristics:

- A water medium containing food (organic waste).
- Dissolved oxygen (for the aerobic types that require it) in sufficient quantities.
- Proper pH—not too acid nor too alkaline—between 6 and 9 on the pH scale.
- Moderate temperature, between 50 °F and 110 °F.

ENZYMES AID IN DIGESTION

An enzyme is a chemical catalyst that breaks up long, complex waste molecules (Hydrolytic Reaction) into smaller pieces, which can then be digested directly by the bacteria.

Enzymes are simply chemicals - they are not living things, and they cannot grow or reproduce themselves. Enzymes are manufactured by bacteria, and used by the bacteria in order to digest waste. The enzymes that are mixed into the products are actually produced by special bacteria, extracted from them in dry form, and blended into the mixture.

Enzyme are added to help them go to work faster. When added to the organic waste, the enzymes immediately go to work breaking down the waste into water - soluble nutrients for the bacteria to digest. The enzymes break the large, complex molecules of starches, proteins, carbohydrates, and cellulose into smaller, simpler pieces. These enzymes act like chemical "knives", chopping the large molecules of waste into smaller pieces of water - soluble nutrients for the bacteria. The growing bacteria will then start to produce more enzymes on their own, creating a continuing cycle of enzyme production.

The Role of Bacteria in the Sewage Treatment Process

One area of sewage treatment that is not well understood is the bacterial decomposition process. Bacteria may be aerobic, anaerobic or facultative. Aerobic bacteria require oxygen for life support whereas anaerobes can sustain life without oxygen.

Facultative bacteria have the capability of living either in the presence or in the absent of oxygen. In the typical sewage treatment plant, oxygen is added to improve the functioning of aerobic bacteria and to assist them in maintaining superiority over the anaerobes. Agitation, settling, pH and other controllable are carefully considered and employed as a means of maximizing the potential of bacterial reduction of organic in the wastewater.

Single-celled organisms grow and when they have attained a certain size, divide, becoming two. Assuming an adequate food supply, they then grow and divide again like the original cell. Every time a cell splits, approximately every 20 to 30 minutes, a new generation occurs. This is known as the exponential or logarithmic growth phase. At the exponential growth rate, the largest number of cells are produced in the shortest period of time.

In nature and in the laboratory, this growth cannot be maintained indefinitely, simply because the optimum environment of growth cannot be maintained. The amount of growth is the function of two variables: - environment and food. The pattern which actually results is known as the bacterial growth rate curve. Initially dehydrated products (dry) must first rehydrate and acclimate in a linear growth phase before the exponential rate is reached.

Microorganisms and their enzyme systems are responsible for many different chemical reactions produced in the degradation of organic matter. As the bacteria metabolise, grow and divide they produce enzymes. These enzymes are high molecular weight proteins.

It is important to recognise the fact that colonies of bacteria are literally factories for the production of enzymes. The enzymes which are manufactured by the bacteria will be appropriate to the substrate in which the enzyme will be working and so you have automatic production of the right enzyme for the biological reduction of any waste material, provided you have the right bacteria to start with. Enzymes do not reproduce whereas as bacteria do.

Enzymes in biochemical reactions act as organic catalysts. The enzymes actually become a part of the action, but after having caused it, split off from it and are themselves unchanged. After the biochemical reactions are complete and products formed, the enzyme is released to catalyse another reaction. The rate of reaction may be increase by increasing the quantity of the substrate or temperature up to a certain point, but beyond this, the rate of reaction ceases to increase because the enzyme concentration limits it.

All treatment plants should be designed to take advantage of the decomposition of organic materials by bacterial activity. This is something you can equate to lower costs, increased capacity, and an improved quality of effluent; even freedom from bad odours which may typically result when anaerobe bacteria become dominant and in their decomposition process, produce hydrogen sulfide gas and similar by-products. Consider the fact that the total organic load of wastewater or sewage is composed of constantly changing constituent, it would be quite difficult to degrade all of these organics by the addition of one enzyme, or even several enzymes. Enzymes are specific catalysts and do not reproduce. What is needed is the addition of an enzyme manufacturing system right in the sewage that can be pre - determined as to its activity and performance and which has the initial or continuing capacity to reduce waste.

At the present time, the addition of specifically cultured bacteria seems to be the least expensive and most generally reliable way to accomplish desirable results. When you add the right bacteria in proper proportions to the environment, you have established entirely new parameters of potential for the treatment situation.

WASTEWATER TREATMENT

Wastewater is water that has been used and must be treated before it is released into another body of water, so that it does not cause further pollution of water sources. Wastewater comes from a variety of sources. Everything that you flush down your toilet or rinse down the drain is wastewater. Rainwater and run-off, along with various pollutants, go down street gutters and eventually end up at a wastewater treatment facility. Wastewater can also come from agricultural and industrial sources. Some wastewaters are more difficult to treat than others; for example, industrial wastewater can be difficult to treat, whereas domestic wastewater is relatively easy to treat (though it is increasingly difficult to treat domestic waste, due to increased amounts of pharmaceuticals and personal care products that are found in domestic wastewater.

RESPONSIBILITY FOR MAKING SURE THAT WASTEWATER IS TREATED PROPERLY

Similar to drinking water provisions, the federal government has delegated responsibility for wastewater treatment to the provinces and territories.

There are two federal acts, however, that may apply to wastewater. The Fisheries Act prohibits the release of harmful substances into waters that fish live in. The Canadian Environmental Protection Act governs the release of toxic substances into the environment and allows the federal government to develop regulations for the use of toxic substances.

Most provincial and territorial governments have legislation regarding wastewater treatment standards and requirements. Operators of wastewater treatment facilities must obtain permits or licenses from the provincial or territorial government, and these permits may also require additional treatments or limits on effluent discharges. For example, in British Columbia, all municipalities are required to have a Liquid Waste Management Plan; without an approved plan, discharges are illegal. Provincial and territorial governments generally assist municipal governments with funds to build and maintain infrastructure.

Municipal governments directly oversee the wastewater treatment process, and are able to pass additional by-laws. For example, the Regional Municipality of Ottawa-Carleton has developed a programme to eliminate toxic substances from the wastewater treatment system, requiring all industrial, institutional and commercial facilities to limit the amount of certain pollutants that are allowed into sewers.

Treatment of Wastewater, to Make it Safe for Discharge

There are several levels of wastewater treatment; these are primary, secondary and tertiary levels of treatment. Most municipal wastewater treatment facilities use primary and secondary levels of treatment, and some also use tertiary treatments. The type and order of treatment may vary from one treatment plant to another, but this diagram of the Ottawa-Carleton wastewater treatment plant illustrates the basic components.

The primary level of treatment uses screens and settling tanks to remove the majority of solids. This step is extremely important, because solids make up approximately 35 per cent of the pollutants that must be removed. The screens usually have openings of about 10 millimetres, which is small enough to remove sticks, garbage and other large materials from the wastewater. This material is removed and disposed of at the landfill.

The water is then put into settling tanks (or clarifiers), where it sits for several hours, allowing the sludge to settle and a scum to form on the top. The scum is then skimmed off the top, the sludge is removed from the bottom, and the partially treated wastewater moves on to the secondary treatment level.

The primary treatment generally removes up to 50 per cent of the Biological Oxygen Demand (BOD; these are substances that use up the oxygen in the water), around 90 per cent of suspended solids, and up to 55 per cent of fecal coliforms.

While primary treatment removes a significant amount of harmful substances from wastewater, it is not enough to ensure that all harmful pollutants have been removed.

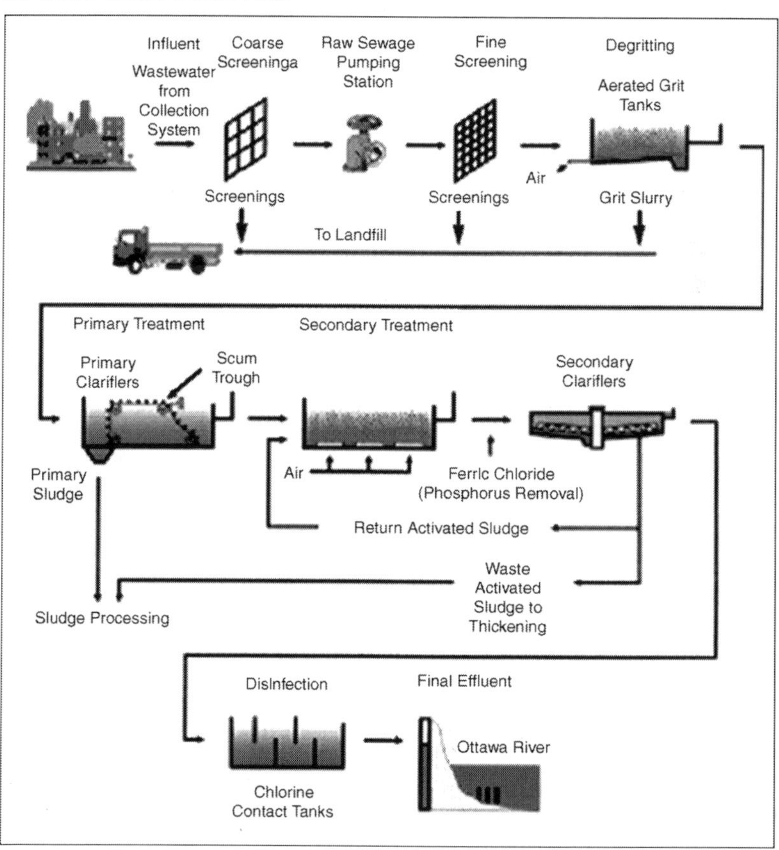

Secondary treatment of wastewater uses bacteria to digest the remaining pollutants. This is accomplished by forcefully mixing the wastewater with bacteria and oxygen. The oxygen helps the bacteria to digest the pollutants faster.

The water is then taken to settling tanks where the sludge again settles, leaving the water 90 to 95 per cent free of pollutants. The picture below shows the settling tanks in the Winnipeg Wastewater Treatment Plant. Secondary treatment removes about 85 to 90 per cent of BOD and suspended solid, and about 90 to 99 per cent of coliform bacteria.

Some treatment plants follow this with a sand filter, to remove additional pollutants. The water is then disinfected with chlorine, ozone, or ultraviolet light, and then discharged.

The sludge that is removed from the settling tanks and the scum that is skimmed off the top during the primary steps are treated separately from the water. Anaerobic bacteria (anaerobic bacteria do not require oxygen) feed off of the sludge for 10 to 20 days at temperatures around 38 degrees Celsius.

This process decreases the odour and organic matter of the sludge, and creates a highly combustible gas of methane and carbon dioxide, which can be used as fuel to heat the treatment plant. Finally, the sludge is sent to a centrifuge, like the one shown in the picture below. A centrifuge is a machine that spins very quickly, forcing the liquid to separate from the solid. The liquid can then be processed with the wastewater and the solid is used as fertilizer on fields.

Tertiary (or advanced) treatment removes dissolved substances, such as colour, metals, organic chemicals and nutrients like phosphorus and nitrogen. There are a number of physical, chemical and biological treatment processes that are used for tertiary treatment. One of the biological treatment processes is called Biological Nutrient Removal (BNR). This diagram shows the treatment steps that Saskatoon wastewater goes through.

In this treatment plant, wastewater first undergoes primary and secondary treatment. For the tertiary treatment, the BNR process occurs in the bioreactors. The BNR process uses bacteria in different conditions in several tanks, to digest the contaminants in the water. The three tanks have unique environments, with different amounts of oxygen. As the water has passes through the three tanks, the phosphorus is removed and the ammonia is broken down into nitrate and nitrogen gas, which other bacterial processes can not do. The BNR process can remove over 90 per cent of phosphates, while traditional processes remove much less than 90 per cent. The water spends approximately nine hours in the bioreactors, before entering the secondary clarifier, which is a settling tank, where the bacteria-laden sludge settles to the bottom of the tank.

Small Communities Treat Waste Ewater, to Make it Safe for Sischarge

In small communities, wastewater treatment facilities may consist of individual septic systems, simple collection systems that directly discharge effluent to surface waters, or municipal lagoons that are emptied annually. These facilities usually treat and disperse the waste as close as possible to its source, thus minimizing operational costs and maintenance requirements. The longer the waste can sit in a lagoon before being discharged, the less likely it will be to contaminate drinking water sources. Some communities store the waste in lagoons, but others release the waste directly into water sources.

Lagoons are reservoirs in the ground that store waste for a time until it is discharged, either to the soil or a water body. Shallow lagoons, that are less than 1.5 metres deep, are used for primary treatment, which allows the solid waste to settle to the bottom of the lagoon over a period of 6 to 20 days. Shallow lagoons, however, cannot effectively remove the majority of contaminants that pose problems for ground and surface waters. Deep lagoons, which are more than three metres deep, can provide long-term storage and treatment for six months to one year.

Many lagoons in small communities are emptied once per year. Rural communities often make use of surrounding land to dispose of wastewater. When the soil is adequate, and there are no water sources nearby, the bacteria in the soil can remove and break down the contaminants in wastewater. Due to the availability of land in many rural areas, this can be an effective method to treat wastewater. However, there are other communities that dispose of waste in a way that threatens the quality of the lake, river or groundwater source that provides drinking water.

The Environmental Protection Agency estimates that between 10 and 20 per cent of small community wastewater treatment facilities in the United States are not operating properly; state water quality agencies have identified malfunctioning wastewater treatment systems as the second greatest threat to water quality (after underground storage tanks). When the inadequate wastewater treatments are combined with ineffective drinking water treatment, the result is a serious contamination issue for a great number of rural communities.

Rural communities typically find it difficult to install and maintain wastewater treatment operations. And while many communities have inadequate methods of treating wastewater, there are some communities that are leading the way with innovative methods of treatment and water conservation measures. In several Arctic communities, including Iqaluit, Nunavut, the high cost of water has led to wastewater treatments that allow water to be reused. Wastewater is passed through a septic tank, filtered, and disinfected with ozone treatment; it is then reused for non-consumptive uses, such as toilets and laundry. These conservation measures allow them to reuse up to 55 per cent of wastewater, while decreasing pressure on wastewater treatment and storage processes. For more information about water conservation, including the ways in which rural and First Nations communities are leading efforts to reduce water use.

WORKING PROCESS OF SEPTIC SYSTEMS

There are many people living in rural areas that are not served by wastewater treatment plants. In fact, according to Environment Canada, as of 2000, only 57 per cent of Canadians were served by wastewater treatment plants, compared with 74 per cent of Americans, 86.5 per cent of Germans, and 99 per cent of Swedes. Many people in rural areas use septic systems to safely store waste. Wastewater travels through pipes, from the house to a buried septic tank. The diagram below illustrates the basic components of a septic system.

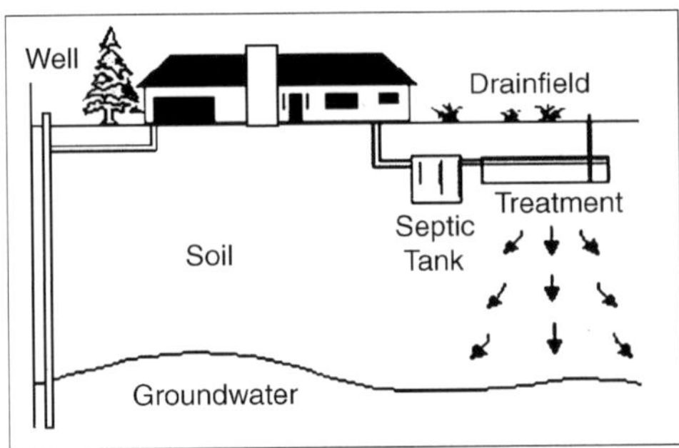

Fig. Septic Tank

The diagram below illustrates the tank in more detail. In the septic tank, the solids settle to the bottom and a scum forms on the top, similar to the process that occurs in settling tanks in municipal wastewater treatment plants. Once separated, the water flows out to the drainfield, and screens and compartments keep the sludge and scum inside the tank, where bacteria begin to partially digest the sludge. When the partially treated wastewater enters the drainfield, it begins to infiltrate the soil and percolate downwards. So long as the soil is appropriate, the microbes in the soil digest the pollutants, removing the bacteria, viruses and excess nutrients by the time the water reaches the source.

When the soil is not suitable, or there are nearby water sources, an alternative system may be used, so that water sources do not become contaminated. The alternative system may use sand, peat, or plastic instead of soil. Constructed wetlands, lagoons, aerators, or disinfection devices are also effective in treating the wastewater.

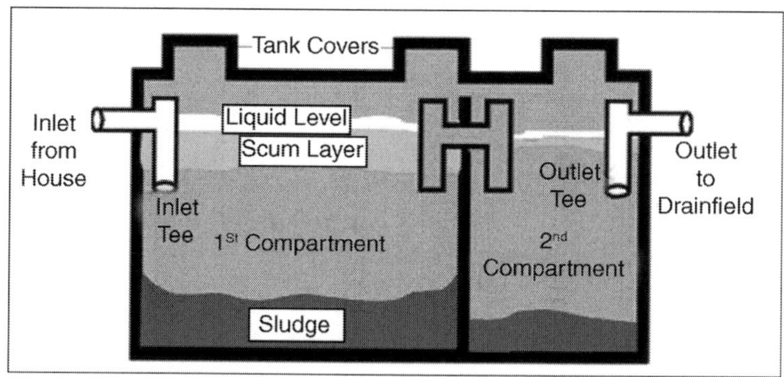

Fig. Inside of Septic System.

It is estimated that around half of all rural wells are contaminated, many from septic tanks. The United States Centers for Disease Control and Prevention suggests that wells should be at least 15 metres from septic tanks, but this distance also varies according to the type of soil.

In a recent study of groundwater sources in southeastern Michigan by the United States Geological Survey, 38 wells were tested between 1999 and 2001. Of the wells that were near sewerlines, viruses were detected in only two of the 18 wells. Of the 20 wells that were near septic systems, viruses were found in seven wells.

This suggests that septic systems are a major cause of groundwater contamination. Previous studies of contaminated wells that were cited by the USGS study found coliforms in up to 80 per cent of the wells, as well as some with significant numbers of the E. coli bacterium.

If you are using a septic system, it is important to maintain it properly, as failure to do so could result in the leakage of pollutants into the soil or water sources. The United States Environmental Protection Agency (EPA) recommends that you have your septic system inspected at least once every three years, so that it can be checked for leaks and malfunctions, and also be pumped out when it gets full (typically once every three to five years).

Following some water conservation practices can greatly reduce pressure on your septic system.

Here are a few things that you can do to care for your septic system:

- Do not use your drain or toilet as a garbage disposal; avoid putting dental floss, diapers, coffee grounds and paper towel down the drain, as they can clog up your septic system.
- Spread your loads of laundry out over the week. When too much water is added to the septic tank, it does not have time to treat wastes, and you could be flooding your drainfield with wastewater.
- Plant grass on your drainfield, but keep trees and shrubs away from it, because roots can clog the system and cause damage.

- Do not drive on your drainfield, because this can compact the soil and damage the septic system components.

NATURAL WAYS TO TREAT WASTEWATER

If nature itself can cleanse water, then imitating nature's processes may be the most effective and sustainable ways of treating wastewater. A great deal of water renewal occurs naturally in wetlands.

Constructed wetlands consist of a lined cell, which the water flows into. Plants are planted in the cell and the roots filter the contaminants out of the water. Below is a diagram of a constructed wetland. Notice that many of the processes in a wetland are similar to the Biological Nutrient Removal process that was described above.

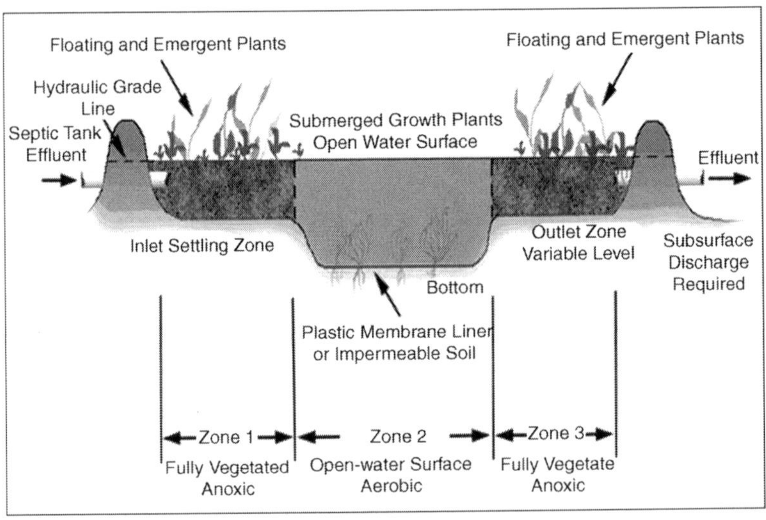

Fig. Constructed Wetland

Another natural method is called rapid infiltration, which is a process where a basin is filled with wastewater, which has already gone through a pre-treatment. The ground acts as a filter and removes the pollutants from the water. This method is similar to what happens in a septic system. A third "natural" process is overland flow, which is used in regions of nearly impermeable ground. The water flows down a sloped surface that is planted with thick grasses. Because the soil is highly impermeable, the water is forced through the vegetation, which effectively removes the pollutants.

Slow rate irrigation is a process that uses a portion of land, and allows the water to flow slowly enough that the land's capacity to infiltrate the water and remove the impurities is not overburdened. Silviculture is similar to slow rate irrigation, in that it uses a large amount of land to treat wastewater, by planting crops or trees that will flourish during the treatment process. Aquiculture uses aquatic plant and animal species to treat wastewater, similar to the constructed wetland process.

There are also alternative separation systems that can conserve water. One such system separates blackwater (from toilets) from greywater (from showers and dishwashers), so that greywater can be minimally treated and used for watering the lawn. As well, there are incinerating, chemical, or composting toilets that release the waste when it is safe.

WASTEWATER IN AQUACULTURE

SOIL-AQUIFER TREATMENT (SAT)

Where soil and groundwater conditions are favourable for artificial recharge of groundwater through infiltration basins, a high degree of upgrading can be achieved by allowing partially-treated sewage effluent to infiltrate into the soil and move down to the groundwater. The unsaturated or "vadose" zone then acts as a natural filter and can remove essentially all suspended solids, biodegradable materials, bacteria, viruses, and other microorganisms. Significant reductions in nitrogen, phosphorus, and heavy metals concentrations can also be achieved.

After the sewage, treated in passage through the vadose zone, has reached the groundwater it is usually allowed to flow some distance through the aquifer before it is collected. This additional movement through the aquifer can produce further purification (removal of microorganisms, precipitation of phosphates, adsorption of synthetic organics, etc.) of the sewage. Since the soil and aquifer are used as natural treatment, systems are called soil-aquifer treatment systems or SAT systems. Soil-aquifer treatment is, essentially, a low-technology, advanced wastewater treatment system. It also has an aesthetic advantage over conventionally treated sewage in that water recovered from an SAT system is not only clear and odour-free but it comes from a well, drain, or via natural drainage to a stream or low area, rather than from a sewer or sewage treatment plant. Thus, the water has lost its connotation of sewage and the public see it water more as coming out of the ground (groundwater) than as sewage effluent. This could be an important factor in the public acceptance of sewage reuse schemes.

SAT SYSTEM LAYOUTS

Various types of SAT system, the simplest being where the sewage effluent is applied to infiltration basins on high ground from where it moves down to the groundwater and eventually drains naturally through an aquifer into a lower area. This lower area can be a natural depression or seepage area, a stream or lake, or a surface drain. SAT systems as in Figure also serve to reduce the pollution of surface waters. Instead of discharging wastewater directly into streams or lakes, it is applied to infiltration basins at a higher elevation so that it receives soil-aquifer treatment before entering the stream or lake.

Where the groundwater is too deep to collect the renovated sewage water by gravity, pumped wells must be used and there are two basic layouts. In one, the infiltration basins are arranged in two parallel strips and the wells are located on the line midway between the two strips. In the other, the infiltration basins are located close together in a cluster and the wells are on a circle around this cluster.

The wells pump essentially all renovated sewage water and no native groundwater from the aquifer outside the SAT system. A mixture of renovated sewage water and native groundwater. Systems 11C and 11D can be used both for seasonal underground storage of sewage water, allowing the groundwater mound to rise during periods of low irrigation water demand (winter), and for pumping the groundwater mound down in periods of high irrigation water demands (summer). The type of SAT system would be suitable for small systems where there are only a few basins around a centrally located well.

WASTEWATER REUSE FOR AQUACULTURE

Wastewater reuse for aquaculture has been practised in many countries for a considerable period of time. It has the potential of wider application in the tropics. There is great diversity of systems involving cultivation of aquatic species, (mainly fish) and plants (mainly aquatic vegetables such as water spinach).

Farmers and local communities have developed most reuse systems; the primary motivating factor has been reuse of nutrients for food production rather than wastewater treatment, and with scant attention to either waste treatment or to public health. In most aquaculture systems, wastewater is not reused directly in aquaculture and the nutrients contained in the wastewater are used as fertilizer to produce natural food such as plankton for fish. These nutrients, mainly nitrogen and phosphorus, are also taken up directly by large aquatic plants such as duckweed which is cultivated for animal feed, and aquatic vegetables such as water spinach and water mimosa cultivated for human food.

As wastewater provides a source of nutrients for aquaculture, it is technically feasible to link it up with most sanitation technologies, providing that land is available at reasonable cost. Farmers have learned by experience how to culture fish, first in static-water nightsoil-fed ponds and more recently in conventional wastewater-fed fishponds. Research has provided a scientific basis for the key parameters in wastewater-fed aquaculture practice developed earlier by farmers and these can be found in the Source Book, published by IWA and IETC.

BIOTA IN AQUACULTURE PONDS

FOOD CHAINS

The objective in fertilizing an aquaculture pond with excreta, nightsoil or wastewater is to produce natural food for fish. Since several species of fish feed directly on faecal solids, use of raw sewage or fresh nightsoil as influent to fish ponds should be prohibited for health reasons.

Edwards has represented the complex food chains in an excreta-fed fish pond, involving ultimate decomposers or bacteria, phytoplankton, zooplankton and invertebrate detritivores. Inorganic nutrients released in the bacterial degredation of organic solids in sewage, nightsoil or excreta are taken up by phytoplankton.

sZooplankton graze phytoplankton and small detritus particles coated with bacteria, the latter also serving as food for benthic invertebrate detritivores. Plankton, particularly phytoplankaton, are the major sources of natural food in a fish pond but benthic invertebrates, mainly chironomids, also serve as fish food, although they are quantitatively less important. To optimise fish production in a human waste fed pond, the majority of the fish should be filter feeders, to exploit the plankton growth.

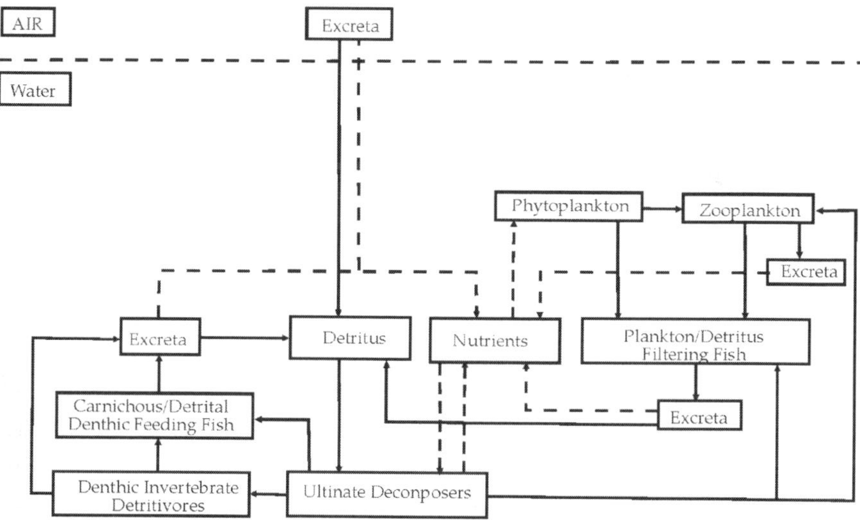

Fig. Food chains in an excreta-fed aquaculture system

A wide range of fish species has been cultivated in aquaculture ponds receiving human waste, including common carp *(Cyprinùs carpio),* Indian major carps (*Catla catlax, Cirrhina mrigala and Labeo rohita),* Chinese silver carp *(Hypophthalmichthys molitrix),* bighead carp *(Aristichthys nobilis),* grass carp *(Ctenopharyngodon idella),* crucian carp (*Carassius auratus),* Nile carp *(Osteochilus hasseltii),* tilapia *(Oreochromis spp.),* milkfish *(Chanos chanos),* catfish *(Pangasius spp.),* kissing gouramy *(Helostoma temmincki),* giant gourami *(Osphronemus goramy),* silver barb *(Puntius gonionotus)* and freshwater prawn *(Macrobrachium lanchesterii).*

FISH SPECIES

The selection reflects local culture rather than fish optimally-suited to such environments. For example, Chinese carps and Indian major carps are the major species in excreta-fed systems in China and India, respectively. In some countries, a polyculture of several fish species is used. Tilapia are generally cultured to a lesser extent than carps in excreta-fed systems although, technically, they are more suitable for this environment because they are better able to tolerate adverse environmental conditions than carp species. Milkfish have been found to have poorer growth and survival statistics compared with Indian major carps and Chinese carps in ponds fed with stabilisation pond effluent in India. Edwards gives a thorough review of current knowledge on the various fish species which can be cultured in ponds fed with human waste. It would appear that considerable confusion still exists with regard to fish feeding on natural food. Although fish are generally divided into types according to their natural nutritional habits - those that feed on phytoplankton, or zooplankton or benthic animals - several species are known to feed on whatever particles are suspended in the water.

There is also uncertainty about the types of phytoplankton fed upon by filter-feeding fish. For example, although blue-green algae are thought to be indigestible to fish, Tilapia have been shown to readily digest these algae and there is evidence that silver carp can do the same.

AQUATIC PLANTS

Aquatic macrophytes grow readily in ponds fed with human waste and their use in wastewater treatment has been discussed. Some creeping aquatic macrophytes are cultivated as vegetables for human consumption in aquaculture ponds and duckweeds are also cultivated, mainly for fish feed. Among the aquatic plants grown for use as vegetables are water spinach *(Ipomoea aquatica),* water mimosa *(Neptunia oleracea),* water cress *(Rorippa nasturtium-aquaticum)* and Chinese water chestnut *(Eleocharis dulcis).* The duckweeds *Lemna, Spirodela* and *Wolffia* are cultivated in some parts of Asia in shallow ponds fertilized with excreta, mainly as feed for Chinese carps but also for chickens, ducks and edible snails.

TECHNICAL ASPECTS OF FISH CULTURE

ENVIRONMENTAL FACTORS

In a successful aquaculture system there must be both an organismic balance, to produce an optimal supply of natural food at all levels, and a chemical balance, to ensure sufficient oxygen supply for the growth of fish and their natural food organisms and to minimize the build-up of toxic metabolic products.

Chemical balance is usually achieved through organismic balance in waste-fed ponds because the most important chemical transformations are biologically mediated. It is now recognised that depletion of dissolved oxygen in fertilized fish ponds is due primarily to the high rates of respiration at night of dense concentrations of phytoplankton. Romaire *et al.* introduced Equation to cover the factors influencing waste-fed fish pond dissolved oxygen (DO) at dawn:

$$DO_{dn} = DO_{dk} \pm DO_{df} - DO_{m} - DO_{f} - DO_{p}$$

where:

DO_{dn} = DO concentration at dawn
DO_{dk} = DO concentration at dusk
DO_{df} = DO gain or loss due to diffusion
DO_{m} = DO consumed by mud
DO_{f} = DO consumed by fish
DO_{p} = DO consumed by plankton

Bacterial respiration is not specifically mentioned in this equation but is included in the mud consumption of DO and in the planktonic DO consumption. In a well-managed waste-fed fish pond the DO in the morning should be only a few mg/l whereas in late afternoon the pond should be supersaturated with DO.

Mud respiration probably lowers DO by less than 1 mg/l overnight and a fish population weighing 3000 kg/ha would also lower DO by only about 1 mg/l overnight. Phytoplankton photosynthesis is the major source of oxygen during daylight hours and, during the night, the major cause of oxygen depletion is respiration. It has been estimated that respiration of plankton (bacterioplankton, phytoplankton and zooplankton) can lower pond DO by 8-10 mg/l overnight. By far the greatest proportion of the DO depletion overnight is caused by the respiration of the phytoplankton that develops as a result of the nutrients contained in the waste.

Phytoplanktons provide feed for the largest percentage of fish farmed in Asia. They also exhibit a positive net primary productivity on a 24-hour basis and are net oxygen contributors to a fish pond. The objective in a waste-fed fish pond should be to maintain an algal standing crop at an optimum level for net primary productivity by balancing the production of phytoplankton biomass, in response to waste fertilization, with the grasing of phytoplankton biomass by filter-feeding fish.

Fish mortality in a waste-fed pond can result from at least three possible causes. First, the depletion of oxygen due to bacterial oxygen demand caused by an increase in organic load. Second, the depletion of oxygen overnight due to the respiratory demand of too large a concentration of phytoplankton, having grown in response to an increase in inorganic nutrients, caused by an organismic imbalance. The third possible cause is high ammonia concentration in the waste feed. All three causes of fish mortality have been reported in respect of sewage-fertilized fish ponds. The sensitivity of fish to low levels of DO varies with species, life stage (eggs, larvae, adults) and life process (feeding, growth, and reproduction). A minimum constant DO concentration of 5 mg/l is considered satisfactory, although an absolute minimum consistent with the presence of fish is probably less than 1 mg/l.

Fish cultured in waste-fed ponds appear to be able to tolerate very low DO concentrations, for at least short periods of time, with air-breathing fish (such as walking catfish *(Clarias batrachus)* being the most tolerant, followed in decreasing order of tolerance by tilapia, carps, channel catfish and trout. Reducing phytoplankton biomass to maintain a reasonable DO in the early morning hours might well depress fish growth more than exposure to a few hours of low DO. A wastewater fertilized aquaculture system might occasionally require a stand-by mechanical oxygenation system for use during periods when DO would otherwise be very low. However, if the system is well managed to avoid overloading, this expense can be avoided.

Unionised ammonia (NH_3) is toxic to fish in the concentration range 0.2 - 2.0 mg/l. However, the tolerance of different species of fish varies, with tilapa species being least affected by high ammonia levels. Bartone *et al.* found that satisfactory growth and survival of tilapia was possible in fish ponds fed with tertiary effluent in Lima, Peru when the average total ammonia concentration was less than 2 mg N/l and the average unionised ammonia concentration was less than 0.5 mg N/l, with the latter only exceeding 2 mg N/l for short periods. In ponds receiving large quantities of organic matter, sediments tend to accumulate and release anaerobic breakdown products, such as methane and sulphides, which can inhibit fish growth. Bottom feeding fish, such as the common carp (*Cyprinus carpio),* are most affected by such conditions, especially if the macrozoobenthos disappear.

FISH YIELDS AND POPULATION MANAGEMENT

A wide range of yields has been reported from waste-fed aquaculture systems, for example: 2-6 tons/ha yr in Indonesia, 2.7 - 9.3 tons/ha yr in China and 3.5 - 7.8 tons/ha yr in Taiwan. Although the majority of waste-fed fish ponds stocks carps, research in Peru and Thailand has demonstrated the potential of tilapia for such systems. Management of fish ponds can have a significant effect on fish yields but the maximum attainable yield in practice is of the order of 10 - 12 tons/ha yr.

Increase in weight of small fingerlings stocked in a pond follows a sigmoidal curve. The first phase of growth is slow, so a high stocking density can be adopted to better utilise the spatial and nutritional resources of the pond. Alternatively, this can be achieved by stocking with larger fish having a higher initial weight, following growth in nursery ponds.

Fish yield is positively correlated with the size of the stocked fish at a given stocking density. In South China, tilapia are stocked once a year at rates of either 30g fish and $0.15/m^2$ or 1.3g fish at $2.3 - 3.0/m^2$ stocking density. An increase in weight of fish in a pond leads initially to an increase in yield or production but there is subsequently a reduction in the growth rate of individual fish because of the limitation of natural food production in the system.

The third phase of slow growth in Figure is because the total weight of fish in the pond is approaching the carrying capacity. Intermediate harvesting when the rapid growth ceases, at the end of phase 2, should lead to significant increases in total yield. The high yields of tilapia reported in South China sewage-fed ponds are due to high stocking density and frequent harvesting.

Clearly, the key to achieving high yields in a waste-fed pond is to determine the carrying capacity of the pond, the maximum standing stock of fish.

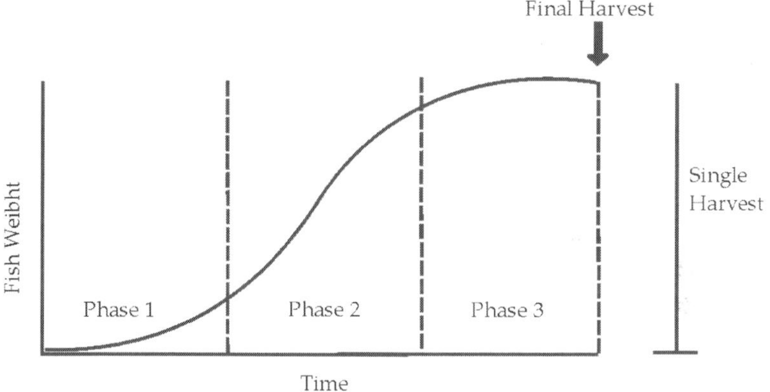

Fig. Fish growth cycle

This can be assessed by varying the waste load and determining the maximum production of natural food consistent with satisfactory water quality, sustainable through a fish culture cycle. Fish stocking density is related to carrying capacity according to the desired weight of individual fish at harvest, as follows:

Fish stocking density,

$$\text{(number/ha)} = \frac{\text{Carrying capacity (kg/ha)}}{\text{Harvesable weight of individual fish (kg)}}$$

Experience has shown that there is a limit to the fish yield attainable from a waste-fed fish pond. Higher yields can be achieved by addition of energy-rich supplementary feed, such as cereals, cereal brans or pelleted-feed. The highest yields are only achieved with a sufficiently high fish stocking density to benefit from the improvement in pond nutrition. There appears to be increased efficiency of utilisation of supplementary feed by fish in ponds receiving sewage effluent. Marketable weights of fish vary with species and local market preferences but, in general, desirable sizes of the following fish range from 0.25-0.6 kg for tilapia, 0.5-1.5 kg for Indian major carps (mrigal 0.5, rohu 1.0, catla 1.5 kg) and perhaps 1-2 kg for Chinese carps. Thus, for a particular carrying capacity, Chinese carps should be stocked at an intermediate density. The length of culture cycle, or frequency of harvesting, depends on the time it takes stocked fish to reach marketable size. It should be recognised that the size of individual fish is only significant if the product is to be consumed by humans. When fish are raised as high-protein feed for carnivorous fish or livestock, size is relatively unimportant. Nevertheless, it is now appreciated that sustainable yields of even high densities of small-size fish with a high specific growth rate are not significantly different from the yield of table fish for human consumption (6.2-7.8 tons/ha yr).

HEALTH RELATED ASPECTS OF FISH CULTURE

Although it is good practice to limit the discharge of toxic materials to sewerage systems, inevitably some of these materials gain access and heavy metals and pesticides are frequently present in municipal sewage. This gives rise to concern about bioaccumulation when sewage effluent is used in aquaculture. Algae are known to accumulate various heavy metals but, with the possible exception of mercury, fish raised in sewage-fed ponds have not been observed to accumulate high concentrations of these toxic substances.

It would appear that the concentrations of heavy metals in the pond water may be accumulated at slower rates than new tissues develop in rapidly growing fish, such as tilapia. In the case of mercury, the position of fish in the food chain seems to be important in determining their mercury uptake, with carnivorous fish accumulating more than herbivores.

Fish, apparently, have the ability to regulate the heavy metal content of their tissues, except for mercury, and tend to accumulate metals in parts other than muscle tissue. There is little information on the uptake of toxics other than heavy metals but a high phenol content in the sewage fed to fish ponds in Wuhon, China caused the fish flesh to become unpalatable due to the odour of phenol. Weis *et al.* have reported on the effects of treated municipal wastewater on the early life stages of three species of fish and indicated that moderately toxic effluent (organic fractions) caused cardiovascular and skeletal defects, depression of heart rate and poor hatching, larval and juvenile growth rates. The health effects of aquacultural use of human wastes in respect of pathogenic organisms have been discussed. Depuration was mentioned as a means to decontaminate fish grown in waste-fed aquaculture. It is generally believed that holding fish in clean-water ponds for several weeks at the end of the growing cycle will remove residual objectionable odours and pathogens and provide fish acceptable for market.

FRESHWATER FISH

Freshwater fish are fish that spend some or all of their lives in fresh water, such as rivers and lakes, with a salinity of less than 0.05 per cent. These environments differ from marine conditions in many ways, the most obvious being the difference in levels of salinity. To survive fresh water, the fish need a range of physiological adaptations.

41.24 per cent of all known species of fish are found in fresh water. This is primarily due to the rapid speciation that the scattered habitats make possible. When dealing with ponds and lakes, one might use the same basic models of speciation as when studying island biogeography.

PHYSIOLOGY OF FRESHWATER FISH

Freshwater fish differ physiologically from salt water fish in several respects. Their gills must be able to diffuse dissolved gasses while keeping the salts in the body fluids inside. Their scales reduce water diffusion through the skin: freshwater fish that have lost too many scales will die. They also have well developed kidneys to reclaim salts from body fluids before excretion.

MIGRATING FISH

Many species of fish do reproduce in freshwater, but spend most of their adult lives in the sea. These are known as anadromous fish, and include, for instance, salmon, trout and three-spined stickleback. Some other kinds of fish are, on the contrary, born in salt water, but live most of or parts of their adult lives in fresh water; for instance the eels. These are known as catadromous fish.

Species migrating between marine and fresh waters need adaptations for both environments; when in salt water they need to keep the bodily salt concentration on a level lower than the surroundings, and vice versa. Many species solve this problem by associating different habitats with different stages of life. Both eels, anadromous salmoniform fish and the sea lamprey have different tolerances in salinity in different stages of their lives.

Status in North America

About four in ten North American freshwater fish are endangered, according to a pan-North American study, the main cause being human pollution. The number of fish species and subspecies to become endangered has risen from 40 to 61, since 1989.

MAJORITY OF FRESHWATER FISH PONDS

RENOVATION OF EXISTING PONDS

The majority of freshwater fish ponds in the Indian subcontinent are the dugout ponds of an undrainable nature which at times lack proper embankments. During the course of culture operations, such ponds receive huge amounts of feed, fertilizers and manures as critical inputs and sediment particles carried down by rain water from the catchment area. A portion of the organic production in the pond also undergoes death and decay and gradually adds to the pond bottom sediment. Thus, with the advancement of time, a thick sediment layer is formed reducing the depth of the pond. They are quite rich in organic and inorganic nutrients, but due to slow bacterial action under prevailing anaerobic conditions the nutrients are almost locked up in the sediment and are not available for primary production. Further, the anaerobic decomposition of the organic matter accumulated in the sediment releases harmful gases and depletes dissolved oxygen level in the water. Thus, it becomes necessary to renovate the existing ponds periodically every 4–6 years by removing sediment from the pond bottom, redressing and repairing the dykes, etc., in order to make the ponds more suitable and to regain their fertility. For this, the following practical measures are recommended.

DEWEEDING

It has been observed that most of the rural ponds are not properly managed and become weed-infested in course of time. Before dewatering the pond, large floating weeds such as water hyacinth should be eradicated by pulling them out manually or mechanically. Otherwise, collection and removal of such weeds will require more labour and time. Other rooted emergent or submerged weeds can be taken care of only after draining the pond.

WHEN TO TAKE UP THE RENOVATION WORK

As soon as the water table of the area surrounding the pond goes down the renovation work can be initiated. Summer is the most suitable period for this Purpose as complete drying of the water body is possible. In this period pond renovation can be carried out efficiently and economically. Removal of slushy silt from the partially dried pond bottom is difficult, laborious and expensive.

DEWATERING AND DRYING

Dewatering of the existing pond is possible either by draining the water after cutting a portion of the embankment or by pumping out. If the water table in the surrounding area is high, there is considerable inflow of water from the pond bottom. This phenomenon of sub-surface secretion is called percolation. In case the rate of percolation is high, several furrows or ditches may be made towards the lowest contour point where a pit may be dug out to drain all the percolated wall. Periodical pumping of water from the pit facilitates keeping the bed dry.

DESILTING

After complete dewatering, the pond bed is allowed to dry and develop cracks in the silt mass. The texture of silt is different from that of the bottom hard soil and cracks quickly. At this stage dried silt is cut and removed manually or mechanically and heaped at a suitable place for its utilisation in agricultural fields. Where complete drying is not possible due to high rate of percolation, walking platforms made up of bamboos or wooden planks may be put on the slushy bed to facilitate desilting work.

In some larger ponds it becomes difficult to dry the central portion of the pond bottom as it is nearer to underground water table. In such cases the slushy and loose silt should be scrapped and spread to the sides with the help of wooden planks tied with ropes for pulling. This helps in drying the silt and easy removal thereafter.

CONTOURING

Where the bed is found to be uneven, contouring is necessary to estimate the amount of silt to be removed. Itis done by taking the level measurements at certain spots on the pond bed. It will also help in redesigning the pond taking into consideration the highest flood level and maximum rain water level.

MAINTENANCE OF DYKES

In general, rural ponds lack proper embankments. During high rainfall or peak irrigation periods in canal-irrigated areas such ponds get inundated with water from the neighbouring agricultural fields causing stocked fish to escape, predators and unwanted species to enter and at times results in mass fish kills due to pesticide pollution. Hence, provision of proper dykes is a must. Existing pond dykes should be repaired every year after the monsoon.

Rats and crabs cause great harm to pond dykes by making holes. Such holes allow serious leakage and if not checked immediately, may endanger the stability of the dykes.

Periodically and especially at the time of renovation, such spots should be properly repaired by stuffing binding clay, claylime mixture or any other locally cheap cementing material.

Due to poor consolidation, erosion from the top of the dyke during heavy rains usually results in grooving out of small channels. These areas should be covered with earth, levelled, thoroughly rammed and grass turfed. In relatively larger ponds, wave action due to wind also causes large-scale dyke erosion.

By putting large floating aquatic plants such as water hyacinth along the sides of the dykes exposed to wave action during the windy season such erosion can be checked. Frequent erosion in steep dykes during heavy rain or wind can be avoided by strengthening the inner sides of the dykes with poles or bamboos or corrugated cement planks.

Most of the traditional pond dykes are below the required height; as a result, overflow of water occurs during heavy rains or flood. These dykes should be properly raised and the height may be kept at a minimum of one meter above the maximum water level recorded in that area. While raising the dykes, the top width may be kept at a minimum of 1.5 m with 2:1 slope (horizontal: vertical).

Cutting the dyke to allow water into the pond from the surrounding area without any secured screening is a normal practice, which however creates many management problems. The silt mass is very rich in organic and inorganic nutrients making it most suitable for application in agriculture and horticulture. Being non-cohesive and unstable, it is unsuitable for making dykes as it may be washed back in the pond.

RECLAMATION OF DERELICT WATER BODIES

Derelict waters in millions of hectares, lying unutilised, are common sights in most of the South Asian countries. Such untapped water bodies with potential for aquacultural production may be reclaimed and made suitable for fish culture by adopting more or less similar procedures.

In case of larger water areas, it would be better if they are connected temporarily to nearby natural or man-made drainage systems having relatively lower bed level for complete dewatering by gravity and making the entire area completely dry. However, if such topographic facilities are not available, heavy duty water pumps may be put into use for quicker dewatering.

In extensively large areas dewatering by draining or by pumping is not feasible. Moreover, the dry period of the year also may not last long enough to permit the work to be completed. It has been experienced that such areas can also be successfully reclaimed and renovated by partitioning into smaller units by raising cross bundhs, farm roads, etc. Each newly formed unit then can be dewatered, dried and desilted.

URBAN WASTEWATER MANAGEMENT AND POLLUTION CONTROL

A "new agenda" of environmentally sustainable development has emerged forcefully, and appropriately, in recent years. One aspect of sustainable development is the quality of the water environment which is seen as a global concern about sustainable water resources. The situation in cities in developing countries is especially acute. Even in middle-income countries, sewage is rarely treated. Buenos Aires, for example, treats only 2 per cent of its sewage, a percentage that is typical for the middle-income countries of Latin America. There is also the problem of uncontrolled industrial discharges into municipal sewers, increasing organic loads and introducing a range of chemical contaminants that can damage sewers, interrupt treatment processes, and create toxic and other hazards.

Water quality is far worse in developing countries than in industrialised countries. Furthermore, while environmental quality in industrialised countries improved through the 1980s, it did not improve in middle-income countries, and even declined sharply in lower-income countries. The costs of this degradation can be seen in many ways.

The vast majority of rivers in and around cities in developing countries are little more than open sewers. Not only do these degrade the aesthetic quality of life in the city, but they constitute a reservoir for cholera and other water-related diseases.

The cause of the major outbreak of cholera in Peru in 1991 could be traced to inadequate urban sanitation and water contamination. It cost the Peruvian economy over US$ 150 million in 1991-92 in direct and indirect health impacts. Similarly, the otherwise inexplicable persistence of typhoid in Santiago over four decades has been attributed to the pollution of irrigation waters by untreated metropolitan discharges.

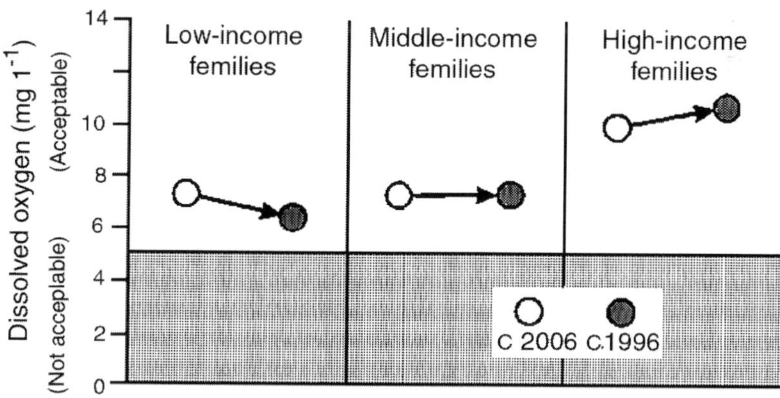

Fig. Dissolved Oxygen Concentrations in Rivers in Developing and Developed Countries.

Energetic emergency measures, taken as a result of the Latin American cholera outbreak in 1991, prevented the spread of cholera in Santiago and brought typhoid under control with estimated savings in direct and indirect health costs in the order of US$ 77 million.

The costs of urban water pollution also create an additional burden for cities in the form of higher water supply costs. In metropolitan Lima, for example, the cost of upstream pollution has increased water treatment costs by about 30 per cent. In Shanghai, China, water intakes had to be moved upstream more than 40 km at a cost of about US$ 300 million.

STRATEGIC PLANNING AND POLICIES FOR SUSTAINABLE SANITATION SERVICES

Applying a strategic planning approach to urban sanitation problems should result in choosing the right policy instruments, agreeing priorities, selecting appropriate standards for service provision, and developing strategic investment and cost recovery programmes. The question of appropriate service standards is a particularly vexing one that, in the end, should be answered by considering user preferences and willingness-topay. In a large city with many pockets of poverty, service standards are likely to be spatially differentiated because many households cannot afford conventional sewerage without massive government subsidies.

The Kumasi Strategic Sanitation Plan provides an example of a differentiated plan matching housing types, income levels and user preference; the plan recommends that sewers be used in tenement areas, latrines in the indigenous areas, and flush toilet/septic tank systems in high income and new government areas.

Willingness-to-pay surveys were carried out, and the results were used to help define differentiated financing options.

Explicit subsidies were targeted to the city's low-income population. Municipal wastewater treatment is a particularly costly and long-term undertaking so that sound strategic planning and policies for treatment are of special importance.

The recently endorsed Environmental Action Programme for Central and Eastern Europe (CEE), formulated with the assistance of the World Bank, recognises that the CEE countries will require a plan to move towards Western European standards over a period of 15-25 years as financial resources become available. Although urban sewerage levels in the CEE are generally adequate, 40 per cent of the population are not, at present, served by wastewater treatment plants. The domestic pollution load represents 60-80 per cent of the combined municipal and industrial organic waste load in many CEE cities. Furthermore, many of the existing plants are currently overloaded, poorly operated and maintained, or bypassed.

The following is a checklist of policy questions posed in the CEE Action Programme to be answered before proceeding with municipal waste-water investments:

- Have measures been taken to reduce domestic and industrial water consumption?
- Has industrial wastewater been pre-treated?
- Is it possible to reuse or recycle wastewater?
- Can the proposed investment be analysed in a river basin context? If so, have the merits of the investment been compared with the benefits from different kinds of investments in other parts of the river basin? (Note that a least-cost solution to achieve improved water quality may involve different, or no, treatment at different locations.)
- Has the most cost-effective treatment option been used to achieve the desired ambient water quality?
- Has there been an economic analysis to assess the benefits (in terms of ambient water quality) that could be achieved by phasing investments over 10 years or more?

COST-EFFECTIVE TECHNOLOGIES

Developing country cities are beginning to recognise that poor urban residents cannot afford, nor do they necessarily want or need, costly conventional sewerage. Beyond the dense urban centres, the average household cost of conventional sewerage may range from US$ 300-1,000. This is clearly too expensive for many households with annual incomes well below US$ 300. Fortunately, a broad range of cost-effective technological options are available to respond to the demands of urban consumers beyond the urban centre, with the potential to reduce costs to the order of US$ 100 per household.

The UNDP/World Bank, Water and Sanitation Programme has worked with many countries over the past decade to develop, demonstrate, document and replicate many of these lowcost sanitation options. The examples drawn upon throughout this chapter illustrate many of the options available to households (*e.g.* ventilated improved pit (VIP) latrines in Lesotho, Sulabh pour-flush latrines in India, condominial sewers in Brazil and simplified sewerage in Pakistan), as well as the supporting institutional and financial systems that make possible the wide-scale application of these options. Wastewater treatment technologies also have a wide range of costs.

Conventional treatment processes may cost US$ 0.25-0.50 per cubic metre. If non-conventional options can be used, it may be possible to cut these costs by at least onehalf.

Promising low-cost treatment approaches, especially for small and intermediate cities, range from natural treatment systems (such as waste stabilisation ponds, engineered wetlands systems and even ocean outfalls), to decentralised treatment systems (such as are used in Curitiba, Brazil), to new treatment processes. In large cities, land or other constraints may result in conventional treatment being the most cost-effective approach for achieving the desired water quality objectives, although this should always be a decision resulting from an economic analysis.

Lifetime costing should always be used to compare and to choose among treatment options, because operations and maintenance constitute a major share of the costs.

CONSERVATION AND REUSE OF SCARCE RESOURCES

Cornerstone ecological principles for sustainable cities include the conservation of resources and the minimisation and recycling of wastes. Translating these principles into urban policies for wastewater management should emphasise the strategic importance of water conservation and wastewater reclamation and reuse in cities. Successful conservation and reuse policies, moreover, need to achieve a balance between ecological, public health and economic and financial concerns.

Pricing and demand management are important instruments for encouraging efficient domestic and industrial water-use practices and for reducing wastewater volumes and loads.

Water and sewerage fees can induce urban organisations to adopt water-saving technologies, including water recycling and reuse systems, and to minimize or eliminate waste products that would otherwise end up in the effluent stream.

In addition to pricebased incentives, demand management programmes should include educational and technical components, such as water conservation campaigns, advice to consumers, and promotion, distribution or sale of water-saving devices like "six-litre" toilets which use less than half the volume of water per flush than a standard toilet.

Wastewater reclamation and reuse is increasingly recognised as a water resources management and environmental protection strategy, especially in arid and semi-arid regions.

The use of reclaimed urban waste-water for non-potable purposes, such as in-city landscape irrigation and industry or for peri-urban agriculture and aquaculture, offers a new and reliable resource that can be substituted for existing freshwater sources.

Water pollution control efforts can make available treated effluents that can be an economical source of water supply when compared with the increasing expense of developing new sources of water. Conversely, in developing countries only recently embarking on major wastewater treatment investments, reuse has the potential to reduce the cost to municipalities of wastewater disposal.

A framework for the economic and financial analysis of reuse projects has been provided by Khouri *et al.* in a planning guide that integrates economic, environmental and health concerns with agronomic concerns for the sound management of crops, soil and water.

CONNECTION BETWEEN SANITATION SERVICES AND ENVIRONMENTAL ISSUES

To understand the connection between sanitation services and environmental issues, it is necessary to consider the sequence in which people demand water supply and sanitation services. For a family which migrates into a shanty-town, the first environmental priority is to secure an adequate water supply at reasonable cost. This is followed shortly by the need to secure a private, convenient and sanitary place for defecation.

Families show a high willingness to pay for these household or private services, in part because the alternatives are so costly. Accordingly, they pressure local and national governments to provide such services, and in the early stages of economic development much external assistance goes to meeting the strong demand for these services.

The very success in meeting these primary needs, however, gives rise to a second generation of demands, namely for the removal of wastewater from the household, then from the neighbourhood and then from the city. As cities succeed in meeting this demand another problem arises, namely the protection of the environment from the degrading effects of such large and concentrated pollution loads.

Thus it is no surprise that the portfolio of external assistance agencies has focused heavily on the provision of water supply.

For example, World Bank lending for water and sanitation over the past 30 years has only included about 15 per cent for sanitation and sewerage, with most of this spent on sewage collection and only a small fraction spent on treatment. In a description of the Orangi Pilot Project in Karachi, Pakistan, Hasan describes how forcefully poor people demand environmental services, once the primary demand for water supply is met, and how it is possible to respond to the challenge of these new demands.

THE FINANCIAL CHALLENGES

Completing the supply of basic sanitation services and making progress on wastewater management and pollution control creates major financial challenges for developing countries. Mobilising the necessary financial resources requires both recognising the need for an urban sanitation subsector and reliance on new ways of financing urban sanitation, sewerage and wastewater management.

RESPONDING TO THE DEMANDS OF HOUSEHOLDS AND COMMUNITIES

In recent years there has been a remarkable consensus on market-friendly and environment-friendly policies for managing water resources and for delivering water and sanitation services on an efficient, equitable and sustainable basis. At the heart of this consensus are three closely related guiding principles expressed at the 1992 Dublin International Conference on Water and the Environment, namely:

- *The Ecosystem Principle:* Planners and policy makers at all levels should take a holistic approach linking social and economic management with protection of natural systems.
- *The Institutional Principle:* Water development and management should be based on a participatory approach, involving user, planners and policy makers at all levels, with decisions taken at the lowest appropriate level.
- *The Instrument Principle.* Water has an economic value in all its competing uses and should be recognised as an economic good.

The challenge facing the urban sanitation subsector is to put these general principles into operation and to translate them into practice on the ground. The new consensus gives prime importance to a central principle of public finance, *i.e.* that efficiency and equity both require that private resources should be used for financing private goods and that public resources should be used only for financing public goods.

Implicit in this principle is a belief that social units themselves, whether households, commercial organisations, urban communities or river basin associations, are in the best position to weigh the costs and benefits of different levels of investment.

The vital issue in the application of this principle to the urban sanitation subsector is the definition of the decision unit and the definition of what is internal (private) and external (public) to that unit. For each level, the demand for sanitation services must be understood, and each social unit should pay for the direct service benefits it receives. To illustrate the application of this emerging ideal, it is necessary to consider how urban sanitation should be financed.

SANITATION, SEWERAGE AND WASTEWATER MANAGEMENT

The benefits from improved sanitation, and therefore the appropriate financing arrangements, are complex. At the lowest level, households place high value on sanitation services that provide them with a private, convenient and odour-free facility which removes excreta and wastewater from the property or confines it appropriately on-site.

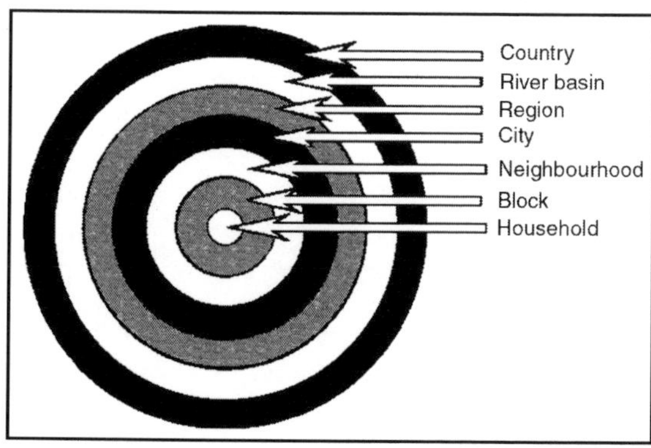

Fig. Levels of Dicision-making on Water and Sanitation.

However, there are clearly benefits which accrue at a more aggregate level and are, therefore, "externalities" from the point of view of the household. Willingness-to-pay studies have shown consistently that households are willing to pay for the first category of service benefits, but have little or no interest in paying for external (environmental) benefits that they consider beyond their concern. At the next level (*i.e.* the block) households in a particular block value services which remove excreta from the block as a whole. Moving up a level, to that of the neighbourhood, residents value services which remove excreta and wastewater from the neighbourhood, or which render these wastes innocuous through treatment. Similarly, at the level of the city, the removal and/or treatment of wastes from the city and its surroundings are valued. Cities, however, do not exist in isolation - wastes discharged from one city pollute the water supply of downstream cities and of other users.

Accordingly, groups of cities (as well as farms and industries and others) in a river basin can perceive the collective benefit of environmental improvement. Finally, because the health and well-being of a nation as a whole may be affected by environmental degradation in one particular river basin, there are sometimes additional national economic, health and environmental benefits from wastewater management in that basin. The example of typhoid in Santiago illustrates the latter point. The fundamental principle of public finance is that costs should be assigned to different levels in this hierarchy according to the benefits accruing at the different levels.

This suggests that the financing of sanitation, sewerage and wastewater treatment should be allocated approximately as follows:

- Households pay the cost incurred in providing on-site facilities (bathrooms, toilets, sewerage connections).
- The residents of a block collectively pay the additional cost incurred in collecting the wastes from individual homes and transporting these to the boundary of the block.

- The residents of a neighbourhood collectively pay the additional cost incurred in collecting the wastes from blocks and transporting these to the boundary of the neighbourhood (or of treating the neighbourhood wastes).
- The residents of a city collectively pay the additional cost incurred in collecting the wastes from blocks and transporting these to the boundary of the city (or of treating the city wastes).
- The stakeholders in a river basin (cities, farmers, industries and environmentalists) collectively assess the value of different levels of water quality within a basin and decide on the level of quality they wish to pay for, and on the distribution of responsibility for paying for the necessary treatment and water quality management activities.
- The nation, for the achievement of broader public health or environmental benefits, may decide to pay collectively for meeting more stringent treatment standards.

Sanitation and Sewerage

Although there are complicating factors to be taken into account (including transaction costs of collection of revenues at different levels and the inter-connectedness of several of the benefits), the principles discussed above are reflected both in the way some industrialised countries finance sewerage investments and in the most innovative and appropriate forms of subsector financing observed in developing countries. In many communities in the USA, for example, households and commercial organisations pay for sewer connections, primary sewer networks are financed by a sewer levy charged to all property owners along the streets served, and secondary sewers and major collectors and interceptors are often financed by improvement levies on all property owners in the serviced areas.

Innovative sewerage financing schemes are now being observed in developing country cities. In Orangi, an informal urban settlement in Karachi, a hierarchical scheme for financing sewerage services has developed in which households pay the costs of their "on-lot" (*i.e.* on-site) services (*e.g.* latrines and septic tanks), the primary sewers are paid for by the households along the "lane" (public passageway between rows of houses), contiguous "lanes" pool their resources to pay for neighbourhood sewers, and the city (via the Municipal Development Authority) pays for trunk sewers.

The arrangements for financing condominial sewers by the urban poor in Brazil follow a remarkably similar pattern; households pay for the on-site costs, blocks pay for the block sewers (and decide what level of service they want from these), with the water company or municipality paying for the trunk sewers. Lack of access to credit may impede investment in sanitation, drainage and other essential urban environmental services, especially in small cities and towns.

This problem has been overcome in some cases by creating special municipal development funds or rotating funds to finance environmental investments. For example, the World Bank has supported the creation of municipal development funds in the State of Minas Gerais, Brazil, for environmental improvements in small cities and towns, and in Mexico for municipal water supply, sewerage and solid waste investments in intermediate cities. Similarly, poor urban households need mechanisms to finance sewer connections and in-home sanitary facilities.

Some cities provide credit to poor households for these investments that can be paid off in instalment payments (not subsidised) over periods of three to five years. Where there are well-managed water and sewerage utilities, the instalment payments can be collected as part of the monthly water bill. In some cases, households can provide "sweat equity" (labour inputs provided by the community for self-help construction schemes) or even make partial payment in the form of construction materials.

A special sanitation credit fund has been established in Honduras for poor urban households, fashioned along the lines of the well-known Grameen rural credit bank in Bangladesh. Such experiences show that the urban poor will invest in a healthier environment if they can spread the initial costs over time. Similarly, innovative schemes for providing urban households access to credit for sanitation investments have been demonstrated in Lesotho and in Burkina Faso.

FINANCING AND INSTITUTIONAL PRINCIPLES OF WASTEWATER TREATMENT

Even when the appropriate financing and institutional principles are followed, very difficult issues can still arise with respect to the financing of wastewater treatment facilities. In industrial countries, two very different models are used.

In many industrialised countries, the approach followed has been to set universal environmental standards and then to raise the funds necessary to finance the required investments. It is becoming increasingly evident that such an approach is proving to be very expensive and not financially feasible, even in the richest countries of the world.

In the UK, the target date for compliance with the water quality standards of the European Union (EU) is being reviewed as customers' bills rise astronomically to pay the huge costs involved. In the USA, US$ 56,000 million in federal construction grants were provided to local governments from 1972-89 to build mandated secondary treatment facilities, but these grants have now been eliminated (and replaced by State revolving funds for loans to municipalities) at the same time that increasingly stringent environmental standards are being proposed.

Many local governments are now refusing to comply with the unfunded mandates of the Federal Government. The city of San Diego, for example, has refused to spend US$ 5,000 million on federally-mandated secondary treatment, arguing that it is more cost-effective to use long, coastal outfalls for sewage disposal. San Diego brought suit against the Federal Government and recently won its case in the federal courts.

The US National Research Council has advocated a change in which costs and benefits are both taken into account in the management of sewage, with a shift to a water quality-based approach at the coastal zone, watershed or basin level. In a few countries, a different model has been developed. In these countries, river basin institutions have been put into place which:

- Ensure broad participation in the setting of standards, and in making the trade-offs between cost and water quality.
- Ensure that available resources are spent on those investments which yield the highest environmental return.
- Use economic instruments to encourage users and polluters to reduce the adverse environmental impacts of their activities.

These institutional arrangements are described more fully below. In river basins in Germany and France, and more recently in Brazil, river basin financing and management models are applied in order to raise resources for wastewater treatment and water quality management from users and polluters in the basin. The stakeholders, including users and polluters as well as citizens' groups, are involved in deciding the level of resources to be raised and the consequent level of environmental quality they wish to "purchase". This system has proved to be efficient, robust and flexible in meeting the financing needs of the densely industrialised Ruhr Valley for 80 years, and for the whole of France since the early 1960s. There is growing evidence that if such participatory agencies were developed, people would be willing to pay substantial amounts for environmental improvement, even in developing countries.

In the state of Espirito Santo in Brazil, a household survey showed that families were willing to pay 1.4 times the cost of sewage collection systems, but 2.3 times the higher cost of a sewage collection and treatment system. In the Rio Doce Valley, an industrial basin of nearly three million people in south-east Brazil, a river basin authority is in the process of being developed. Stakeholders have indicated that they are willing to pay about US$ 1,000 million over a five-year period for environmental improvement.

In the Philippines, recent surveys show that households are often prepared to make substantial payments for investments which will improve the quality of nearby lakes and rivers. For developing countries, the implications of the experience of industrialised countries are clear. Even rich countries manage to treat only a part of their sewage, *e.g.* only 52 per cent of sewage is treated in France and only 66 per cent in Canada. As in the USA, Japan and France, most countries have provided some form of environmental grants to municipalities in order to achieve their present levels of treatment. Given the very low initial levels in developing countries (*e.g.* only about 2 per cent of wastewater was treated in Latin America at the beginning of the decade) and the vital importance of improving the quality of the aquatic environment, an approach is needed that simultaneously makes the best use of available resources and provides incentives to polluters to reduce the loads they impose on surface and groundwaters. An effluent tax is one form of incentive that is used in many countries, ranging from France, Germany and The Netherlands to China and Mexico.

It can be applied to any dischargers, cities or industries, with two benefits; it induces waste reduction and treatment and can provide a source of revenue for financing wastewater treatment investments. The dramatic impact of the Dutch effluent tax on industrial discharges is described by Jansen. The overall industrial effluent loads decreased by two-thirds between 1969, when an effluent tax was first applied, and 1985 (falling from 33 million to 11 million population equivalents).

The experience of China in the application of an industrial effluent tax for financing industrial wastewater management improvements has been described by Suzhen. In France and Mexico, the effluent tax is applied equally to municipal and industrial effluents, thus encouraging local investment in municipal wastewater treatment plants. An effluent tax, however, should be used in combination with municipal sewer use charges in order to ensure that industries do not escape paying for their discharges by passing the cost on to the municipality, as well as to ensure that the municipal sewerage authority has sufficient revenues to build and to operate sewerage and treatment works.

COMMUNITY PARTICIPATION

The aspiration of most urban households, including the urban poor, is to have access to cost-effective and affordable sanitation services via public or private utilities. Consequently, they would be willing to participate, as responsible users, by paying the appropriate service charges. In the cities of many developing countries, however, such services are not yet universally accessible and poor communities must, themselves, get involved in the planning and delivery of sanitation and sewerage options.

The examples of the condominial sewer system in Brazil and the Orangi Pilot Project indicate an important institutional approach to community participation in which a productive partnership is formed between community groups and the municipal government or the utility. Often, such a system involves public provision of the external or trunk infrastructure, which may be operated by either the public or private sector, and the community providing and managing the internal or feeder infrastructure. The link between feeder and trunk infrastructure is essential for the evacuation and disposal of human waste collected by the community, but it is too easily overlooked. Many forms of community participation are possible for the provision of sanitation and sewerage services, such as:

- Information gathering on community conditions, needs and impact assessments.
- Articulation of, and advocacy for, local preferences and priorities.
- Consultations concerning programmes, projects and policies.
- Involvement in the selection and design of interventions.
- Contribution of "sweat equity" or management of project implementation.
- Information dissemination.
- Monitoring and evaluation of interventions.

Promoting and enabling community participation can take many forms. Where political will exists, governments may promote participation and create the conditions under which communities and households, as well as NGOs and the private sector, can play their appropriate roles. The World Bank-financed PROSANEAR project in Brazil for example, provides a framework and the resources for municipalities and utilities to experiment with innovative technical and institutional arrangements for providing sanitation services to the urban poor. When such government support is absent, alternative approaches have commonly been used to stimulate community involvement and to build the necessary political will.

First, NGOs or community-based organisations (CBOs) often play a catalytic role in mobilising communities and forming partnerships. In one of the largest scale examples involving an NGO, Sulabh Shauchalaya International began, in 1970, promoting the construction of pour-flush latrines in Delhi and other Indian cities, and over a period of 20 years assisted in building over 660,000 private latrines and 2,500 public toilet complexes with community participation and government support.

Second, consultations and town meetings are increasingly used as a forum to discuss and agree on environmental priorities, and to propose participatory solutions. Finally, communities may engage in public protests or legal actions as a means of building a constituency of the urban poor, and applying pressure on local governments and utilities for dialogue and action. The Orangi Pilot Project had its origins in the discontent of local residents with excreta and wastewater overflowing in the streets as a result of the failure of the Karachi Development Authority to provide adequate sewerage.

A ROLE FOR THE PRIVATE SECTOR

Financial resources can also be mobilised through the private sector; poor service provision by the public sector often suggests a need for increasing partnerships with the private sector. Private sector participation, however, is only one possible opportunity; it is not a panacea. In situations in which existing sanitation service delivery is either too costly or inadequate, private sector participation should be examined as a means of enhancing efficiency and lowering costs, and of expanding the resources available for service delivery. In deciding whether to involve the private sector, it is important to assess several key factors which have been summarised by the *Infrastructure for Development: World Development Report, 1994*. Introducing competition is the most important step in creating conditions for greater efficiency by both private and public operators; some services can be split into separate operations to help create contestable markets.

The principle of accountability to the public should be maintained through transparent contractual agreements that are open to public scrutiny and should help to minimize risks to public welfare, create real competition, ensure efficiency, and promote self-financing.

Paradoxically, public sector capacity may have to be strengthened in order to achieve effective private sector participation which requires public sector agencies with sufficient capacity to prepare bidding documents and performance indicators, assess proposed outputs and costs, administer the contracting process, and regulate contract performance.

In Mexico, municipalities are granting concessions to the private sector to build and operate wastewater treatment plants, both as a means of financing investments in plants through the private sector and to overcome problems with weak local operating capacity.

The Puerto Vallarta wastewater treatment plant was the first of many new plants to come on line in the past few years. An important point to remember in cases such as Puerto Vallarta is that the private sector performs the necessary function of mobilising financing for needed investments, but the investments made together with operations, maintenance and depreciation costs will all have to be recovered through tariffs charged to domestic and industrial customers. Another innovative example is a concession to 26 industries in the Vallejo area of Mexico City to form a new enterprise, Aguas Industriales del Vallejo, to rehabilitate and expand with its own funds an old municipal wastewater treatment plant, treat up to 2001 s-1 of sewage, and sell the treated water to shareholders at 75 per cent of the public utility water tariff.

CHEMICAL POLLUTANTS

Pollutants pose a real or potential threat to wildlife on many industrial sites. Many substances have been identified as being toxic to plants and animals, and some of these are likely to occur in industrial effluents or are used in industrial processes. Major groups of toxic pollutants include various metals (including mercury, lead and cadmium), a host of organic compounds, reactive gases such as ammonia, anions such as cyanide and fluoride, acids and alkalis. Dissolved substances present a particular problem as they are readily taken up by aquatic life, often passively.

Pollutants need be present only in minute quantities to have an effect; heavy metal concentrations of only a few parts per million may inhibit root growth. Polluted waters support an impoverished fauna, although the few tolerant species can occasionally be numerous owing to reduced competition and predation in such situations.

The toxicity of many substances has often only been demonstrated in controlled laboratory experiments; in the field apparently polluted waters have often been found to support life. Where more than one pollutant is present in the water, as is often the case, they may interact, either within the water or within the organism. The effects of several pollutants together may be additive, antagonistic (where the combined effect on an organism is less than predicted by each pollutant's effect when found alone) or synergistic (where the combined effect is greater than predicted from the effects of each substance when found alone). In general it has proved difficult to predict accurately the effects of a potential pollutant in the field.

The effects of a pollutant may also be modified by environmental factors. A recent review found that pH was the factor most likely to influence toxicity (affecting 20 per cent of 410 chemicals investigated), that increasing temperature generally increased toxicity and that water hardness had little effect on organic chemicals. The same review found that insects seemed to be the most sensitive group, followed by crustaceans, fishes and amphibians. Birds, which pick up pollutants mainly through consumption of contaminated prey, appear only rarely to die from excessive levels of pollutants (lead being an exception), and apparently absorb only limited quantities of some pollutants such as heavy metals. However, the metabolism of such substances probably puts those birds living in polluted environments under much greater physiological stress, making them much more susceptible to cold weather and disease, and potentially affecting their reproductive success.

Should water quality improve in a previously polluted wetland, invertebrate populations can recover quite rapidly, while higher plants respond much more slowly and fish populations are the last to recover.

It may be that only a particular stage in the life cycle of an organism is susceptible to a pollutant. A review of toxicity tests on fish demonstrated that the early life stages were particularly susceptible: hatchability of eggs was affected in 19 per cent of tests, survival of larvae in 57 per cent, growth of larvae in 36 per cent, reproduction in 30 per cent, adult survival in 13 per cent and adult growth in only 5 per cent. So, while individuals of a species may survive in polluted waters the species as a whole may die out if those conditions persist.

SHOULD WILDLIFE BE ATTRACTED TO CONTAMINATED WETLANDS

Before all else, consideration needs to be given to whether the water available to create a wetland is of an appropriate quality to warrant encouraging wildlife. Unfortunately, our understanding of the way pollutants affect organisms and interact with each other is far from comprehensive, making it difficult to predict the problems that an industrial wetland might pose to wildlife.

In trying to assess whether wildlife will be at risk at a particular site, consideration must be given to a variety of factors:

- The types of wildlife that might use a site;
- The chemistry and characteristics of the water;
- The characteristics of any potentially toxic substances in the wetland - toxicity, persistence, bio-availability, and the potential for bio-accumulation.

Different groups of plants and animals vary greatly in the way they respond to the presence of contaminants. Organisms living in the water column, such as aquatic plants, fish and invertebrates, are likely to be significantly affected by water chemistry. These organisms often take up pollutants dissolved in the water, plants occasionally accumulating Very high concentrations, and are vulnerable to oxygen depletion resulting from high BOD.

Submerged plants are also adversely affected by reduced light penetration caused by suspended solids; Fennel Pondweed seems to be the most tolerant species in this respect.

By contrast, emergent plants absorb most substances, including pollutants, from the sediment in which they are rooted. Reedmace can apparently become acclimatised to sediments contaminated with metals, despite metal concentrations sometimes accumulating in the root system (very little is stored in the above-ground portions of the plant). Many metal compounds probably pass straight through the guts of birds undigested, while most other metals can apparently be excreted by birds. Complex organic substances, such as organochlorines, certainly can cause chronic conditions in birds, while organo-lead compounds are lethal in even modest concentrations. It is, therefore, difficult to generalise as to whether a water source will be harmful to wildlife;

in some wetlands aquatic plants and many invertebrates may be excluded owing to the pollution levels while birds apparently prosper.

Probably the factor that should be given most attention is the potential bio-availability of known toxic substances. Inert, immobile forms of such substances may not present a problem to wildlife. Metals such as lead and copper, for example, will remain as insoluble and immobile sulphides as long as they are trapped within anoxic sediments. The pH will be critical in this respect as it affects the mobility and bio-availability of most metals, many of which can go into solution under acid conditions. The activities of benthic invertebrates may lead to the disturbance or chemical transformation of contaminated sediments. Consequently, it is possible for the bio-availability of a substance to change with time, where, for instance, the water chemistry is affected by a fluctuating management regime. A possible example of this effect was seen in the Mersey Estuary where there was a series of bird kills between 1979 and 1981 thought to have been caused by discharges of alkyl lead compounds. These discharges had been on-going for many years, suggesting that some other factor must have triggered the sudden lethal effects. One possibility is that a reduction in general pollution levels within the estuary resulted in increased invertebrate populations in the discharge area which in turn increased the birds' consumption of prey contaminated with the lead compounds.

The likelihood of a substance passing up a food-chain also varies tremendously. Sampling undertaken at Werribee wastewater treatment works in Australia demonstrated that although metal contamination in the wastewater was taken up by the plants growing in the grass plots, very little of this accumulated in the tissues of the livestock that grazed them, and that copper levels were actually depressed in these stock.

Ingeneral, it is the lipid-soluble toxins, such as the methylated forms of mercury and lead and organochlorines, that show a tendency to accumulate (bio-magnify) as they pass up a food-chain, and hence pose most concern with regard to the welfare of vertebrates.

Polluted wetlands obviously are not universally good for wildlife, as evidenced by the impoverished species diversity that is often associated with them.

That is not to say, however, that contaminated wetlands cannot provide valuable habitat for some forms of wildlife, as demonstrated by Features 12.1 Some effluents will contain such high levels of toxic substances that common sense will dictate that they are dealt with sensitively and in such a way that wildlife should not come into contact with them. A more difficult ethical issue is whether wildlife should be deterred or excluded from sites where they might be exposed to substances that can cause chronic rather than lethal conditions.

At the present time there are no hard and fast rules and each situation should be considered individually.

Until such time as our knowledge suggests otherwise, it is recommended that wildlife is not attracted, or is even deterred from, situations where:

- The water contains substances in concentrations that are likely to be lethal to birds and mammals;
- Sediments are likely rapidly to accumulate toxic substances in forms that are, or are likely to become, soluble or otherwise mobile and therefore available for biological up-take. (Sites where accumulation of such substances is likely to occur only at a slow rate, should be monitored to ensure that critical levels are not reached. If such levels are reached then the contaminated sediments should be removed or the site design or management modified to deter these groups of wildlife);
- Known toxic substances, present in significant concentrations, are likely to bio-magnify as they are passed up a food-chain.

DESIGNING AND MANAGING WETLANDS TO IMPROVE WATER QUALITY

If, as is likely on many industrial sites, there are any doubts over water quality, there are a number of mechanisms that can be incorporated and approaches adopted in order to bring about improvements, as briefly summarised in the following paragraphs.

SUSPENDED SOLIDS AND ASSOCIATED CONTAMINANTS

Many metals as well as phosphates are often bound to clay and organic sediments. As some 40-90 per cent of pollutants are thought to be associated with sediment particles up to 0.2 mm in size, silt traps offer a very simple but effective means of improving water quality. They function by slowing down the flow of water; silt starts to settle out where the flow is less than 0.2 m per second. They are best located just above the inflow of a waterbody or wetland that needs safe-guarding. Silt traps of all sizes need to be cleaned out regularly in order to prevent sediments going back into suspension every time flows increase. Silt traps should, therefore, be designed to make dredging as simple as possible by, for instance, providing a concrete approach and floor in order to ease access for machinery.

HIGH NUTRIENT LEVELS

The stripping of plant nutrients from water is not easily achieved. It is always better, where possible, to try to restrict the inputs of nutrients into a wetland by, for instance, controlling the application of fertilizers within the catchment. Most cases of eutrophication result from high concentrations of phosphate, and controlling phosphate levels may be sufficient to remove or prevent the worst symptoms. There are a number of methods that have been used with varying degrees of success for reducing concentrations of dissolved phosphates and/or overcoming the problems of eutrophication which are discussed in Refs. 18 and 79. The most widely applicable techniques are summarised below:

Chemical treatment

Aluminium and iron salts and lime have all been used to precipitate out dissolved phosphates. The chemical reaction is pH dependent, being most effective at pH 6-7. The chemicals can be added directly into a waterbody or inflow stream. However, better results have been obtained in the more controlled conditions associated with water treatment plants, especially where the effluent has been passed through filters. Good results have recently been obtained by passing water through an aluminium oxide filter. These methods pose potential problems in terms of the toxicity of the chemicals used and the need for regular inputs.

Holding ponds

Incoming water can be passed through various forms of treatment ponds and wetlands prior to entering the main wetlands Phosphates are readily adsorbed onto sediment particles under the right conditions and can therefore be removed in silt traps and reedbed treatment systems. The RSPB reserve at Rye House Marsh is fed almost entirely by wastewater that has received tertiary treatment at the adjacent sewage works. In the early years of the reserve a gradual improvement in water quality was observed as the water passed through the long, shallow wetland complex encouraging the development of a spectrum of wetlands, including fen-like communities which require relatively pure water. More recently nutrient levels within these wetlands have increased suggesting that the system's ability to absorb such substances has been exceeded. Additionally, in ponds with a significant retention time (at least three days), nutrients will be taken up by algal blooms. In properly designed ponds (sometimes referred to as 'bioreactors') the dead algae settle on the bed and much of the phosphate is added to the sediment. The effectiveness of this process is inevitably affected by light and temperature and hence varies seasonally.

Dilution

Sources of nutrient-poor water can be used to flush out algal blooms or dilute concentrations of nutrients.

Harvesting the Biota to Remove Nutrients

Various workers have looked at the potential for cropping an element of the food web within eutrophic waters in order to reduce nutrient levels. As yet, no one has come up with an option that would be commercially viable in a temperate climate. Algae and non-rooted aquatic plants are most effective at removing nutrients from water. Algae often dominate in the most eutrophic waters but are difficult to collect and as yet there are no markets for a mixed crop of algae.

Submerged plants are more easily harvested but care is needed to ensure that the ecology is not altered to such an extent that algae are then favoured. Emergent plants, as with other rooted plants, gain most of their nutrients from the substrate and therefore have little potential when it comes to removing dissolved nutrients. If left unharvested a buildup of dead emergents may even increase nutrient levels within a wetland. Fish are relatively ineffective at removing nutrients, but some benefits may result -where the population can be completely removed on a regular basis..

Dredging

Sediments often contain a high proportion of a wetland's nutrient load. These nutrients are derived both from the decay of organisms within the wetland and from sediments and detritus brought in by inflowing water. Dredging can be used to limit the accumulation of nutrient- rich sediments.

ACIDITY

A combined treatment of lime and sewage sludge has been used successfully to raise the pH in previously acidic waters spread over the bed of a waterbody acts as a chemical filter, removing acidic sulphate as it enters and converting it into neutral sulphide. The sludge also prevents groundwater coming into contact with oxygen thus slowing down the production of further sulphate.

When the pH is artificially raised by liming, the additional nutrients from the sewage sludge encourage plant growth together with associated animal populations. The increased productivity enables an organic-rich sediment to be maintained which in turn sustains a stable, roughly neutral pH. Before applying this technique, consideration needs to be given to the levels of contaminants within the available sludge and any problems they might pose.

FLOATING SUBSTANCES AND DEBRIS

Booms can be placed around inflows in order to trap oils and floating objects. These devices need to be checked regularly and appropriate action taken when required. At the British Steel plant at Shotton (Clwyd), site run-off drains into a series of lagoons where up to c.300 pairs of Common Terns breed. The three inflows are protected by floating booms which are inspected daily, enabling any oil to be dealt with before it disperses across the lagoons.

Screens and filters can be placed across inflows to trap solid objects. Debris should be removed regularly in order to prevent flooding and erosion

BENEFITS OF WATER-POLLUTION CONTROL

This chapter presents two studies that endeavor to develop methods for assessing the *national* benefits associated with improvements in, or maintenance of, the quality of surface waters. The first focuses exclusively on freshwater fishing and builds up a national total from regional estimates. The second uses a national sample survey technique to elicit individual's valuation of some broad national water-quality goals.

NATIONAL FRESHWATER RECREATION BENEFITS

Among the more important pieces of national environmental legislation created during the 1970s were the comprehensive amendments to the Federal Water Pollution Control Act. These amendments, signed into law in 1972 and further amended in 1977, in reality constituted a major piece of legislation in their own right, dramatically redirecting the nation's efforts at water-pollution control and setting out ambitious national goals, expressed both in terms of discharge controls and of resulting water quality.

Criticism of the amendments and debate over their goals and requirements began during the legislative process and has continued, with more or less heat, to the present. Some critics argue that the goals are too ambitious, that is, the benefits of meeting the goals (and related requirements) are thought to be too small to justify the costs of compliance. This argument over the balance of benefits and costs can never be resolved entirely by research, but the RFF project described here was undertaken in the conviction that it should be possible to improve methods for estimating at least some of the benefit categories associated with waterpollution control, in this case, the benefits from recreational fishing in freshwater bodies.

From the outset the intent was to design a method for estimating benefits for the nation as a whole rather than benefits for particular sites. In this respect, it resembles the study discussed in the last part of chapter. In undertaking this project, a primary question concerned the ways in which water-quality improvement would favourably affect freshwater fishing. Two major ways were identified.

First, it tends to increase the total availability of fishable freshwater bodies by reducing the incidence of conditions such as low dissolved oxygen that results from the bacterial degradation of organic materials and heavy sediment loads that make it difficult for fish to survive.Second, it produces changes in the *types* of fish that can survive in particular water bodies.Simply put, clean water means "game" fish such as trout or bass, and dirty water means rough fish such as carp or buffalo. In general, fishermen prefer game fish.

Therefore, pollution control tends to increase the amount of water yielding high-quality fishing relative to that yielding low-quality fishing.Given this view of the benefit-producing mechanisms, one can work towards a methodology for making national benefit estimates based on it. As explained earlier, benefit estimation for environmental improvement requires the understanding of a number of links. For this particular study, the following questions should be considered:

- How will implementation of the law affect pollution discharges by location, quantity, and pollutant type across the entire nation?
- How will the pre- and postpolicy discharge levels affect ambient water quality? Or how does ambient quality change as discharges
- Change not only in terms of such familiar indicators as dissolved oxygen, but also in terms of supportable fish population types?
- How will increases in total amounts of water supporting recreational fishing and shifts in the composition of that water towards more highly valued fish species affect the number of anglers and the amount of time they spend fishing?
- In addition, one needs to be able to value fishing activity of various kinds—that is, for practical purposes, how many days are spent fishing for various species—rough fish versus game fish?

The novelty of this study and its main contribution to methodological development lies in the ingenious way it is able to link models together to structure these linkages and how it is able to take existing and newly developed data sets to estimate them quantitatively. I turn now to a discussion of each step in the procedure.

DISCHARGE REDUCTIONS AND LINKS TO AMBIENT QUALITY AND FISH

Initially, one must have an understanding of the "fishability" of the nation's water prior to the implementation of the Federal Water Pollution Control Act. A data base is available from the Fish and Wildlife Service that permits estimates of fishable water by state (the state is the basic geographic unit on which this study is operated), but these data do not provide a basis for the breakdown between rough fish and game fish that is basic to the methods used in this study. For this reason, the researchers surveyed state fish-and-game officials asking them for a breakdown by species category within their own states. Using these data, they found that for the contiguous forty-eight states and the District of Columbia, there are about 30.6 million acres of fishable fresh water consisting of about 20.4 per cent cold-water game fisheries, 68.4 per cent warm-water game fisheries, and 11. 2 per cent rough fisheries.

To determine how the implementation of discharge controls would affect the current status requires a knowledge of the amount and location of discharges prior to, and following, the implementation of the 1972 amendments. Then it is necessary to estimate how this change will affect ambient conditions in water courses, and how, in turn, these will affect fishability. The first three kinds of information have been established by the use of RFF's Water Quality Network (WQN) model. This model, designed specifically to answer those questions, was run for four scenarios representing—albeit roughly in some cases—stages in the implementation of the law. In what follows, I will focus on only one of these stages—the Best Practical Control Technology Currently Available.

This is for simplicity and also because the quantitative benefits still must be regarded as experimental. The Best Practical Control Technology Currently Available (BPT for short) requirement was to be achieved by all point sources (that is, discharges from confined channels, such as pipes) of wastewater discharge. This unmet goal may reflect where we currently are in our control efforts.

At best, the WQN model provides a reasonable estimate of the impact of policy changes on one important aspect of ambient conditions: dissolved oxygen. However, it does not translate directly into fishability. Indeed, making that step is an undeveloped discipline, calling for heroic measures.

Fortunately, a fisheries biologist, willing to use his knowledge and skill to survey the literature, developed a set of rules that appear to capture whatever consensus exists on the water-quality conditions appropriate to the survival and reproduction of various fish populations. These rules can be applied to the results of the WQN model to provide estimates of the acreages of different kinds of fishing availability by state, and by aggregation, for the nation as a whole. The reader may be struck by how small the increases in total fishable water are—only about 100,000 acres from a base of more than 30 million. This is because a very large proportion of U.S., fresh waters already was fishable before implementation of the water-pollution law. However, at the same time, it is projected that the waters regarded as unfishable or capable of supporting rough fish only will decline dramatically.

This does not mean a proportionate decline in rough fish populations, but rather a large increase in the water that rough fish will share with warmand cold-water game fish. The next step is to devise ways of converting the water-quality results into changes in fishermen's participation in various kinds of fishing. Before proceeding, however, it is pertinent to note that what has been discussed so far is not types of research and modeling that are in the usual purview of economics. But the situation here, is reflective of the fact that existing models of natural systems rarely fit the needs of the economist who would estimate the benefits of environmental improvement. Accordingly, he is often forced into disciplinary imperialism.

Behavioral Economic Aspects of the Study

I now turn to steps in the analysis that are more clearly economic in character. In order to estimate total activity in various types of fishing, the individual fisherman's chain of decision about recreational fishing must be broken down into several logical stages.

The first choice is whether to do any fishing at all. The researchers' hypothesis is that the decision of whether to fish is sensitive, among other things, to the opportunity to fish, represented by the quantity of fishable water. The object of this first stage of the research is then to quantitatively estimate how the decision to fish is influenced, in the population at large, by the availability of fishable water. Regression analysis is the method used to determine the separate influences of availability of fishing opportunity and those other factors that might affect the decision.

The indicators of existing availability of fishable water are the statelevel estimates divided by the state population to get a per capita measure. This is rather crude, but a more refined indicator was not available at the time. The other data needed for this stage of the research were obtained from a very large survey conducted by the U.S. Department of the Interior, Fish and Wildlife Service. The first or screening stage of this survey was conducted by telephone interview of more than 100,000 households (300,000 individuals). Its primary intent was to determine whether individuals participated in hunting, fishing, and other recreational activities associated with wildlife.

The survey also contained information on other pertinent variables such as age, sex, income, and other factors so that it was possible to include them in the regression analysis and control for their possible effects on participation. The dependent variable was the decision to fish or not to fish. Since the availability of fishable water was included among the independent variables, once the coefficients of the equation have been estimated, the size of the availability variable can be changed and the corresponding change in participation calculated.

We have seen regression analysis results used in a similar way in other chapters, for example, in projecting the effect of air-quality improvement. So far, all the analysis permits us to do is to project fishing in general as a function of water quality. But since, as I have indicated, different types of fishing (warm-water game fishing, cold-water game fishing, and rough fishing) probably differ in value, we must also be able to project how likely a representative individual is to pick each of these types if he or she does decide to fish.

For this purpose, data obtained by the Fish and Wildlife Service in the second stage of the 1975 survey was used. A questionnaire was mailed to more than 50,000 persons who had declared themselves to be hunters or fishermen in the screening stage. For this subgroup, detailed information was gathered on their participation patterns, socioeconomic characteristics, and preferences. Data for the fishermen only was used in analysing the second stage in the decision chain—namely, once a person has decided to fish how likely is he or she to participate in each of the three types of fishing given the availability of water suitable for each type?

Because doing some trout fishing, for example, does not rule out doing some bass or rough fishing as well during the course of the year, the regression equations for the type of fishing decision might best be characterised in "some-of" terms. Either a person did some cold-water game fishing or he or she did not. But the individual also might have done some bass fishing. In any case, whether some of a particular kind of fishing was done was hypothesised to be a function of the availability of water suitable for that kind of fishing as well as other characteristics of the participant.

The final stage in the decision chain is the decision on how much time (how many days) will be spent in that activity. The same set of survey data was used in the analysis of this question, and regression analysis was the tool for connecting reported decisions on days of fishing to the independent variables, including the availability of water suitable for the fishing in question. The drift of the analysis is now clear. The steps are as follows: the amount of increase in total fishable water and fishable-type water associated with water-pollution control is given for the nation as a whole from the models of the previous sections. Given this, the results of Stage 1 are used to calculate how much fishing participation will increase in general.

Then, the results of Stages 2 and 3 are used to calculate how this increase in participation will be distributed across the fishing types and how many days of increased fishing of each type will occur nationally as a result of the pollution-control policy. The final problem confronted by this research on the benefits from improved freshwater fishing opportunities is how to assign dollar-value benefits (that is, willingness to pay) to the increase in each category of fishing activity. The approach adopted estimated a demand curve for fishing days for each category and used those to calculate the average consumer's surplus per day.

The travel-cost method, described generally in earlier chapter, was the technique selected. I now turn to a brief discussion of how it was applied in this study. Recall that the basic assumption of the travel-cost method is that higher costs of access, as reflected in distance from a recreational site, will have the same effect on visitation as an equivalent admission fee assuming zero distance from the site. I presented a very simple example of how this relationship can be used to develop a demand curve by assuming successively higher admissions fees and using information on access costs to estimate their effects on visitation.

This establishes points on a demand curve, that is, the relationship of price to the number of visitor-days. The area under the demand curve, by principles discussed in chapter, is the total willingness to pay of participants for the total number of visitor-days to the site, say, a trout fishery. If one then divides the number of visitor-days into this number, one obtains the average willingness to pay for a day of fishing for trout. The researchers who conducted the study collected data from a large number of fishing sites around the country which permitted them, by statistical means, to make exactly such a calculation yielding average willingness to pay per visitor-day for each type of fishery.

ESTIMATING NATIONAL WATER-QUALITY BENEFITS

We are now at a point where a national benefits estimate can be made. All the earlier machinations were designed to estimate how many days of increased recreational fishing of each type would correspond to the water-quality changes resulting from a reduction of wastewater discharges corresponding to the implementation of a pollution-control policy. Having these numbers in hand, it is a simple matter to multiply them by average willingness to pay for a day by fish type and get a total benefit number for freshwater fishing in the United States. When this is done, the following results are obtained for Best Practical Control Technology Currently Available.

Valuation base	*Total Annual Benefits over base (millions)*
Low	307
High	683

A few words of explanation are needed about the difference between the low and the high estimates. For the low estimate, travel cost is based only on out-of-pocket expenses—gasoline, restaurant food, motels, and others. This is the conventional method. The higher estimate takes account of the fact that the fisherman may also attach a cost to the time it takes to get to the site. For the higher figure, an estimate of this cost is made by attaching average wage rates to the travel time needed to reach the site.

Needless to say, large uncertainties attend these numbers and, because of this, they must be regarded as largely experimental. Nevertheless, in view of the heavy costs of the national programme for water-quality improvement they may strike the reader as being quite low. There are several things to be said in this connection. First, the reader should recall that in terms of the availability of fish species the vast majority of the nation's fresh water was already fishable prior to the 1972 Amendments. Second, these estimates are partial in the sense that they consider only the fresh waters and even then they do not include values that may accrue to fishermen from the possible effects of pollution control on the aesthetic aspects of the fishing experience. At present, research is under way to extend the methodology developed in this study to effects of pollution control on marine (saltwater) recreational fisheries, and on both marine and freshwater swimming and recreational boating.

METHOD FOR ESTIMATING NATIONAL WATER-QUALITY BENEFITS

The research reported in the previous section was designed to yield national recreational fishing benefits of water-quality improvement. Basically, it used subregions as units of analysis and aggregated them by adding up the results. Thus it can be described as a large-scale simulation falling somewhere between a particular site (or micro) study and a national survey that asks respondents directly about their willingness to pay for national programmes of pollution control. This last procedure has been called the "macro" approach. Among other potential advantages of such an approach, two are especially important.

First, a randomised national sample of persons can be interviewed which permits the use of well-established statistical procedures to extrapolate the results to the entire population. Second, one can enquire about "intrinsic" or existence benefits as well as user benefits. The second reason invites more explanation.

Because the U.S., population politically supports very expensive programmes of water-pollution conrol—much more costly than the benefits estimated for recreational users in the previous section—the researchers were led to believe that there must be some form or forms of benefits accruing to persons who do not actually use particular water bodies. We have termed such benefits variously as intrinsic or existence benefits. These benefits may accrue because persons value the options for possible use that are opened to them when water bodies are cleaned up.

This type of value, discussed widely in the economics literature, has come to be called the option value. Other intrinsic values may accrue from a sense of national pride or rectitude associated with having clean waters. One of the main conclusions of the research reported in this chapter and in the following one is that intrinsic benefits definitely exist with respect to environmental improvements or maintenance. Moreover, and with the usual caution about accuracy of results, not only do they exist, but they are large, perhaps even larger than user benefits in some instances. Some aspects of water quality make it more appropriate than air quality for an experimental application of the macro approach. Chiefly, goals of our national policy are set out in a manner that would let most of the population understand what they mean in terms of ordinary experience.

The objectives are to make all the nation's water fishable and swimmable in successive stages. Furthermore, much of the cost of these programmes is to be paid from taxes levied at the national levels (taxes financing subsidies to local governments) so that respondents can be realistically asked how much in added tax burden they are willing to pay for improved water quality across the whole nation. Neither one of these situations holds with respect to air quality, so it would be much harder to pose understandable and realistic alternatives in a national clean air survey.

A macro study, then, is potentially useful for doing a benefit-cost analysis for national water programmes. It should be noted, however, that it is *not* a substitute for site-specific studies in other applications. For example, determining whether the benefits outweigh the costs of a programme for water-quality improvement in the Potomac estuary would require a site-specific study.

RESEARCH PROCEDURES

One problem with national surveys is that they are quite expensive. What made it possible to conduct an experiment with the macro approach, given available resources, was that the researchers were able to add some water-quality questions onto a survey being funded by another source. After the interview for the other survey was completed, the interviewers administered a sequence of benefits questions that had been carefully pretested by researchers on the benefits project. From the respondents' perspective, the two interviews appeared as one long interview. In all, 1,576 personal interviews of a national probability sample of persons eighteen years of age and older were completed. The sample was designed and the interviews were conducted by Roper and Cantril, a national polling firm.

A penalty of this add-on approach proved to be that an unfortunately large number of persons failed to complete all of the questions. In part this was because they came at the end of an already fairly lengthy survey and in part because it was not possible to undertake special training of the interviewers to administer the benefits section. Because of the likelihood of item-response bias (caused by respondents failing to answer individual items), the researchers regard their estimates as only suggestive and warn against accepting them as definitive. The main intent of the experiment was not to develop definitive estimates at this stage but to test whether a macro approach is applicable to an investigation of waterquality benefits. The low response rate presumably can be cured by an improved questionnaire and by training of the interviewers. A study is currently being planned in which both of these elements will exist.

THE WATER-POLLUTION LADDER AND VALUE LEVELS

The levels of water quality for which the research team sought willingness-to-pay estimates are "boatable, " fishable," and "swimmable." These levels are described in words and depicted graphically by means of a "water-quality ladder". Use of these categories, two of which are embodied in the law mandating the national programme for water-pollution control, permitted avoidance of the communications problems associated with describing water quality in terms of the numerous abstract technical measures of pollution (oxygen depletion, for example).

Although the boatable-fishable-swimmable categories are widely understood by the public, they did require further specification to ensure that different people perceived them in a similar fashion. *Boatable water* was defined as an intermediate level between water which "has oil, raw sewage and other things in it, has no plant or animal life and smells bad" on the one hand, and water which is of fishable quality on the other. As discussed earlier, *fishable water* covers a fairly large range of water quality. Game fish such as bass and trout cannot tolerate water in which certain rough fish such as carp and catfish flourish.

In pretests, experiments were made with two levels of fishable water-one for rough fish like carp and catfish, and the other for game fish like bass—but a single definition of fishable was adopted as water "clean enough so that game fish like bass can live in it," under the assumption that the words "game fish" and "bass" had wide recognition and denoted water of the quality that Congress had in mind. *Swimmable water* appeared to present less difficulty for popular understanding since the enforcement of water-quality standards for swimming by health authorities has led to widespread awareness that swimming in polluted water can cause illness.

Because willingness-to-pay questions have to describe in some detail the conditions of the "market" for the good, they are inevitably longer than the usual survey research questions. Respondents quickly become bored and restless if material is read to them without giving them frequent opportunities to express judgements or to look at visual aids. The questionnaire for this experiment was designed to be as interactive as possible by interpreting the text with questions which required the respondents to use the newly described water-quality categories. They were also handed a card depicting the water-quality ladder which was referred to constantly during the sequence of benefits questions.

WILLINGNESS-TO-PAY QUESTIONS AND ANSWERS

Questions about willingness to pay should seem realistic to respondents. Accordingly, they were couched in terms of annual household payments in higher prices and taxes because this is the way people do pay for waterpollution control. A portion of each household's annual federal tax payment goes towards the expense of regulating water pollution and providing construction grants for sewage-treatment plants. Local sewage taxes pay for the maintenance of these plants.

Those private users, such as manufacturing plants, who incur pollution-control expenses ultimately pass much or all of the cost along to consumers in higher prices. Thus, this payment method has a ring of truth to the respondents. As explained earlier "starting-point bias" can be an important problem in bidding games and surveys. That is, a high starting bid from an interviewer may elicit a higher bid from a respondent than a low starting bid.

A major methodological innovation of the research reported in this chapter is the development of a device for eliminating such a bias, the "payment card." In this technique, the respondent is given a card which contains a menu of alternative amounts of payment beginning at $0 and increasing by a fixed interval until an arbitrarily determined large amount is reached. When the time comes to elicit the amount one is willing to pay, the respondent is asked to pick a number from the card (or any number in between) which "is the *most* you would be willing to pay in taxes and higher price *each year*" (italics in the questionnaire) for a given level of water quality. Thus, the interviewer suggests no bid at all. It turns out, however, that this presents some problems of its own. In initial pretests, it was found that the respondents had considerable difficulty in determining their willingness to pay when a card was used which only presented various dollar amounts.

A number of them expressed embarrassment, confusion, or resentment at the task, and some who gave amounts indicated they were very uncertain about them. The problem lay with the lack of benchmarks for their estimates. People are not normally aware of the total amounts they pay for public goods even when that amount comes out of their taxes, nor do they know how much such goods cost.

Without a way of psychologically anchoring their estimate in some manner, they were not able to arrive at meaningful estimates. They needed benchmarks of some kind which would convey sufficient information without biasing their responses. Their most appropriate benchmarks for willingness to pay for water-pollution control would appear to be the amounts they are already paying in higher prices and taxes for other non-environmental, publicly provided goods and services.

Amounts were identified on the card for several such goods, and further pretests were conducted, indicating that the benchmarks made the task meaningful for most people. But the use of payment cards with benchmarks raises the possibility of introducing its own kind of bias. Are the respondents who gave amounts for water-pollution control using the benchmarks for general orientation or are they basing their amounts directly on the benchmarks themselves in some manner? In the former case, respondents would be giving unique values for water quality; in the latter case, they would be giving values for water quality relative to what they think they are paying for a particular set of other public goods.

If the latter case holds and their water-quality values are sensitive to changes in the benchmark amounts, or to changes in the set of public goods identified on the payment card, their validity as estimates of consumer surplus for water quality are suspect. A test for this kind of bias was conducted in the pretest by using different versions of the payment card with the amounts paid for other publicly provided goods changed by modest amounts. No bias was found, and so the "anchored" payment card was deemed to be a suitable device for the full-scale experiment. Tests were also conducted to attempt to discover if any of the other sorts of bias were inherent in the questionnaire. Again, none was found.

A final point should be made regarding the payment card. What people actually pay for publicly provided goods varies with their income. To correct for this, four different payment cards were developed corresponding to four income classes. At the appropriate point in the interview, the interviewer gave the respondent the payment card for his or her income category, which had been established by a prior question.

As already discussed, the respondents valued three levels of water quality which were described in words and depicted on the water quality ladder. They were first asked how much they were willing to pay to maintain national water quality in the boatable level. Subsequent questions asked them their willingness to pay for overall water quality to fishable quality and swimmable quality. The average willingness-to-pay amounts given by the respondent for the two higher levels consists of the amounts they offered for the lower levels plus any additional amount they offered for the higher level.

The average annual amounts per household for those respondents who answered the willingness-to-pay questions turned out to be:

Water quality	Total $	Marginal $
Boatable	152	152
Fishable	194	42
Swimmable	225	31

The most substantial benefit is for boatable water. The respondents are willing to give about 20 per cent more for fishable water than boatable water, but only an additional 15 per cent to make the water swimmable.

The data also permitted one to make a rough distinction between the type of recreation and the intrinsic values discussed earlier. Since the willingness-to-pay questions measure the overall value that respondents have for water quality, the amount given by each respondent represents the combination of recreational and intrinsic values held by that person. But it was possible to tell from the questions whether a person actually engaged in water-based recreation. It was reasoned that the values expressed by the respondents who do not engage in in-stream recreation should be almost purely intrinsic in nature. In calculating the average willingness-to-pay amount for the non-recreationists alone, therefore, we get an approximation of the intrinsic value of water quality. By subtracting this amount from the total the recreationists are willing to pay, one can estimate, in a rough way, the portions of the recreationists' benefits which are attributable to recreation and intrinsic values.

When this is done, it is found that intrinsic value constitutes about 45 per cent of the total value for recreationists, 100 per cent for the non-recreationists (by assumption), and about 55 per cent for the sample as a whole. If this is a correct reflection of reality, it is a major finding and may have large implications for the future study of benefits from environmental improvement. It was noted earlier that, while the sample of persons interviewed was initially chosen at random, quite a few respondents failed to give usable answers. Any aggregate national benefit estimate based on these data therefore could not be put forward as accurate. Thus, I make such an estimate simply to illustrate that the results of this experiment imply very large values.

There are about 80 million households in the United States. Assume that the sample results imply that to have high-quality recreational waters throughout the country there is an annual willingness to pay of $200 per household.

This would imply a total willingness to pay of $16 billion. According to the earlier discussion, this would divide about equally between user and non-user values. At first this might seem out of line with the value of well under the billion dollars that was calculated for recreational fishing. But this is not necessarily the case. Recall that that estimate is for a relatively small *increase* in the nation's fishable waters over the actual conditions of the early 1970s, and that the estimate from the national survey is the value people attach to making and *maintaining* the whole of the nation's fresh waters of high recreational quality where the alternative is almost total degradation of most of the nation's watercourses. In other words, both the baselines and the routes of benefit accrual considered are different in the two studies.

A somewhat closer comparison, though still not a perfect one, is between the survey's reported willingness to pay for an improvement from boatable to fishable water and the largest value found in the fishing study for essentially complete cleanup (in fishing terms) of the nation's *fresh* water—roughly $1 billion. The objective of this experiment was not to produce an accurate estimate of national benefits, rather it was to test the feasibility of using a macro approach to the estimation of water-quality benefits. In that, it succeeded.

Bibliography

Chiles, T. H., & Choi, T. Y.: *"Theorizing TQM: An Austrian and Evolutionary Economics Interpretation"* Journal of Management Studies 37(2), 2000.

Cowen, Tyler and David Parker.: *Markets in the Firm: A Market Process Approach to Management,* London: The Institute of Economic Affairs, 1997.

Dominick Salvatore and Ravikesh Srivastava.: *Managerial Economics: Principles and Worldwide Applications*, Oxford University Press, 2008.

Dulbecco, Philippe and Pierre Garrouste.: *"Towards an Austrian Theory of the Firm"* Review of Austrian Economics 12, 1999.

Ellig, Jerry.: *"Organizational Economics and the Market-Based Management Framework: Toward a Common Research Agenda,"* Journal of Private Enterprise12:1, 1996.

Foss, Kirsten and Nicolai Foss.: *"Coase vs Hayek: Economic Organization in the Knowledge Economy"* International Journal of the Economics of Business 9, 2002.

Foss, Kirsten and Nicolai Foss.: *"Economic Organization in a Process Perspective: an Explorative Discussion"* In Jackie Krafft, ed. The Process of Competition, Aldershot: Edward Elgar, 2000.

Foss, Kirsten and Nicolai Foss.: *"Organizing Economic Experiments: Property Rights and Firm Organization,"* Review of Austrian Economics 15, 2002.

Foss, Kirsten, Nicolai J. Foss, and Peter G. Klein.: *"Original and Derived Judgment: An Entrepreneurial Theory of Economic Organization"* Organization Studies 28, 2007.

Foss, Kirsten, Nicolai J. Foss, Peter G. Klein, and Sandra K. Klein.: *"Heterogeneous Capital, Entrepreneurship, and Economic Organization"* Journal des Economistes et des Etudes Humaines 12, 2002.

Foss, Nicolai and Jens Frøslev Christensen.: *"A Market Process Approach to Corporate Coherence"* Managerial and Decision Economics 22, 2001.

Foss, Nicolai J., and Peter G. Klein, eds.: *Entrepreneurship and the Firm: Austrian Perspectives on Economic Organization*, Aldershott, U.K., Edward Elgar, 2002.

Foss, Nicolai J., and Peter G. Klein.: *"Entrepreneurship and the Economic Theory of the*

Firm: Any Gains from Trade" In Rajshree Agarwal, Sharon A. Alvarez, and Olav Sorenson, eds., Handbook of

Foss, Nicolai J.: "*More on Knight and the Theory of the Firm*" Managerial and Decision Economics, 1993.

Foss, Nicolai J.: "*The Use of Knowledge in Firms*" Journal of Institutional and Theoretical Economics 155, 1999.

Foss, Nicolai J.: "*Misesian Ownership and Coasian Authority in Hayekian Settings: The Case of the Knowledge Economy*" Quarterly Journal of Austrian Economics 4, 2001.

Ghoshal, Sumantra, Peter Moran and Luis Almeida-Costa.: "*The Essence of the Megacorporation: Shared Context, not Structural Hierarchy*" Journal of Institutional and Theoretical Economics 151, 1995.

Ionnanides, Stavros.: "*Towards an Austrian Perspective on the Firm*" Review of Austrian Economics 11, 1999.

Klein, Peter G.: "*Economic Calculation and the Limits of Organization*" Review of Austrian Economics 9, 1996.

Klein, Peter G.: "*Opportunity Discovery, Entrepreneurial Action, and Economic Organization*" Strategic Entrepreneurship Journal 2, 2008.

M.Madana Mohan and P.Premchand Babu.: *Managerial Economics and Financial Analysis*, Himalaya Publishing House, Delhi, 2011.

M.S. Bhat and A.V. Rau.: *Managerial Economics and Financial Analysis*, BS Publications, Delhi, 2008.

R.K. Tailor.: *Principles of Managerial Economics*, RBSA Publication, 2012. Robert Waschik, Timothy C.G. Fisher and David Prentice.: *Managerial Economics : A Strategic Approach*, Routledge India, 2011.

S.P. Gupta.: *Managerial Economics*, Deep and Deep Publication, Delhi, 2012.

Shipra Chawla.: *A Textbook of Managerial Economics*, Dominant Publication, Delhi, 2012.

V.P. Raghavan.: *Managerial Economics : The Economic Way of Thinking of Managerial Decisions Theories Applications and Cases*, Kunal Books, Delhi, 2010.

W. Bruce Allen, Neil A. Doherty, Keith Weigelt and Edwin Mansfield.: *Managerial Economics : Theory, Applications and Cases*, Viva Books, 2011.

Index